The CGA-Canada Research Foundation was incorporated and registered as a charitable foundation on May 30, 1979. The creation of the foundation grew from the desire of members of the Certified General Accountants' Association of Canada to make a meaningful contribution to accounting research in Canada by sponsoring research which would advance the accounting community as a whole. It is our desire to encourage pure and applied research in the areas of auditing, accounting and finance.

This monograph is the twenty-first in a series to be published by the CGA-Canada Research Foundation as part of the Association's continuing research effort. Each monograph expresses the viewpoint of its authors, and has been neither approved nor disapproved by CGA-Canada. These monographs are intended to stimulate thought, discussion and debate on matters relating to accounting, auditing and finance. The foundation welcomes comments from readers.

Ronald W. Pickerill, FCGA
President
CGA-Canada Research Foundation
June 1993

MONOGRAPHS PUBLISHED BY THE CGA-CANADA RESEARCH FOUNDATION

No. 1: Historical Cost Accounting and its Rationality, by Yuji Ijiri

No. 2: Accounting for Local Government in Canada: The State of the Art, by Arthur Beedle (Out of Print)

No. 3: Local Government Financial Management and Accounting: A Research Framework, by Katherine Graham (Out of Print)

No. 4: Accountants' Roles in Industrial Organizations and Access to Information, by Michael Newman, Carolyne Smart, Ilan Vertinsky and Vinay Kanetkar

No. 5: The Financial Reporting of Contingencies and Uncertainties: Theory and Practice, by Daniel Thornton

No. 6: Research in Audit Decision Making: Rationale, Evidence and Implications, by Robert Ashton (Out of Print)

No. 7: Modern Accounting Research: History, Survey, and Guide, second edition, by Richard Mattessich

No. 8: International Conflict of Accounting Standards, by Kenneth Most

No. 9: La comptabilité en périodes de changements de prix, deuxième édition, par Daniel Zéghal

No. 10: Risk Assessment in Accounting and Auditing, by Theodore Mock and Ilan Vertinsky

No. 11: The Serviceability of Financial Information: A Survey, by Raymond Chambers and Haim Falk

No. 12: Materiality: An Empirical Study of Actual Auditor Decisions, by Chris Robinson and Len Fertuck

No. 13: Product Differentiation in Auditing: Auditor Choice in the Market for Unseasoned New Issues, by Dan Simunic and Michael Stein

No. 14: Analytical Review Procedures and Processes in Auditing, by Stanley Biggs, Theodore Mock and Paul Watkins

No. 15: Le marché de la vérification au Canada, par Daniel Zéghal

No. 16: The Value of Communication in Agency Contracts: Theory and Experimental Evidence, by Joyce Berg, Lane Daley, Frank Gigler and Chandra Kanodia

No. 17: Accounting Research in the 1980s and its Future Relevance, by Richard Mattessich

No. 18: Accounting for Options: No Longer an Option, by Wanda Wallace and Duane Smith

No. 19: Experimental Tests of Auditing as a Credibility Generating Mechanism, by Nicholas Dopuch and Ron King

No. 20: The Management of Financial Disclosure: Theory and Perspectives, by Michael Gibbins, Alan J. Richardson and John Waterhouse

No. 21: Ethical Reasoning in Accounting and Auditing, by Lawrence A. Ponemon and David R. L. Gabhart

No. 22: The Ethical Foundations of Public Accounting, by James C. Gaa

Acknowledgements and Dedication

This work could not have been completed without the tireless efforts of the many professional auditors from Canada and the United States who participated in this study. Furthermore, the quality of this research has been vastly improved by the intellectual contributions made by Urton Anderson, Donald Arnold, Richard Bernardi, Haim Falk, Michael Fetters, Jim Gaa, Jagdish Gangolly, John Gardner, Joan Grossman, Sandra Kirkby-Gabhart, C.J. McNair, James Rest, Allen Schick, John Wendell and the five anonymous reviewers assigned to this monograph. We also appreciate the generous financial support provided by the CGA-Canada Research Foundation and the KPMG Peat Marwick Faculty Research Fellowship Program. Last, but certainly not least, we are indebted to Stephen Spector and Maxine Glover of the CGA-Canada Research Foundation for their patience, encouragement and immense assistance throughout this project. Thanks again Steve and Maxine!

This book is dedicated to our best friends,
our wives,

Joan Grossman and Sandy Kirkby-Gabhart

Abstract

This monograph extends the work of researchers who have examined ethical reasoning of accounting and auditing practitioners. Its purpose is to explore the influence of ethical reasoning upon domain-specific judgment and behaviour. Drawing upon cognitive-developmental theory, cross-sectional and experimental studies of auditing professionals from the United States and Canada were conducted using a well-known psychometric measure of ethical reasoning called the Defining Issues Test (DIT). The objective of this research is to assess the impact of cross-national differences between the Canadian and American auditing professions upon ethical judgments of individual practitioners. This research also seeks to determine the influence of ethical reasoning on the auditor's ability to frame strategic auditing judgments such as audit risk and the detection of fraudulent financial reporting in client organizations.

The three empirical studies reported in this monograph all employed experienced auditors at various position levels from international public accounting firms located in Ontario, Canada and the Northeast Region of the United States. The first study examined the ethical reasoning of Chartered Accountants (CAs) and Certified Public Accountants (CPAs) from accounting firms in both Canada and the United States, where results suggest differences exist between Canadian and American accounting professionals in terms of the ethical reasoning level of the individual practitioner. In particular, CAs at all position levels in Canadian firms possess higher and less homogeneous DIT P scores than CPAs in American firms. In other words, the process of ethical socialization alluded to in earlier studies for individuals entering and remaining in the accounting profession may not exist in Canadian firms.

Utilizing a field experiment, the second study examined CAs' and CPAs' perceptions of underreporting of billable time, premature sign-off, shirking on the job and shifting time to other billable engagements within the firm. Results show that both CAs and CPAs with relatively low DIT P scores are less likely than high-scoring DIT practitioners to view this behaviour as a negative or dysfunctional reaction to work-related pressure. Similarly, the last study experimentally investigated the relationship between ethical reasoning and the auditor's ability to recognize potentially important attributes of the client organization and its management. Findings show that recognition of ethical cues may be enhanced by the audit practitioner's level of ethical reasoning. In particular, auditors with higher DIT P scores were found to more effectively frame competence and integrity characteristics of client management than auditors with lower DIT P scores, especially when management were believed to possess low integrity and high competence.

Results of all three empirical studies corroborate the importance of ethical reasoning as a determinant of ethical choice and professional behaviour in a wide array of decisions, including the assessment of client competence and integrity, audit materiality and audit risk. These findings should be of consequence to auditing researchers and practitioners alike because they suggest that the examination of task performance in accounting and auditing would be incomplete without also considering the ethical reasoning of the individual practitioner. Thus, the present collection of work may explain salient performance differences, heretofore not explained by experience or expertise alone, on tasks requiring the accountant or auditor to exercise professional judgment when evaluating the client organization and its management.

It is our hope that this work will be beneficial to graduate students and experienced researchers doing research in ethics or moral psychology, especially in the domain of professional accounting and auditing. The findings of this research also should be of value to auditing firms in their attempt to continuously improve the quality of professional judgement when providing attestation and consulting services to client organizations. To this end, we hope this monograph will be beneficial to all those interested in reading about and advancing ethics in the accounting profession.

Résumé

Cette monographie complète les travaux de chercheurs qui ont étudié le raisonnement déontologique chez les experts en comptabilité et en vérification. Les auteurs cherchent à déterminer l'influence du raisonnement déontologique sur le jugement et le comportement spécifiques à un domaine. En se fondant sur la théorie du développement cognitif, les auteurs ont effectué des analyses en coupe et des études expérimentales portant sur des experts en vérification aux États-Unis et au Canada et utilisant, pour mesurer le raisonnement déontologique, un test psychométrique bien connu pour l'identification des valeurs, le *Defining Issues Test* (*DIT*). L'objectif de la recherche est d'évaluer l'effet, sur le raisonnement déontologique du vérificateur, des différences qui existent au sein de la profession entre le Canada et les États-Unis. Les auteurs cherchent aussi à déterminer l'influence du raisonnement déontologique sur la capacité du vérificateur à formuler un jugement sur des points stratégiques de la vérification, comme le risque lié à la vérification et la détection de pratiques frauduleuses des entreprises clientes en matière d'information financière.

Les trois études empiriques présentées dans cette monographie portaient sur des vérificateurs expérimentés travaillant, à divers échelons hiérarchiques, dans des cabinets d'expertise comptable internationaux situés en Ontario (Canada) et dans la région nord-est des États-Unis. Les résultats de la première étude, qui examinait le raisonnement déontologique de comptables agréés (c.a.) et de *Certified Public Accountants* (*CPA*) exerçant en cabinet tant au Canada qu'aux États-Unis, suggèrent qu'il y a une différence entre les deux pays dans le niveau du raisonnement déontologique des praticiens. En particulier, les c.a. exerçant à tous les échelons hiérarchiques dans des cabinets canadiens obtiennent des «scores de moralité» (*DIT P scores*) plus élevés et moins homogènes au test d'identification des valeurs que les *CPA* des cabinets américains. Autrement dit, le processus auquel font allusion certaines études antérieures, à savoir la socialisation déontologique de toute personne débutant dans la profession comptable et s'y établissant, pourrait ne pas exister dans les cabinets canadiens.

La deuxième étude, consistant en une expérience sur le terrain, examinait la manière dont les c.a. et les *CPA* perçoivent la sous-estimation du nombre d'heures facturables, la conclusion prématurée de missions, le relâchement de l'effort au travail et le transfert d'heures de travail à d'autres missions facturables effectuées par le cabinet. Les résultats montrent que les praticiens (tant c.a. que *CPA*) dont le score de moralité est peu élevé ont moins tendance que ceux dont le score est élevé à considérer ces pratiques comme des réactions négatives ou dysfonctionnelles aux pressions causées par le travail. De même, la dernière étude examinait expérimentalement la relation entre le raisonnement déontologique et l'aptitude du vérificateur à reconnaître les caractéristiques d'une entreprise cliente ou de sa direction qui pourraient être importantes. Les résultats montrent que le niveau du raisonnement déontologique du vérificateur permet à ce dernier de mieux trier les indices déontologiques. En particulier, un vérificateur peut évaluer de façon plus efficace la compétence et l'intégrité de la direction de l'entreprise cliente si son score de moralité est plus élevé, surtout lorsque la direction passe pour avoir beaucoup de compétence mais peu d'intégrité.

Les résultats de ces trois études empiriques confirment que, dans un grand nombre de décisions prises par les vérificateurs, le raisonnement déontologique a un effet déterminant sur les choix déontologiques et le comportement professionnel. Parmi les décisions influencées par le raisonnement, on compte l'évaluation de la compétence et de l'intégrité des clients, l'importance relative en vérification et le risque lié à la vérification. Ces constatations devraient être intéressantes pour les chercheurs et les praticiens qui évoluent dans le domaine de la vérification. En effet, elles laissent entendre que l'évaluation de la performance d'un comptable ou d'un vérificateur ne saurait être complète si l'on ne tient pas compte de son raisonnement déontologique. Les études présentées ici permettront donc peut-être d'expliquer ce que l'expérience et la compétence à elles seules ne semblent pas justifier jusqu'à présent, à savoir les différences marquées qui existent entre les résultats obtenus par les divers comptables ou vérificateurs lorsqu'ils font appel à leur jugement professionnel pour évaluer l'entreprise cliente et sa direction.

Nous espérons que ces travaux seront utiles aux étudiants des deuxième et troisième cycles et aux chercheurs en déontologie ou en psychologie de l'éthique, particulièrement dans le domaine de la comptabilité et de la vérification. Les résultats de cette recherche devraient aussi aider les cabinets d'expertise comptable dans leurs efforts pour constamment améliorer la qualité du jugement professionnel exercé dans le cadre des services d'attestation et de conseil. Enfin, nous espérons que cette monographie sera utile à toute personne désirant s'informer sur la déontologie de la profession comptable et la promouvoir.

Preface

The evolution of the present-day accounting and auditing professions can be traced to the development of banking and commerce in the eighteenth century British Commonwealth (Previts [1986]). A sense of the public sentiment regarding the early accounting profession is illustrated in the following anecdotal commentary by the noted economist John Maynard Keynes [1919, p. 63] in his now famous work entitled *Economic Consequences of the Peace*:

> Watching the company, with six or seven senses not available to ordinary men, judging character, motive, and subconscious impulse and even what each was going to say next, and compounding with telepathic instinct the argument and appeal best suited to the vanity, weakness, or self-interest of his immediate auditor . . .

Over the years, the notion of professional ethics has emerged as the image of accountants was raised from that of financial historian to one of public fiduciary, or what some have termed "corporate watchdog" (Briloff [1966]). In reaction to public mistrust of Corporate America after the great stock market crash of 1929, the Securities and Exchange Commission (SEC) was established to ensure the quality, integrity and consistency of financial reports. Unable to enforce its mandated policy alone, however, the SEC delegated much of its authority and power to the accounting profession.

As a result of these events, an ethics code, including principles of conduct such as independence, objectivity and due professional care, was created with the hope that public accountants or auditors would not be involved with or be financially connected to the clients they were supposed to be auditing.[1] Not only was ethics a "state-of-mind" (Mautz and Sharaf [1961]), but it quickly became a matter of economics because accountants no longer had the ability to invest and prosper by their inside knowledge of the client organization and its management. Over the decades, the role of the auditor has changed in terms of the scope and nature of services provided to audit clients. In light of this changing role, auditors often confront situations that may compromise independence or objectivity, or give an appearance of questionable professional judgment.

In recognition of a changing environment, professional bodies, such as the American Institute of Certified Public Accountants (AICPA), the Institute of Internal Auditors (IIA), the Institute of Management Accountants (IMA), the Certified General Accountants' Association of Canada (CGA-Canada) and the Canadian Institute of Chartered Accountants (CICA), in recent years have attempted to restructure professional ethics in accounting or auditing, as reflected in revised codes of professional conduct for auditors and management accountants as well as new internal and external auditing standards. At the same time, there is also evidence of increasing governmental concern over the possible conflicts of interest between large public accounting firms and the clients they audit, brought about by a litigious business environment, recessions in global financial markets, crisis in the U.S. savings and loan industry and the demise of the seventh largest public accounting firm (Laventhol and Horwath). As a result, in 1990 Congressional legislators proposed radical changes in the way audit firms are selected and compensated for services rendered.[2]

Beyond political sentiment are the ethical demands of accountants and auditors in the professional domain. While it is difficult to assess the effect of an ever-changing business environment on professional judgment, a requisite to public policy should be a fundamental understanding of an individual's ethical choice and action in auditing practice. Thus, one important reason or purpose for exploring the influence of ethical reasoning on individual judgments within the professional domain is to provide evidence to corroborate or refute claims of diminishing ethical propriety as a result of recent changes in the business environment and accounting practice.

This monograph includes and extends the work of researchers who have examined ethical reasoning of auditing practitioners in professional practice. Its purpose is to explore the influence of ethical reasoning upon judgment and behaviour. Drawing upon cognitive-developmental theory, cross-cultural and experimental studies of auditing professionals from the United States and Canada were conducted using a psychometric measure of ethical reasoning. Research findings and corresponding implications for the practice and theory of auditing are reported in this work. In summary, results of these studies corroborate the importance of ethical reasoning as a determinant of ethical choice, professional judgment and behaviour in a wide array of audit decisions including the assessment of client competence and integrity, audit materiality and audit risk. These findings should be of consequence to auditing researchers and practitioners because they suggest that the examination of auditor task performance would be incomplete without considering the ethical reasoning of the individual auditor. Thus, the present collection of empirical studies may explain salient performance differences, heretofore not explained by experience or expertise, on tasks requiring the auditor to exercise professional judgment when evaluating the client organization and its management.

The manuscript is organized into seven chapters, wherein the first three provide the conceptual foundation for our work. Chapter 1 consists of two sections: part one provides the reader with the fundamental literature pertaining directly to the study of ethics in professional accounting and auditing, and part two introduces the cognitive-developmental framework utilized in all ensuing chapters. Chapter 2 describes the situational, environmental and psychological factors that often give rise to the plethora of ethical conflicts that abound in accounting and auditing practice. In Chapter 3, cognitive-developmental theory is applied to ethical judgment and behaviour in current professional practice via the illustration of three auditing cases and a discussion of prior research.

The next three chapters of the monograph report the results of empirical studies that employed experienced auditors at various position levels from international public accounting firms located in Ontario, Canada and the Northeast Region of the United States. Chapter 4 focuses on differences in the ethical reasoning capacities of individual auditing practitioners from public accounting firms in Canada and the United States. Utilizing a field experiment, Chapter 5 studies auditor perceptions of unethical behaviour in the workplace, including the underreporting of time, premature sign-off, slacking on the job and shifting time to another engagement. Chapter 6 examines the relationship between ethical reasoning and the auditor's ability to recognize potentially important attributes of the client organization and its management — culminating in audit risk judgments and the assessment of material error in financial statement information. Chapter 7 concludes the monograph with an in-depth discussion of the implications and limitations of the presented research findings for the practice and theory of auditing, and provides directions for possible future research.

In summary, this monograph is motivated by the work of researchers who have sought empirically to understand the influence of ethical reasoning on the judgment and decision-making abilities of accountants and auditors in professional practice. Its purpose is to assess the impact of cross-cultural differences between the Canadian and American auditing professions in shaping the ethical reasoning characteristics and judgments of individual practitioners in these countries. Taking this one step further, this research seeks to determine the influence of ethical reasoning on the auditor's ability to frame strategic auditing judgments such as audit risk and fraud. It is our hope that this book will be useful to anyone interested in conducting applied ethics research, especially in the fields of accounting, auditing, and business. In addition, the findings of this research may be of value to auditors and auditing firms in their ongoing attempt to improve the quality of audit judgment as well as the services provided to client organizations. To this end, we hope this monograph will be beneficial to all interested readers.

Lawrence A. Ponemon, Director
Center for Study of Ethics
and Behavior in Accounting
State University of New York
Binghamton, NY

David R. L. Gabhart, Professor
Department of Accountancy
Bentley College
Waltham, MA

Contents

Chapter 1

Introduction and Review of Ethics Literature

1.1 LITERATURE REVIEW

This monograph draws upon works in three related fields of study including: professional and business ethics, professional judgment in accounting and auditing, and the psychology of ethical reasoning. The ethical reality of most accounting or auditing practitioners is guided by two major (and often conflicting) factors — namely, professional responsibility and the economic needs of the firm. Thus, to comprehend fully the nature and extent of ethical judgment and behaviour in accounting and auditing, one must first understand the role of ethics in the broader context of professions and business organizations. Accordingly, a summary of important articles pertaining to professional socialization and business ethics is provided in the following subsection. This will be followed by a brief discussion of ethical judgment research in accounting and auditing.

Professional and Business Ethics

Because public accounting is deemed to be a legitimate profession in advanced industrial societies, to study ethics in accounting or auditing practice, one should first consider the role of professional status and stature on ethical behaviour. According to Greenwood [1957], professions are granted much greater control over their work than other occupations. In exchange for this autonomy, members of a profession are expected to obtain specialized training and demonstrate a high degree of ethical conduct. Bayles [1989] and Freidson [1971] also believe that occupations often employ a code of ethics to convince society that they are worthy of professional status. By showing the general public that their ethics codes are vigorously monitored and enforced, occupations such as medicine, law and accountancy have been allowed to practice autonomously. In recent years, society has become more reluctant to grant occupations complete autonomy because many believe that professionals have become more concerned with self-interest than with societal needs (Cullen [1978]; Davis [1982]; Benson [1982]).

A significant body of sociological literature on occupations attempts to differentiate professional from non-professional occupations. Organizational researchers have attempted to categorize occupations as either professional or non-professional based upon the presence of several attributes (Greenwood [1957]; Montagna [1974]; Wilensky [1964]). Sociologists generally agree that the following six attributes should be present for an occupation to be considered deserving of professional status:

- **Autonomy** that grants legitimate control over the work environment.
- **A set of values** that is oriented toward community interest rather than toward individual self-interest.
- **A body of knowledge** that is formulated into a systematic theory or set of theories.
- **A formalized educational process** that imparts a body of knowledge that the professional group decides is necessary.
- **A code of ethics** that governs relations with clients, colleagues, and other organizations.
- **Formal recognition** that grants status to the profession by society through means of licensing, thus limiting entry into the profession.

Autonomy is perhaps the most significant attribute that distinguishes professions from other occupations. Greenwood [1957] and Benson [1982] assert that the only truly important distinction between professions and other occupational groups is that professionals possess legitimate control over their work. The state grants autonomy, including the exclusive right to determine who can legitimately do the work and how the work should be done (Gaa [1986]). Professional autonomy is not absolute, however, since the state has ultimate sovereignty. As Freidson [1971, p. 44] suggests, the profession has, within the state-protected environment, sufficient power to control virtually all facets of its work without serious interference from any lay group.

Through a process of political negotiation and persuasion, members of an occupation may be able to persuade society to confer professional stature and the right to self-govern. To be granted autonomy, an occupation should demonstrate a high level of specialized knowledge and skill, and, perhaps most importantly, trustworthiness. Many emphasize the importance of a code of ethical conduct as a means of persuading the state to grant an occupation professional status (Benson [1982]). Along these lines, Freidson [1971, p. 83] expresses his belief about the implicit role of an ethics code:

> A code of ethics may be seen as a formal method of declaring to all that the occupation can be trusted, and so of persuading society to grant the special status of autonomy. The very existence of such a code implies that individual members of the occupation have the personal qualities of professionalism, the imputation of which is also useful for obtaining autonomy. Thus most of the commonly cited attributes of professions may be seen either as consequences of autonomy or as conditions useful for persuading the public and the body politic to grant such autonomy.

A code of ethics is an important device for persuading the general public to believe that members of an occupation are ethical, but it does not guarantee public support nor does it guarantee that members of the occupation actually comply with the code. Thus, a code of ethics may be seen as an occupation's method of influencing society's opinion about its members without directly affecting their behaviour or professional conduct. Once a profession is established and is granted the protection of autonomy, it should recognize that autonomy is conditional, rather than absolute, since the state has ultimate sovereignty. Consequently, if a profession's work or behaviour is not consistent with societal expectations, the profession may have difficulty surviving.

To complete our understanding of ethics in accounting and auditing, one also must understand the influence of business pressure on the individual practitioner's ethical conduct. As a starting point, consider the field of business ethics, which has been typically studied by the descriptive analysis of human behavioural attributes, including:

1. the values guiding human conduct
2. the obligations and responsibilities of agents and institutions
3. predictable outcomes in human costs and benefits
4. character traits and dispositions (Troy and Jones [1982]).

Underlying these attributes is the promotion of human welfare and the support of principled (moral) reasoning. In essence, business ethics broadly encompasses individual judgment, reasoning and action as well as the policies and practices of an organization. The study of business ethics can be further subdivided into two general components.

The first component, personal ethics, deals with the ethical choices of the individual employee or manager. The second component, social ethics, pertains to the deliberate actions and activities conducted by a business enterprise in its dealings with the public. Most business firms are concerned with personal ethics, which is typically defined as the correctness of an employee's behaviour in terms of some organizational credo or norms of behaviour. Often these norms are formalized into a written standard or code of ethical conduct. As noted by Downie [1971], social ethics pertains to the global activities of an enterprise in its dealings with other businesses, its employees or the final consumer of its products or services. Unlike personal ethics, it rarely conforms to a formalized code of conduct and is usually measured in terms of conformity to other business organizations or is steeped in tradition.

The formal study of business ethics is a relatively new field of social science. Drawing from the Judeo-Christian ethical tradition and common law, the study of business ethics evolved in response to the increased complexity of business organizations. Many managers and business entrepreneurs believed that a more refined, intellectually rigorous, and practical application of ethics to business organizations was required because the traditional means of ethical governance, the marketplace and the law, all ceased to be effective (Galambos [1975]; Galbraith [1976]). Thus, the ambition of early researchers in this area was to develop an optimal set of values that could serve to guide all business decisions (see, for example, Baumhart [1968]).

The universality of ethics in business operates on the fundamental assumption that a human being has a purpose for existing, and one ought to behave in order to realize that purpose (Nozick [1975]). Thus, the search for a purpose in life involves an individual's attempt to discover a relationship between oneself and a larger social context. This extends to daily activities within the work environment where an individual strives to believe that what one is doing is worthwhile (Graham [1986]). Clearly, then the lack of job satisfaction or goal congruity for the individual can be a significant source of emotional stress and conflict. Applied business ethics always involves the study of conflict, and conflict always involves choice. That is, whenever an individual in the business environment considers "what ought to be done?" or "what should be done?" the ethical process is engaged. Here the individual seeks some resolution to a conflict by choosing the "right thing" for that particular situation at that time (Donaldson [1980]). There are many conflicts that managers face within the business environment. For example, an irreconcilable conflict results when a business person ceases to believe in the goodness of the firm or its product. Typical situations causing conflict for the manager include: honesty versus tact, competition versus cooperation and failure versus the abuse of society (Donaldson and Werhane [1979]).

Rapid growth, diversification and expansion of many organizations (including accounting firms), may have contributed to the decline of the individual's sense of ethical responsibility or morality in the workplace. Ethicists argue that the lack of adequate standards of conduct in many corporations is causing the decay of principled behaviour in society by allowing business executives to hide behind a corporate veil (Beauchamp and Bowie [1988]; Brenner and Molander [1977]; Donaldson [1982]; Dunfee [1991]). Even if high ethical standards are encouraged by a corporation, organizational researchers have found that actual ethical choices often follow the norms and conventions established by an immediate reference group rather than the organization as a whole (Greenberger, Miceli and Cohen [1987]; Jansen and Von Glinow [1985]). Taking this one step further, some business ethics practitioners and researchers have sought to find ways of effectively raising the ethical consciousness of work groups in the context of business organizations.

Powers and Vogel [1980] make a distinction between professional and managerial ethics. They state that the profession is an instrument of the practitioner, while the manager is an instrument of the organization. Hence, these authors contend that a member of a profession contributes directly to human welfare through some public or humanitarian service, while a manager contributes indirectly to the social good. Because of the service-to-society relationship, the professional often has much more at stake in the event of ethical impropriety. In contrast, the manager is sheltered, in part, by the corporate entity. Even though the stakes are lower, managers must still be concerned with ethical propriety in their place of business. Taking this idea one step further, Drucker [1981] suggests that the secret of business success involves the integration of the manager's ethic into the philosophies of the organization. When the integration is complete, the organization is capable of maximizing its social welfare as well as the needs of society.

A common theme found in much of the business ethics literature is that ethics start at the level of the individual employee or manager. Here, the ethical concerns of individuals pervade the moral atmosphere of the organization. Thus, the most effective strategy for improving organizational ethics is to raise the ethical consciousness of each individual in the workplace. Knowledge of ethics alone, however, is insufficient to improve the overall level of ethical behaviour. Such knowledge, in conjunction with an integral understanding of human cognition, can prove helpful in developing the ethical or moral reasoning skills of individuals within a business enterprise or when dealing with the public at large.

Ethical Behaviour in Accounting and Auditing

Research on ethical conflict and ethical decision making in auditing has typically focused on environmental or psychological factors that cause dysfunctional behaviour or that bring about compliance with professional standards. Goldman and Barlev [1974] explain conflicts intrinsic to the auditing role and define an imbalance of power between clients and auditors, with management usually having the upper hand. They argue that client management can exert control over audit conflict because they have an ability to hire or dismiss the auditor, determine the audit fees, and determine the work conditions. Following the same line of reasoning, others have found that management is more likely to obtain its preferred resolution in a conflict when it is not dealt with precisely by technical standards (Nichols and Price [1976]). In contrast, some have found that auditor's influence over the client increases if services rendered are nonrecurring and of direct benefit to the client (Knapp [1985]).

Building on this research premise, other studies have used methodologies such as game theory (Antle [1984]; Datar [1985]), positive economics (Watts and Zimmerman [1981], or DeAngelo [1981], and economic analysis (Raghunathan [1986]) to describe accountants' behaviour regarding compliance with the standards of independence and objectivity. Because these studies deal with macro issues within an economic framework, results do not provide many insights into the practitioner's belief system or state of mind prior to framing ethical judgment.

Six doctoral dissertations have attempted to gain a fundamental understanding of the ethical decision-making process in the auditing profession. Works by Loeb [1970], Yerkes [1975], Schilit [1981], Armstrong [1984], Ponemon [1988] and Shaub [1989] provide evidence of problems in the way individual practitioners frame, attend to or resolve ethical issues in professional practice. Stephen Loeb [1970] was the first to investigate factors that could explain unethical behaviour in the professional auditing community by using a survey containing hypothetical ethical scenarios. His findings show that accountants with high-status clients experienced less pressure to violate ethical norms than accountants with low-status clients. In addition, Loeb found that CPAs with marginal auditing practices had greater vulnerability to client pressure and would be more likely to violate the ethics code for economic incentives. He also found that as the CPA's opportunity to violate the code of ethics increased, so did the frequency with which he or she did not comply with the code. Further, a "strict" office attitude was likely to decrease the willingness of its members to violate the code, while a "permissive" attitude was likely to reinforce the accountant's vulnerability to outside pressures to violate it. Finally, and perhaps most importantly, an accountant's ethical behaviour was affected by his or her knowledge of and concern for ethical issues, attentiveness to ethical problems, and membership in the AICPA.

Using a survey instrument similar to that used by Loeb [1970], Russell Yerkes [1975] compared CPAs from large and small accounting firms. He found that accountant's social position within the firm influenced his or her adherence to the code of ethics, though members in larger CPA firms had the highest degree of conformity to the AICPA's rules. He attributed firm differences to the fact that national firms have relatively large auditing departments as compared to local or solo practices. Finally, he found that CPAs and public accountants in very small local firms were least likely to adhere to the ethics code. In a similar study, Schilit [1981] analyzed auditors' independence judgment for a sample of CPAs and found that most CPAs were willing to violate at least one or more independence rulings as prescribed by the AICPA.

Mary Beth Armstrong [1984] attempted to model what she termed the internalized professional ethic of accounting students and practitioners using a psychometric instrument called the Defining Issues Test (DIT) and Loeb's [1970] ethics survey. While DIT results were not correlated to survey responses, she found that the moral reasoning of CPAs and students majoring in accounting tended to conform to lower levels of ethical cognition than the general population of college-educated adults and college seniors, respectively. Apropos of this finding, Armstrong [1984, p. 105] writes:

> One of the greatest contributions of the research study is this identification of the essential differences between Hi P CPAs (e.g., P Scores closer to 1.00 [100%]) and other respondents. How can the research results be used to aid universities and CPA firms in their efforts to enhance the moral development of students and staff? In the researcher's opinion, the results indicate that teaching emphasis should not be placed solely on the content of the AICPA Code of Professional Ethics. To teach CPAs and students how to categorize conflict is sub-optimal, if full moral maturity is considered optimal.

Ponemon [1988] and Shaub [1989] extended Armstrong's dissertation. These studies differ from earlier works in three major respects. First, their research used a measure of ethical reasoning rather than self-reported adherence to a code of ethics as a surrogate (proxy variable) for ethical behaviour in accounting and auditing. Second, both dissertations provided a basis for evaluating the interaction of ethical behaviour to a number of situational or environmental factors in the accounting firm or audit setting. Third, both studies demonstrate the applicability of cognitive-developmental theory to the study of ethical reasoning and moral development in the domain of auditing practice using two different psychometrics of moral development. In summary, both Ponemon [1988] and Shaub [1989] found an association between ethical reasoning and position level in public accounting firms, wherein ethical stages seemed to decrease steadily in the manager and partner ranks. Ponemon [1988] suggests that this net decrease in measured ethical cognition may be caused by self-selection or selection-socialization within the public accounting profession.

Based upon the work of Kohlberg [1969] and Rest [1979a], several recently published empirical studies have also examined accounting and auditing professionals in terms of their level of ethical reasoning (Armstrong [1987]; Arnold and Ponemon [1991]; Lampe and Finn [1993]; Ponemon [1990, 1992a, 1992b]; Ponemon and Gabhart [1990]; Ponemon and Glazer [1990]; St. Pierre, Nelson and Gabbin [1990]). Most of these studies report that professional accountants and accounting students do not develop ethical reasoning capacities commensurate with individuals having similar social, economic, or educational backgrounds. For example, using the DIT on a sample of accounting students and practitioners, Armstrong [1987, p. 33] writes, "CPA respondents appear to have reached the moral maturation level of adults in general, instead of maturing even to the level of college students, much less to the level of college graduates. In other words, their college education may not have fostered continued moral growth."

Ponemon [1990, 1992a] studied accountants at various position levels in public firms. His cross-sectional and longitudinal studies revealed a marked negative association between accountants' position level within the firm and their level of ethical reasoning. Ponemon [1990, p. 206] writes, "This work suggests that differences in ethical behaviour are likely to reflect differences in socialization; thus different positions in a firm's hierarchy are likely to engender different ethical proclivities." He also finds that, by virtue of a strong rule-oriented firm culture, ". . . the ethical values encouraged by (CPA) firm management are inconsistent with higher levels of ethical reasoning. As a result, the ethical development of those entering and remaining in the accounting profession is stymied" [1992a, p.30]. In attempting to explain this finding, Ponemon [1992a, p. 32] suggests that traditional accounting education may constrain moral development and, therefore, he argues that ". . . ethics education in accounting should be replaced by formal courses and programs that foster the highest order of ethical reasoning."

To test the influence of college education on accountants' moral development, Ponemon and Glazer [1990] examined accounting students and alumni from a small liberal arts college and large state university. Using the DIT, they found that only accounting seniors and alumni of the liberal arts college progressed to levels of ethical reasoning comparable to the DIT norms published by Rest [1986]. They conclude [1990, p. 204] that differences in students' moral development, ". . . may be caused, in part, by an educational process that inhibits students' abilities to develop an increasing sense of ethics, integrity or moral beliefs during the college years. These findings suggest that liberal learning in college may be an important factor in the development of students' and accounting practitioners' moral reasoning." Other studies confirm Ponemon and Glazer's findings, showing that students of traditional accounting programs may not be developing to higher levels of ethical reasoning (Holt and Jeffrey [1991]; Lampe and Finn [1993]). The following section briefly describes the underlying theory employed in the aforementioned ethics studies in the accounting and auditing literature.

1.2 THE PSYCHOLOGY OF ETHICAL REASONING

The psychology of ethical reasoning is a field of social science research and theory. Unlike the philosophical treatment of morality where norms are developed and ideals postulated, moral psychology focuses on the individual's conception of ethical behaviour and how one's belief system dictates conflict resolution and problem solving in everyday living. This area of psychology is researched according to two major theoretical approaches:

1. behaviourism
2. cognitive-developmental theory.

Behavioural psychology asserts that all behaviour can be accounted for by operant conditioning, or the modeling of the functional relationships between stimulus conditions and behaviour. Here, moral reasoning is explained as simply a quantitative accumulation of data, organized into a pattern according to the amount and types of reinforcement one has experienced.

Cognitive-developmental theory, which is the basis of this research, is the most widely used approach to the study of ethical cognition and reasoning. The theory is based upon the intellectual processes of assimilation and accommodation from which the individual develops moral reasoning capabilities. In turn, this intellectual capacity forms the governing unit that directs an individual's moral development. Psychologists also theorize that an individual actually proceeds through a series of stages reaching maturity (Kohlberg [1984]).

In this section, significant research of ethical cognition will be examined. Specifically, the works of Jean Piaget, Lawrence Kohlberg and James Rest will be discussed in detail. The next chapter will apply the foundations of this theory to the study of ethics in the accounting and auditing environment.

Jean Piaget and Cognitive Moral Development

Over 50 years ago, the noted psychologist and scholar Jean Piaget explored the moral judgments of children while observing them as they played the game of marbles. From these observations, Piaget gained an insight into a child's developmental process as it pertains to a conception of morality. From this preliminary study, Piaget derived a framework on the consciousness of rules present in children and young adults during the development of their moral judgment. He describes this framework as "stages in conceptualization." According to Piaget, an individual's moral reasoning ability develops through social intercourse in a series of stages over the life cycle, and is particularly vulnerable during adolescence and young adulthood (Piaget 1932 [1966]).

Piaget used a clinical interview technique to determine the underlying structure of children's spontaneous moral reasoning. He typically began his interviews by reading the child a story or a pair of stories about children's transgressions and then proceeded to probe the child's thinking further. For example, he asked who was more mischievous — a boy who unintentionally broke one cup while sneaking a cookie, or eight cups while helping his mother? After his subject responded, Piaget continued to probe, asking "why?" and other questions designed to elicit the world view of the child. Through these conversations with children, Piaget identified two major stages of moral development. The developmentally earlier stage he called "autonomous morality" or a "morality of constraint." The later stage he called a "morality of cooperation," or heteronomous morality. These two stages differ on nine dimensions (Lickona [1976, p. 220]):

1. Absolutism of moral perspective, as opposed to awareness of differing viewpoints.
2. Conception of rules as unchangeable, as opposed to a view of rules as flexible.
3. Belief in inevitable punishment (imminent justice) for wrong doing as opposed to a naturalistic conception of punishment.
4. Objective responsibility in judging blame as opposed to consideration of the actor's intentions.
5. Definition of moral wrongness in terms of what is forbidden or punished, as opposed to what violates the spirit of cooperation.
6. Belief in arbitrary or expurgatory punishment, as opposed to belief in restitution or reciprocity-based punishment.
7. Approval of authority's punishment of peer aggression, as opposed to approval of eye-for-an-eye retaliation by the victim.
8. Approval of arbitrary, unequal distribution of goods or rewards by authority, as opposed to insistence on equal distribution.
9. Definition of duty as obedience to authority, as opposed to allegiance to the principle of equality or concern for the welfare of others.

Piaget held that all children make the transition from a morality of constraint to a morality of cooperation unless their development is retarded by deprivation of opportunities for reciprocal social interaction. Through this same interaction, children acquire a sense of justice, which is the essential element of heteronomous morality. Piaget proposed three steps in the development of this sense of justice or fairness. In the first period, justice cannot be distinguished from an internalized sense of duty or a need to abide by adult authority. The second step is a period of development towards heteronomy where equality gradually supersedes authority. The third and final step is a period in which equity replaces equality. Here equity is similar to the judgment of equality, but it differs in one major respect. That is, equity seeks a classical utilitarian orientation that promotes the greatest good for the greatest number of people, whereas equality seeks to allocate good in equal proportions to everyone.

To summarize, Piaget described the process of moral development in terms of an individual's emerging conception of justice arising from his or her peer interaction. The integration of cognitive and social factors leads to the development of moral heteronomy, and to a mature sense of justice. Piaget's theory, which was based solely on interview data, was the first attempt to view morality as a developmental process. Thus, Piaget is frequently cited as the proverbial father of the field of moral development by most psychologists.

Lawrence Kohlberg and the Six Stages of Moral Development

Lawrence Kohlberg examined the stage theory of moral development as postulated by Piaget. Kohlberg's aim was to define the process by which an individual reasons to act according to some self-chosen moral principle. Based on direct observation of adolescents and young adults and interview data collected for his doctoral dissertation at the University of Chicago, Kohlberg derived a model of the conceptualization of ethical judgment that he defined as a series of developmental stages (Kohlberg [1958]). That is, an individual's moral judgment is developed through a series of six stages somewhat akin to the rungs of a ladder. At any given point in time, each individual is at a specific stage, or step, in the developmental process, and proceeds to the next step at a pace dictated by one's internalized belief system.

Kohlberg developed this model by examining an individual's actual resolution of hypothetical moral conflicts (e.g., the Heinz Dilemma discussed later). From those responses, he noted that each individual's resolution was grounded in some notion of justice. By applying this test in longitudinal and cross-cultural studies, he noted a very broad developmental process (Kohlberg [1969]), which he described as a consecutive series of moral judgment levels. That is, over time, individuals progress upwardly through these developmental levels beginning at what Kohlberg [1969] terms "pre-conventional morality," to the second level termed "conventional morality" and sometimes to the final and highest level called "post-conventional morality."

One way to understand the three levels is to think of them as three different types of relationships between the self and society's rules and expectations. Thus, to the pre-conventional person, rules and social expectations are something external to self; a conventional person identifies self in relation to others; a post-conventional person differentiates himself from the rules and expectations of others and defines his values in terms of self-chosen principles (Kohlberg [1984]).

The basis for evaluating an individual's ethical capacity is a standardized series of hypothetical conflicts. For example, the most well used ethical conflict is called the "Heinz Dilemma" (Colby and Kohlberg [1987, p. 241]):

> In Europe, a woman was near death from a kind of Cancer. There was one drug that the doctors thought might save her. It was a form of radium that a druggist in the same town had recently discovered. The drug was expensive to make, but the druggist was charging ten times what the drug cost him to make. He paid $400 for the radium and charges $4,000 for a small dose of the drug. The sick woman's husband Heinz, went to everyone he knew to borrow the money and tried every legal means, but he could only get together about $2,000 that is half of what it cost. He told the druggist that his wife was dying, and asked him to sell it cheaper or let him pay later. But the druggist said, "No, I discovered the drug and I'm going to make money from it." So having tried every legal means, Heinz gets desperate and considers breaking into the man's store to steal for his wife.

It is assumed that there is only one cure, which is a drug created and owned by the druggist, and that Heinz lacks the money necessary to purchase the drug, and thus must make a choice: should he steal the drug or should he abide by the law? The subjects are asked to resolve the conflict and state their opinions.

Using the Heinz Dilemma as a measure of an individual's conception of ethical behaviour, we might expect the following resolutions to the problems from someone at the three different levels:[3]

- The **pre-conventional** person might believe that stealing the drug is acceptable if the penalties of getting caught are low enough.
- The **conventional** person might believe that stealing the drug is the choice that does the least harm to others — but still believes that breaking the law is unequivocally wrong.
- The **post-conventional** person might declare that stealing the drug is necessary, and would specify that the underlying principle of life is far more important than personal property.

Kohlberg's model then partitions two developmental stages within each of the three levels of ethical judgment, producing a total of six discrete stages. For example, pre-conventional behaviour consists of a lower order belief system termed "Stage 1" where an individual chooses to do right to simply avoid punishment, and a higher order belief system termed "Stage 2" where an individual chooses to do right only when it serves one's own immediate interest. In this model, ethical stage is defined in terms of the individual's recognition of right and wrong. Exhibit 1.1 illustrates the six stages of ethical judgment, showing how individuals at each stage of development perceive an ethical choice and the corresponding reason for choosing an ethical action.

While the theory deals with a mode of thinking, individuals at higher moral stages are not necessarily at higher intellectual states. For example, Kohlberg [1984, pp. 64-65] reports that an individual with a very high IQ could be at the middle or lower stages in this model. It is also important to note that the model is *cognitive* in that it attempts to explain how a person thinks; it is *structural* in that it describes an underlying mental process; it is *developmental* in that the structure develops within an individual over time; it is *sequential* in that the development progresses in order and only in one direction (i.e. one only goes up the ladder and only one step at a time) and consists of six discrete identifiable stages. Rest [1979a], on the other hand, posits that while one stage might dominate an individual's reasoning capacity, he or she is never simply at one stage of cognition.

Standard Issue Scoring was developed by Kohlberg and his colleagues to overcome the limitations of the earlier interview scoring techniques. The major contribution of this method is that it provides greater objectivity and reliability in scoring by specifying structural criteria that clearly and concisely define the moral development sequence. The basis of Standard Issue Scoring is a moral construct that specifies cognition to a particular norm, issue and stage of development. Colby and Kohlberg [1987, p. 40] write:

> This change from an intuitive scoring method to a standard scoring technique maintains the hermeneutic or phenomenological orientation but reflects a change from a view of interpretation as art to a view of interpretation as a science, i.e., as a research activity employing an objective and reliable method of observation. This method, however, still rests on the communicative stance of an interpreter, not on the positivistic stance of someone trying to classify and predict behaviour as distinct from meaning.

Exhibit 1.1

Kohlberg's Six Stages of Ethical Reasoning

STAGE	WHAT IS RIGHT?	REASONS FOR DOING IT
	Pre-conventional level	
Stage 1	Avoid breaking rules backed by punishment	Avoidance of punishment or harm to self
Stage 2	Follow rules if they are in own interest	To serve one's own immediate interest
	Conventional level	
Stage 3	Living up to what is expected by people	Need to be a good person in the eyes of others
Stage 4	Fulfilling agreed-to duties and obligations	To keep the social institutions going
	Post-conventional level	
Stage 5	Upholding non-relative obligations first	Obligation to law before social contracts.
Stage 6	Follow self-chosen ethical principles	Belief in ideal as a rational person

Adopted from Kohlberg [1969].

The scoring technique was constructed from verbal reports (transcript data) collected from a multitude of cross-sectional and longitudinal research studies. Here, the researchers were particularly concerned about the problem of circularity (or theoretical verification as a self-fulfilling prophecy). Keeping this in mind, the technique emerged from clearly defined scoring units that are termed interview judgments. A set of related interview judgments form the basis of the criterion judgment that is the foundation of a stage scoring assignment for a particular individual.[4]

To measure an individual's ethical reasoning capacity, the researcher applies a fairly elaborate scoring technique that carefully examines and analyzes verbal protocols. Each resolution can be defined in terms of three discrete and global aspects that are defined as:[5]

- **Issues:** the broad aspect of a dilemma and is utilized as a cue or signal by the individual in the formation of a judgment.
- **Moral norm:** the frame surrounding an issue or cue, forming a logical structure of judgment.
- **Modal element:** the reason given for endowing the norm with value.

Within each issue, the individual's resolution is grounded in some notion of morality or ethics that is termed the moral norm. The justification behind the norm is the element. In the Heinz Dilemma, the "issue" is simply human life versus the law. The reason for selecting one issue over another is the "moral norm" and the rationale behind this norm is the "modal element". The individual's verbal conclusions are scored by the union of the issue, norm and element forming what is termed an "issue judgment", and the sum of these issue judgments form the "criterion judgment", which is the basis for completing an ethical stage measure. Exhibit 1.2 reports the most frequently cited moral norms and moral elements compiled from a vast body of research and literature (Colby and Kohlberg [1987, pp. 166-168]).[6]

The Moral Judgment Interview (MJI) is used to determine an individual's stage of ethical cognition. As mentioned above, the methodology employs a series of hypothetical dilemmas that are used to evaluate moral thought and cognitive capacity for a single individual. The first series of standardized interviews was developed by Kohlberg in his 1958 doctoral dissertation at the University of Chicago. Here, Kohlberg developed clinical and semistructured "mock" case studies based upon several moral dilemmas. One of these original cases, which is still used in the current version of the MJI interview, is the "Heinz

Exhibit 1.2

Procedural Elements for Standard Issues Scoring

The Moral Norms

1. Life
   a. Preservation
   b. Quality/quantity
2. Property
3. Truth
4. Affiliation
5. Erotic love and sex
6. Authority
7. Law
8. Contract
9. Civil Rights
10. Religion
11. Conscience
12. Punishment

The Moral Elements

Upholding normative order

1. Obeying/consulting persons or deity. Should obey, get consent (should consult, persuade)
2. Blaming/approving. Should be blamed for, disapproved (should be approved)
3. Retributing/exonerating. Should retribute against (should exonerate)
4. Having a right/having no right
5. Having a duty/having no duty

Egoistic consequences

6. Good reputation/bad reputation
7. Seeking rewards/avoiding punishment

Utilitarian consequences

8. Good individual consequences/bad individual consequences
9. Good group consequences/bad group consequences

Ideal or harmony serving consequences

10. Upholding character
11. Upholding self-respect
12. Serving social ideal or harmony
13. Serving human dignity and autonomy

Fairness

14. Balancing perspectives or role taking
15. Reciprocity or positive deserts
16. Maintaining equity and procedural fairness
17. Maintaining social contract or freely agreeing

Based on Colby and Kohlberg [1987, p. 167].

Dilemma". To evaluate each individual's moral resolution to the dilemma, he employed a sentence and story rating technique following the work of Piaget (1932 [1966]) and Weber [1949].

The MJI was constructed in such a way as to maximize the breadth and depth of moral judgments required for evaluation and stage score assignment under Standard Issue Scoring, discussed earlier. The present version of the MJI consists of three parallel forms (A, B, and C). Each form contains three hypothetical moral dilemmas, from which a standardized scoring manual was compiled. Each dilemma is grounded in two significant moral issues, and several underlying moral structures (elements and norms) from which the individual forms his or her judgment. For example, in the Heinz dilemma, the individual must express a broad moral value that is either preservation of life or upholding law. Within this choice are a host of moral structures from which the individual forms a moral thought process. Kohlberg [1984] suggests that these structures are quite diverse, ranging from a grounding that prescribes the avoidance of harm at all costs (Stage 1) to the seeking of universally applicable moral principles (Stage 6).

Diversity of Research

The theory of ethical reasoning and moral development, as advanced by Kohlberg and others, has been shown to be of consequence in applied psychological research, including studies of criminal behaviour (Kohlberg, Hickey and Scharf [1972]), moral atmosphere within organizations (Higgins, Powers and Kohlberg [1984]), whistle-blowing judgment (Brabeck [1984]; Arnold and Ponemon [1991]; Finn and Lampe [1992]) and ethical decision making in the business environment (Carmella [1985]; Derry [1989]; Trevino [1986]; Trevino and Youngblood [1990]). As previously mentioned, several recently completed studies have examined accounting or auditing professionals' ethical reasoning and development.[7]

An interesting area of moral development research that is directly applicable to the study of professional judgment in the accounting or auditing domain is the study of an organization's moral atmosphere. Such research attempts to describe the environmental and situational factors that seemingly promote or curtail an individual's advancement in terms of moral thought, reasoning and capacity. Kohlberg [1984, p. 201] describes moral atmosphere in the context of his work:

> Beyond provision of role-taking opportunities by groups and institutions, how do we define the moral atmosphere of a group or institution? We have said that the core of a specifically moral component of moral judgment is a sense of justice. While role-taking defines the conflicting points of view taken in a moral situation, the "principles" for resolving conflicting points of view at each stage are principles of justice, of giving each his or her due. The core of the moral atmosphere of an institution or environment, then, is its justice structure . . . the way in which social institutions distribute fundamental rights and duties and determine the division of advantages from social cooperation.

The notion of moral atmosphere is based on the principles of justice judgment making. The aims of such research are to determine those external variables that seemingly interact with the individual's moral development process, and to understand the power and relationship of this underlying interaction to various modes of ethical thought. Studies of moral atmosphere apply to a wide variety of organizational and social settings including the U.S. Army during the Vietnam War (Candee [1976]), the federal government during the Watergate investigation (Candee [1975]), the prison system (Kohlberg, Hickey and Scharf [1972]), public schools (Power and Reimer [1978]; Higgins, Powers and Kohlberg [1984]) and, most recently, national public accounting firms (Ponemon [1990, 1992a]).

Critiques of the Theory

Over the years the stage theory and underlying methodology utilized in the measurement and classification of an individual's ethical stage have been refined and enhanced. From the results of longitudinal studies, Kohlberg noted an apparent violation of the invariant stage sequence assumption that states that individuals progress in only one direction throughout their lives. Here the data suggest what Kohlberg termed "retrogression" in responses, or movement from higher to lower stages, in certain subjects. Analyzing these data more closely led Kohlberg and Kramer [1969] to reinterpret the model where such responses represented transitional movement from one ethical level to the next highest level. For example the movement from the conventional level (Stage 4) to the post-conventional (Stage 5) often gives the appearance of lower order ethical behaviour patterns. Such transitional progression to a higher ethical level was incorrectly measured as downward movement (e.g., retrogression) in the six-stage model.

A second problem with the research is the lack of a truly objective measurement-elicitation instrument. Because of overt criticism of Kohlberg's seemingly subjective scoring scheme (Kurtines and Greif [1974]), Kohlberg and colleagues at Harvard set out to develop a more valid and reliable moral development measurement tool (Colby and Kohlberg [1987]). This effort brought about the Standard Issue Scoring System (described earlier), which lends itself to a systematic content analysis of interview data.

The third major criticism of Kohlberg's theory is that his model is based on justice reasoning. Critics argue that this mode of morality is only a subset of the ethics domain (Simpson [1974]). Some believe that such an approach overlooks other moral orientations such as caring or concern for others. As a result, individuals that possess moral values outside the realm of justice, per se, may be incorrectly specified within the six-stage developmental model (see Gilligan [1977]; Lyons [1982]; Murphy and Gilligan [1980]).

A fourth area of contention is the existence of the highest level of ethical cognition. Much of the moral development research provides empirical evidence that individuals tend not to progress beyond a Stage 5 orientation (Kuhn [1980]). Kohlberg, Levine and Hewer [1983] suggest that this occurs for two reasons. First, contextual limitations within the hypothetical dilemma series used to elicit an individual's moral capacity are inadequate for evaluating Stage 6 resolutions. Second, the vast majority of individuals in our society are at the conventional and pre-conventional levels, with very few ever developing beyond the fifth stage. Kohlberg argues that researchers have not had the opportunity to analyze individuals at the highest ethical state because of an inadequate sampling of subjects. According to Colby and Kohlberg [1987, p. 40]:

> The question of whether Stage 6 should be included as a natural psychological stage in the moral development sequence will remain unresolved until research (using more appropriate moral dilemmas and interviewing techniques) is conducted with a special sample of people likely to have developed beyond Stage 5.

James Rest and the Defining Issues Test

Scoring reliability and data collection difficulties using the MJI led to the development of a psychometric instrument that could be scored objectively. James Rest [1979b] developed the Defining Issues Test (DIT), which is a self-administered questionnaire that elicits ethical reasoning and judgment responses and is consistent with the Kohlberg stage-sequence theory [Rest 1979a]. The DIT presents subjects with six hypothetical moral dilemmas and a set of standard responses conforming to the six-stage model. The subject is required to select for each case the four factors that had the greatest influence on his or her resolution.

Each of Rest's responses represents the type of thinking typical in one of the six stages of moral development. In scoring the questionnaire, points are assigned to a subject's responses as follows: 4 points for the most important response, 3 points for the second most important, 2 points for the third most important, and 1 point for the fourth most important response. All other responses are ignored. Points corresponding to Stages 5 and 6 responses are added and that total is divided by the number of dilemmas used. The result is known as the subject's "P" score. Rest describes it as "the relative importance a subject gives to principled moral considerations in making a decision about moral dilemmas" [Rest 1979a, p. 5]. Why does Rest choose a "P" score, which is a continuous number from 0 to 95, instead of identifying a certain stage associated with each subject? His rationale is [1979a, p. 63]:

> The notion that a person either has or has not a stage is wrong. The manifestation of certain thought organization is not an all-or-nothing matter. The question of developmental assessment should not be what state is a person in? But rather, to what extent and under what conditions does a person manifest the various types of organizations of thinking?

In addition, Rest [1979a, pp. 63-64] states:

> Developmental assessment is probabilistic .... No pure, direct assessment of cognitive structure exists that is unaffected by the specific task, content, and response characteristics of the situation .... Therefore the manifestation of a particular cognitive structure in a particular set of tasks gives us only a probabilistic indication whether that cognitive structure would be manifest in any other set of tasks.

Clearly, a continuous rather than discrete form of measurement is a radical departure from Kohlberg's [1984] theory in that individuals can possess the capacity to reason at more than one cognitive stage for any given moral dilemma in any particular situation.

The Four-Component Model

In addition to the DIT, Rest develops a broader concept of ethical capacity. Rest [1986, pp. 3-15] defines the "Four-Component Model" as four basic psychological processes that underlie all moral behaviour and action:

- **Component 1** describes how the individual interprets the situation surrounding a particular set of ethical actions and alternatives. Here the individual considers the welfare of those affected by possible actions.

- **Component 2** describes the process from which an individual selects among the various courses of action available, a single "best" ethical choice. Rest suggests that the works of Piaget and Kohlberg have primarily focused on this aspect of moral reasoning.

- **Component 3** describes the assigning of "moral value" among other values to the moral course of action selected. Rest [1986, p. 9] writes:

> Moral values are not the only values that people have. People value advancement in their careers, art, projects that they have worked long and hard on — many things besides fairness or morality. It is not unusual for non-moral values to be so strong and attractive that a person will choose a course of action that pre-empts or compromises the moral ideal.

- **Component 4** describes the process by which an individual follows through on a particular ethical choice. Many factors will foster or hinder an individual's ethical perseverance. Rest [1986, p. 11] states:

> Component 4 involves figuring out the sequence of concrete actions, working around impediments and unexpected difficulties, overcoming fatigue and frustration, resisting distractions and allurements, and keeping sight of the eventual goal. Perseverance, resoluteness, competence and character are attributes that lead to success.

In summary, the Four-Component Model provides a useful means of analyzing the present field of research and theory. It also provides a realistic mechanism for integrating the complex process of ethical cognition with ethical behaviour and action.

DIT Validity

Because the DIT is scored objectively, reliability and validity can be assessed more rigorously than is possible with Kohlberg's test. Test-retest reliability for the "P" score is generally in the high 70s or 80s and Cronbach's alpha index of consistency is generally in the high 70s (Rest [1979a]). Validity has been assessed in a number of ways (pp. 64-66):

- **Criterion-group validity** demonstrates that groups of subjects who ought to have different scores on a measure do in fact have different scores. For example, criterion group differentiation in some studies has accounted for nearly 50% of the variance scores.

- **Longitudinal change validity** shows changes in the direction of "higher stages" for subjects who are repeatedly retested over time. Several longitudinal studies are reported by Rest, all of which show significant upward trends. Cohort-sequential and time-sequential analyses indicate that this upward movement cannot be attributed to generational or cultural change as opposed to individual ontogenetic changes, neither can it be attributed to testing effects or sampling bias.

- **Covergent-divergent correlational validity** shows that variables that are theoretically more similar to moral judgment will have higher correlations with the DIT than variables that are theoretically dissimilar. In his 1979 and 1986 research monographs, Rest presents hundreds of correlations with other measures. With other measures of moral reasoning (Kohlberg's and others), the correlations are as high as the 60s and 70s, averaging about 0.50. With other measures of cognitive development and intelligence, the correlations are generally in the 20s to 50s range, averaging 0.36. With various measures of attitudes and personality, the correlations are usually nonsignificant or inconsistent, as are the correlations with demographic or sociological variables.

- **Validation through experimental enhancement studies** was also reported. If the DIT is measuring moral judgment, and if moral judgment is a distinctive domain of development, then experiences that focus on structural aspects of moral reasoning ought to be more effective in increasing DIT scores, in contrast to other kinds of experiences. At the same time, if the DIT is measuring underlying conceptual organization and not the mere learning of slogans, special vocabulary, or easily learned ideas, then progress in stimulation development will be slow and gradual, even if effective. Intervention studies clearly document the difficulty of artificially changing DIT scores.

- **Validation through experimental manipulation of test-taking sets** has also been reported. In some studies, one group of subjects is asked to "fake good answers" on the DIT, another group to "fake bad answers" and a third group is used as a control. These studies, with several variations, have shown that under the "fake bad" condition, scores were lower than under the usual conditions; but under the "fake good" condition, scores were no higher than under the normal condition. These findings would suggest that subjects can recognize items that are developmentally less advanced because presumably they had used that way of thinking at some previous time and had subsequently given it up. However, they cannot recognize items more advanced than their cognitive development.
- **Validation through studies of internal structure**, using multidimensional scaling and latent trait theory to scale the DIT items, has shown that the average scale value of items grouped according to their theoretical stage were ordered in the theoretical order: Stage 2 had the lowest average value, then Stage 3, and so on. This internal structure of the scale values of the stages was found on a sample of 1,080 subjects and replicated on a sample of 160.

To summarize, the main difference between Kohlberg's moral judgment interview and Rest's DIT questionnaire is that Kohlberg defines responses in terms of a series of discrete and invariant transitional stages, while Rest's approach is founded on a continuous variable that is termed the "P" score, which is the median representation, or most likely measure, of higher order ethical capacity (Colby and Kohlberg [1987]). Rest [1986] suggests that each individual operates using a range of possible cognitive structures that can span more that one developmental stage for any given ethical judgment. The development of ethical reasoning in this context can be thought of as an upwardly shifting distribution of cognitive structures rather than a single global shift in stages over an individual's life cycle. The "P" score is presented in a percentage form and can be thought of as the individual's utilization of Kohlberg's post-conventional or principled stages of moral reasoning, where a "P" score approaching 100% implies the highest achievable cognitive stage. Clearly, then, higher P scores are analogous to Kohlberg's higher stages of development (Rest [1986]). In response to the success of the DIT instrument and the usefulness of the "P" statistic, Kohlberg and colleagues developed the "Mean Moral Score" (MMS) that has psychometric properties similar to the "P" statistic (see Colby and Kohlberg [1987]).

Concluding Thoughts

It is our belief that the research and cognitive-developmental theory espoused by Kohlberg [1969], Rest [1979a] and many others applies to a broad class of social and professional conflicts, including those ethical considerations faced every day by members of the accounting and auditing community both in the United States and elsewhere. For example, the mere existence of objectivity and independence rules create, exacerbate or reduce ethical tension for accounting and auditing practitioners. On one hand, individuals are supposed to maintain a position of strict objectivity and independence, yet their relationship with clients is dictated by economics — or the fees collected for services rendered. Accountants and auditors are like all other individuals, facing the same set of social and moral conflict in their everyday lives. The objective of the proposed line of research is to connect the professional accountant's or auditor's ethical judgment to the cognitive-developmental theory of ethical reasoning postulated above, with the hope of gaining a greater understanding into the reality and complexity of professional practice.

Chapter 2

Factors Affecting Ethical Reasoning in Accounting and Auditing

In this chapter we attempt to describe the ethical reasoning and judgment-making process in the context of accounting and auditing by defining the various economic, social and psychological factors that affect ethical reasoning. As noted by Rawls [1971], the ethical domain can be thought of as an open and interactive system of beliefs wherein the individual builds a complete repertoire of philosophical and psychological skills to deal with everyday problems. This repertoire is constantly changing, being modified, updated and improved by the many interactions encountered in life. Like all individuals, accountants or auditors deal with conflict according to their cognitive capacities and ethical sensibilities.

In this monograph, we advance the idea that an individual's ethical reasoning capacity, as represented by cognitive-developmental theory, is an important determinant of ethical judgment and behaviour in accounting and auditing. To understand how an accountant's or auditor's underlying ethical reasoning skill affects professional judgment, one must first understand the domain in which ethical decisions are made. In this chapter, we provide a brief description of the many factors that can influence ethical judgment and behaviour in the practice of accounting and auditing. Such factors have been studied by researchers. For example, Farmer, Rittenberg and Trompeter [1987] provide a framework that incorporates five factors that could potentially influence auditor independence when attesting to client financial statement information. These factors are (Farmer, Rittenberg and Trompeter [1987, p. 5]):

- **Psychological factors:** for example, mental attitude and sense of idealism.
- **Economic factors:** such as pressure to subordinate judgments, freedom from

economic influences of retaining a client, and economic independence of the individual auditor.

- **Third-party influences:** such as a sense of being a public servant, existence of an audit committee, and existence of legal liability.
- **Technical competence:** including a thorough knowledge of auditing and accounting standards, computer systems and statistics.
- **Standard-setting structure:** for instance, a standard-setting organization that enforces narrowly focused accounting and auditing principles, thus reducing the ambiguity of judgments.

Farmer, Rittenberg and Trompeter [1987] tested several hypotheses regarding auditor independence using a hypothetical case experimental design, and found that certain non-accounting variables can have a profound effect on audit judgment concerning the implementation of a particular accounting rule or the treatment of an accounting issue. Other authors have dealt with those areas of conflict that have the most negative impact on the auditor's independence in his or her dealings with a client (Goldman and Barlev [1974]; Knapp [1985], Dunmore and Falk [1992]). These works suggest that to gain an appreciation for the accountant's ethical judgment, it is necessary to understand and carefully evaluate the many elements that can mitigate or worsen professional conflict in everyday practice.

According to social psychologists (e.g., Argyris [1982] and Argyris and Schon [1974]), the elements of social conflict typically include:

- **Actor:** the person perceiving the problem in terms of his or her moral domain who is forced to deal with it in some fashion. In this chapter, the primary actor will always be an accountant or auditor.
- **Recipient(s):** including all others that, according to the actor, will be affected by some judgment or action. The domain of recipients can be grouped in two camps, namely internal and external parties.
- **Internal party(s):** those who instigate, either intentionally or unintentionally, an ethical dilemma for the actor.
- **External party(s):** those bystanders who happen to be affected by the actor's or recipient's judgment or action concerning the conflict.
- **Situational forces:** that either influence the conflict or affect its resolution. Forces can be described as either instigating or mitigating in terms of the conflict at hand.

Ethical conflict is a form of social conflict because it always involves one or more affected parties, including work groups (e.g., the audit team), organizations (e.g., the accounting firm and the client entity), or society as a whole. For example, the accountant may perceive a conflict in terms of a particular employee at the client organization or the entire organization. External parties are a particularly salient factor in the study of ethical conflict in accounting and auditing because the existence of an independent public accounting profession is based upon the need to protect parties who are external to an organization. In other words, there would be no point in having audits if external parties (such as shareholders or creditors) could not be harmed by the wrongful or unethical acts of internal parties (such as an organization's management).

An ethical dilemma occurs whenever the accountant or auditor believes that dissonance exists between his or her self-chosen beliefs or values and those espoused by peers, the accounting firm, the profession, or society as a whole. Clearly, the magnitude of an ethical conflict is a function of the actor's perception of all parties involved as well as the possible consequences to the actor and the players. To facilitate our understanding of the ethical domain in terms of accounting or auditing practice, we must define:

1. the many players (e.g., recipients, internal parties, external parties) that relate the nature of ethical conflict for the individual practitioner
2. those forces that tend to instigate unethical behaviour in terms of the ethical norms of the firm and the profession
3. those forces that tend to curtail unethical or noncompliant behaviour.

2.1 SOURCES OF ETHICAL CONFLICT

Professional practice requires the accounting practitioner to deal with various individuals, entities and organizations. Many times, such interactions will result in conflict, causing the accountant to behave in a way that will compromise professional conduct according to the norms as espoused by the firm or the profession. The profession is becoming increasingly concerned about such interactions. Governmental organizations and various professional bodies that oversee and regulate the accounting profession have applied more stringent controls over the most salient and damaging relationships that could give rise to the appearance of ethical impropriety. (See NCFFR (Treadway) [1987]; U.S. Congress (Dingell) [1988]; AICPA [1988]; U.S. Congress (Wyden) [1992]). In terms of the social conflict model presented above, potentially damaging relationships for the accounting or auditing professional can be described in terms of the players as well as situational forces that affect the nature and severity of ethical conflict.

Players in the ethical domain of accounting or auditing generally include the following constituent groups:

1. the client organization, including management personnel and members of the audit committee
2. the accounting firm, which is typically represented by the collective interests of firm management within the firm, or personnel in a particular office, or individuals at the same social level in the firm's formal hierarchy (e.g., staff, seniors, managers, partners)
3. the accounting profession, including various self-governing professional bodies and regulatory authorities in the United States and elsewhere
4. society as a whole, including all key people within the client organization and the public accounting firm.

In this regard, the role of an independent public accounting or auditing profession is defined in the context of the many conflicts of interest caused by the different and competing objectives of various players.

Client-Centred Conflict

The conflict caused by responsibility to the profession and the economic needs of the public accounting firm is at the core of many ethical problems in the accounting and auditing environment. The fact that accountants and auditors are paid a fee directly by the client organization for so-called "independent" services often causes a perception of possible bias or conflict of interest (Rhode [1978], National Commission on Fraudulent Financial Reporting (NCFFR) (Treadway) [1987]). This problem is especially salient when the client organization represents a significant source of revenues for the public accounting firm, or when the firm has a long-standing professional or social relationship with the organization and its management.

As recent cases of audit litigation suggest, non-traditional accounting or consulting services, coupled with unorthodox fee arrangements between the public accounting firm and the client organization, can cause the appearance of ethical shenanigans in accounting and auditing (see Rhode [1978]; Previts [1986]). However, firm profitability is not the only factor affecting ethics in public accounting. Variables such as firm reputation, legal liability, and the stringent enforcement of standards and rules over unethical acts offset the temptation by some practitioners to seek unbridled profits without regard to professional or societal consequences.

Client-centred conflicts are probably the most publicly conspicuous and highly sensitive ethical problems confronting the public accounting profession (see Palmrose [1988]). To illustrate such conflict, imagine that the controller of the fairly sizable audit client asks the audit senior in charge of the engagement to pass on a highly questionable accounting transaction that could materially impact the company's financial statements. Furthermore, suppose that the audit senior defies the controller by requiring that the material entry be recorded, thus having a negative impact on the reported profitability of the organization.

In spite of good intentions, the audit senior soon learns that requiring this entry could jeopardize the auditing firm's continuing relationship with the client organization. In addition, restating the financial statements to reflect what the audit senior believes is economic reality or by qualifying the audit opinion can cause a proverbial "self-fulfilling prophecy" problem for the client organization (Solomon and Krogstad [1988]; Sullivan [1992]). This, in turn, can exacerbate its fiscal problems and perhaps even lead to allegations of audit failure and litigation for the auditing firm. However, *not* requiring the client to book the adjustment is a violation of the auditor's professional and ethical responsibilities. This too can cause litigation problems for the auditing firm if the stakeholders of the client organization believe that the financial statements were materially misleading.

Despite the costly problems that can arise when accounting or auditing professionals do not choose the ethical high road, practice development activities still remain the most important aspect of performance appraisal as individuals enter the management ranks of the public accounting firm (McNair [1987, 1991]). In particular, attaining partnership in large public accounting firms means that the individual has proven his or her ability to effectively manage client relations. All too often, however, managing the client relationship means that the accounting or auditing practitioner has learned to trade professional responsibility for fee potential. Only those individuals who have developed the ability to resolve client-centred ethical conflict without harming the economic relationship between the client and the audit firm will be given the opportunity to advance to the partner ranks. Because ethical compromises such as these may be very difficult for many individuals, some may actually choose to leave the profession rather than be placed in the position of making unethical choices (see, for example, Ponemon [1990, 1992a]).

Firm-Centred Conflict

Due to economic limitations of the practice environment, the accountant is often forced to make compromises. Sometimes concession-making on the part of the individual accountant is done with members of the firm, rather than with members of the client's organization. For instance, an audit manager may tacitly agree to look the other way when evaluating a poorly implemented accounting information system by members of a consulting team from the same accounting firm (see Coreless and Parker [1987]). Another common example of this behaviour involves the audit budget activities of individual auditors assigned to a client engagement. As Dirsmith and Covaleski [1985a] and McNair [1991] observed, audit seniors may encourage staff-level auditors to underreport their effort in order to properly complete audit tasks within the allotted time budget. Obviously, to be successful in any organization, an individual must learn to balance his or her personal beliefs and needs against those of the firm. The balancing of personal beliefs with those of an organization has been examined by cognitive-developmental researchers in studies of the moral atmosphere within organizations (see, for example, Higgins, Powers and Kohlberg [1984]). Such research suggests that emotional distress and ethical conflict emerges for individuals when their personally-held beliefs or values are not consistent with the goals or needs of the organization as a whole. The organization also may experience ethical conflict when choosing how to accommodate the potentially conflicting interests and concerns of employees or constituent groups.

Profession-Centred Conflict

The rules and principles advocated by the profession and those believed to be ethical by the individual accounting practitioner in a particular situation may not be congruent. The usual source of rules regarding ethical behaviour can be found in codes of conduct published by professional accounting organizations (including those in private industry, education and government). For example, an audit partner may believe that participating in the management of an audit client in financial distress may be very helpful, even though it jeopardizes the independence and objectivity of the firm in terms of the auditing engagement. In contrast, another partner in the same firm may believe that abiding by the code of conduct is more important than helping a client in a management capacity.

For example, an accountant may have knowledge of certain facts regarding the plans and policy of one client that may devastate the operations of another audit client. Since client confidentiality prevents the disclosure of this information, the accountant must choose between the code of conduct and his or her ethical beliefs and responsibilities (see, for example, Fund of Funds Ltd. v. Arthur Andersen & Co. discussed in endnote 10). Clearly, if such beliefs are consistent with those espoused by the profession, a conflict will not occur. If beliefs and the code are inconsistent on this matter, an ethical conflict may emerge for the accounting practitioner.

In another example, suppose that an auditing partner has to choose between rendering a qualified audit report for going concern uncertainties rather than a clean opinion. Assume that the facts obtained on the audit substantiate the substantial doubt criterion required in applicable auditing standards, but the partner realizes that such an audit report could hurt the client's organization, and may in fact exacerbate its financial demise (e.g., the "self-fulfilling prophecy" problem). Although the correct action in this matter is clearly defined by auditing standards, the partner may have some reservations regarding such action. Here again, if the partner's beliefs are consistent with the course of action mandated by the auditing standards, a conflict will not emerge.

Society-Centred Conflict

There are many reasons why one chooses a career in public accounting: a desire to earn a fairly generous income, a desire to become a member of a profession, or a desire to serve the public at large. As discussed earlier, a profession is differentiated from other occupations by having certain obligations to society. Such an obligation may at times cause conflict for the accounting professional. The accountant may believe that the correct accounting treatment of a particular transaction according to generally accepted accounting principles (GAAP) results in a misrepresentation of facts, and thus could potentially harm those who rely on such information for making decisions.

For example, supporters of social cost accounting believe that recording the full costs of cleaning up a nuclear power plant at the end of its useful life should be recorded on the balance sheet as a liability. Others criticize such accounting treatment, since these costs are based on estimated clean-up activities and resources using today's technology, which at the end of the plant's useful life may be outmoded. They argue that the cost of a megabyte of computer storage thirty years ago and the cost of this capacity today is equivalent to what may happen to the costs of nuclear clean-up as technologies advance. Others believe that the final consumer of such information is receiving an incorrect picture regarding the costs to society associated with nuclear power. For some accountants, the need to present a fair and useful financial picture to the public may give cause to reconsider his or her allegiance to the principles or guidelines as espoused by the profession.

At a more tacit level, the accounting practitioner may at times question the validity of his or her role as a public servant. Increasing competition for clients, more accounting and auditing regulations and the threat of costly litigation makes the chore of being a public accountant more like a business and less like a profession. Briloff [1966] predicted this phenomenon over twenty-five years ago in his book describing the changing orientation of public accounting firms. According to Briloff, as the accounting profession matures and becomes more competitive in terms of the demand for primary (auditing) services, it will lose much of the rights and privileges accorded to a profession. Research has shown that this may be happening in other professions as well (Gormley [1988]).

The changing tides of public accounting may mean that the society-serving aspects of the profession will cease to be important, and will be substituted by an ever-increasing need for income and market share. For those concerned about the quality of the profession, this can cause extreme pressure. To make matters even worse, negative economic trends in the profession today may force many practitioners to choose between ethical responsibilities to the general public and loyalty to the public accounting firm so that it can continue as a viable economic entity.

2.2 INSTIGATING FORCES

In each of the preceding potential sources of conflict, the nature and magnitude of the particular conflict is grounded in the perceptions of the individual practitioner, which in turn are influenced by a wide array of normatively important factors that could influence the nature and outcome of ethical conflict for a particular situation in the accounting or auditing domain. In terms of Rest's [1986] four-component model, the relationship between ethical reasoning and ethical behaviour can be mediated by the way an individual prioritizes ethical values over other personal values (e.g., Component 3) as well as his or her ethical perseverance (e.g., Component 4). Thus, in cases involving bribery, the individual accountant may feel a need to stand firm on his or her ethical conviction despite the possible consequences. However, as the value of the bribe increases, the ethical perseverance of some may start to weaken. Perhaps Sir Robert Walpole's famous quote (Bartlett [1968, p. 397]) "All those men have their price" is applicable here. Given the rash of bad press and the rising incidence of malpractice litigation against auditing firms, this statement may be especially true of accountants and auditors in today's business climate.

Clearly then, the degree to which a practitioner upholds the ethical principles of the profession is a function of many factors. Certain factors tend to encourage compliance with an ethical standard, while others abet the practitioner's noncompliance. In the literature, the most commonly cited forces that tend to induce conflict in the public accounting environment include:

1. fees paid by clients
2. extent of non-audit and management advisory services (MAS) work provided to auditing clients
3. status and career attainment within the firm
4. affiliation or tenure with the client
5. affiliation with work associates and colleagues
6. competition
7. job security.

Fees Paid by Clients

At the centre of many conflicts confronting the accounting practitioner is the desire to earn ample income while upholding the high ethical standards as advanced by the profession. To some, the concepts of making money and high ethical standards are mutually exclusive (Briloff [1972]). For others, a high ethical standard is a part of being successful in public accounting. They argue that as competition increases, only the firms with the greatest integrity and best reputation will survive and prosper (Walters [1986]). For many practitioners, the truth probably lies somewhere between these two extremes. Earning a reasonable livelihood is a necessity for most accounting professionals. The pursuit of greater income may at times jeopardize the appearance, or reality, of ethical propriety. According to Goldman and Barlev [1974], the public accountant is a servant to any master that pays the bill. In most cases, the master is the auditing client. According to these authors, however, this master-servant relationship is often ameliorated by stringent and enforceable rules or guidelines.

For many firms, fees paid by a single client for audit, consulting and tax services can easily amount to millions of dollars a year. Thus, such a client is very important to the wealth of the firm and the success of all accounting staff involved. Obviously, if a single client represents a significant part of the firm's overall revenue, it is more risky for the firm to pursue issues or concerns that may jeopardize this relationship. On the other hand, if a client's total contribution to the firm's overall revenues are relatively small, the firm and its management may be more likely to stand fast on its ethical principles.

MAS Services to Audit Clients

Management advisory services (e.g., non-audit accounting services) being rendered to auditing clients have caused a great deal of concern for those who regulate the accounting profession (see U.S. Congress (Moss) [1976]; U.S. Congress (Metcalf) [1977]; U.S. Congress (Dingell) [1988]. The basis of such concern is that as the firm plays more of a management role in the audit client's organization, it is less able to render an independent and objective opinion regarding the financial position of the company. Also of concern to those outside the profession are the comparative growth and profitability aspects of consulting versus traditional auditing services. For some large public accounting firms, consulting services contribute as much as forty percent of the total revenues, and perhaps a much higher percentage to their bottom-line net income.

The following examples illustrate the typical concerns associated with MAS involvement on auditing clients. In the performance of a consulting engagement, an individual practitioner may have access to information unavailable to him during the normal course of an audit. At times, this new information might cause conflict for the practitioner, especially if such data would compromise the results of an audit. Similarly, an auditor might find fault in the underlying system of accounting controls developed and implemented by a member of the same firm working in a consulting capacity. In this case, commenting on such weaknesses may cause serious problems for the firm in its continuing role as consultant and perhaps auditor for the client.

As the competition for new auditing clients increases, and as legal liability costs for audit failure rise, many firms may be forced to expand outside the domain of traditional accounting services. Thus, many smaller accounting firms are becoming authorized dealers for various brands of microcomputer accounting software. While the sale of software applications can generate a fair profit to the firm's pre-existing accounting and auditing clients, such a business enterprise can place the accounting practitioner in an interesting predicament. Not only is he or she responsible for making a reasonable recommendation regarding the selection of the system, but now, as the vendor, becomes liable for the proper functioning of each software application. If, during the course of an audit or a review, the practitioner uncovers a significant problem with the accounting software generating the financial statements, will the practitioner render an honest opinion regarding the system?

Some may argue that most accounting firms are departmentalized, and the services performed in another department are treated by the auditor in much the same way as he or she would handle outside services. It is interesting to note that Coreless and Parker [1987, p. 29] examined this issue, and found that auditors are more skeptical of consulting work performed by members of the same firm than identical work completed by another public accounting firm. Although such findings ease the concern of auditor bias over MAS activities in the large firm environment, problems may still exist in smaller firms, as well as small practice offices of large firms, especially when the practitioner acts in the capacity of consultant and auditor on the same client engagement.

Status and Career Attainment

Most individuals entering the professions today are eager to learn and are often hungry for success (Lawrence [1990]). Early in one's career, success equates with obtaining promotion and greater responsibilities quickly. This is often referred to as the "fast track". For example, those granted in-charge responsibilities first among their cohorts in the junior ranks are said to have the greatest status among peers in that work group (Dirsmith and Covaleski [1985a, 1985b]; McNair [1991]). Thus, the association between the perception of status within the firm and job responsibilities and promotion is highly significant. As individuals move up the public accounting career ladder, they become more concerned about client relations, spending relatively little effort on technical matters. This requires the skillful practitioner to balance the wishes of the client with the needs and requirements of his or her firm and the profession itself. Skillful negotiation requires the accountant or auditor to negotiate and sometimes compromise on issues regarding accounting or auditing standards. For instance, an audit partner may permit the client to take an aggressive stance on the treatment of a particular revenue item as long as it is disclosed in the footnotes to the financial statements. Unskilled negotiation, however, often means that the practitioner merely concedes to the demands of client management (see Goldman and Barlev [1974]).

To understand fully situations in which the accountant or auditor feels compelled to concede to a client on an ethical issue, one must first understand the causes behind ethical behaviour. Among the most important motives is the practitioner's inner drive to succeed, which is conveyed by status, praise and early promotion within the firm. If the firm measures success by client relations, the accountant or auditor is more likely to bend to the demands of client management. If, on the other hand, the firm places high regard on personal integrity, the individual may be more likely to stand steadfastly on his or her principles, even at the expense of harming the client-audit firm relationship. While the practitioner's behaviour may be influenced by his or her internalized ethic or capacity to reason morally (Armstrong [1984]; Ponemon [1988, 1992b]), other factors enter into the process, including ethical sensitivity, the individual's priority to moral courses of action over other personal needs and desires, and the ability to follow through on his or her moral intentions (see Rest [1986]).

Client Tenure

Many believe that the longer the accountant or auditor serves a client, the less able he or she is to render services independently and objectively. As a result of controversy, the AICPA developed standards that encourage partner rotation every five years on audit engagements involving publicly traded organizations. Typically, the rotation only involves the shifting of management responsibilities within the same firm. The firm keeps the client while maintaining the appearance of independence and objectivity to the public at large. Some argue that such a process is insufficient (NCFFR (Treadway) [1987]; U.S. Congress (Dingell) [1988]). They suggest that rotation should be a supervised process of changing audit firms, not merely alternating partners within the same firm.

In terms of ethical conflict, the longer accounting or auditing professionals are associated with the same client organizations, the more they are likely to empathize with its management (Levinthal and Fichman [1988]). In the event of a moral dilemma involving long-standing clients, a practitioner might find it difficult to separate his or her professional responsibilities from the needs of the client organization and its key personnel. Nevertheless, the benefits of having tenure with an auditing client at times may outweigh the risks. For example, the audit firm with tenure has a greater understanding of the client's organization and should accomplish an audit more efficiently. Moreover, if ethical conflicts emerge during the course of an audit, the practitioner with more experience might have greater sensitivity to such issues.

Affiliation within the Firm

Like all organizations, a public accounting firm contains an informal system tied together by a series of relationships and work groups. Affiliation is the process by which a single individual learns to "fit in" to his or her immediate work group. Noted organizational theorist Abraham Maslow [1970] described such affiliation, or a need to belong, as a primary motivator for every employee. According to Maslow [1970] and Greenberger, Miceli and Cohen [1987], not being able to conform to the standards of an immediate work group can cause difficulties, and perhaps an impossible existence for a single individual, when he or she is labelled an outcast by the work group.

Since a typical public accounting firm is organized hierarchically into levels by years of experience and area of specialization, most individuals entering a firm identify their immediate work group by the level at which they are hired. To illustrate, an employee hired directly from college will usually define his or her work group as all other junior (inexperienced) staff level accountants. In a larger firm, the level might be segmented by years with the firm, such as first-year staff or second-year staff. In a very large office, the group might be further subdivided by specialization or the type of industry experience.

While informal standards can be set by any group of individuals within the organization, norms and conventions that establish guidelines for affiliation are typically set by peers in a work group. Conflict is least likely for any individual when these informal rules are congruent to those of the firm and the profession. When such conventions or rules are not consistent with either the firm or the profession, conflict will be more prevalent for some individuals. This is especially true when the accountant's or auditor's personal beliefs are inconsistent with those held by others in the work group. Such a situation was illustrated in the audit budget example discussed later, wherein peer pressure and an unrealistic audit budget may cause some to underreport their billable time in order to appear efficient. Obviously, the degree to which such conflict becomes a moral dilemma is again a function of many variables, including the individual's ethical reasoning abilities.

Competition

In the public accounting environment, competition comes from two sources: external competition among accounting firms vying for clients in the marketplace, and internal competition among work associates in the same firm vying for position, status or job security. The first kind of competition is typically an area of major concern for the management of an accounting firm, since public accounting is a profit-making business enterprise. Like all businesses, a firm must remain competitive if it is to survive. External competition implies that at times the management of the accounting firm must be price- and quality- sensitive to the demands of their clients. With the advent of merger and acquisition activity in the 1980s, there are substantially fewer large client organizations to audit. In light of the dwindling supply of lucrative audit clients, accounting firms are competing in many other ways, including introducing new and innovative consulting and tax services. To maintain growth and market share, some international firms have merged while others have actively sought to acquire smaller firms.

Internal competition among work associates also can be fierce, especially when the individual accountant or auditor assumes managerial responsibilities within the firm (Marxen [1990]; McNair [1991]). As the individual progresses in his or her career, there are greater demands and responsibilities. Such pressure can lead to emotional stress and work-related conflict (McNair [1991]; Lord [1990]; Ponemon [1992b]). Only those that can best tolerate the pressures and demands of their jobs are considered eligible for partnership. Furthermore, making it to partner is not the end of these work-related pressures. A partner is responsible for many aspects of the practice, including the maintenance of the client base, as well as marketing and promotion activities. As a result of such pressure, many partners may experience burn-out at a fairly young age relative to others in other high stress occupations or professions.

In light of both the internal and external competitiveness associated with public accounting practice, many individuals find the environment too demanding. Some accountants become disillusioned early in their career. To them, the business aspects of public accounting practice more than offset the various benefits of continuing in the profession. Many accountants or auditors at times will experience conflict because of such demands. For example, a senior auditor might believe that a certain auditing engagement requires substantially more time to complete, but because of budgeting pressures created by management, is unable to do so. If the auditor puts in too much effort on the job, such "excess time" may appear as a negative entry on his or her personnel record. On the other hand, if the auditor missed something of significance, it may cause a severe penalty for the individual some time in the future in the form of legal liability or diminishing professional reputation.

Job Security

Experience in public accounting provides opportunities both within the profession and outside in the fields of business, education and government. Executives in the field of accounting or finance are often recruited directly from public accounting firms. Often, various members of the audit team are targeted by a client organization's recruitment activities. In fact, once individuals earn their professional certification, job opportunities seem to abound. As the practitioner progresses to higher income brackets and experiential levels, however, it is often more difficult to find suitable employment elsewhere. Hence, by virtue of certification and a sufficient level of job expertise, individuals in public accounting firms may be most marketable somewhere between the third and fifth year in the profession (McNair [1987]). With too much public accounting experience, the practitioner may have difficulty if he or she suddenly wants to leave the firm and seek employment outside the profession. In other words, as the practitioner progresses in his or her career, there is certainly more at stake.

The availability of job opportunities within and outside the firm can impact on the practitioner's ethical resolve and perseverance. For example, if the practitioner has career mobility outside the firm, his or her ability to withstand pressure to engage in unethical acts within either the firm or the client organization might be quite different if job opportunities were not available. As the individual joins the partnership ranks of a firm, the loss of a substantial client will lower partnership earnings, and ultimately reduce his or her share of these profits. Hence, the practitioner's feelings about job security, as well as his or her position within the firm, play a pivotal role in resolving ethical conflict.

In summary, what has been described as the "instigating factors" do not represent an exhaustive list of every possible variable creating ethical conflict in accounting and auditing. However, it is maintained that these factors all play a very instrumental role in the process by which the public accountant forms his or her ethical judgment and chooses to take some course of action. As shown in Exhibit 2.1, each of these factors work collectively to create potential conflicts for individuals working in public accounting firms. The next section discusses several factors that tend to reduce ethical conflict in the profession.

Exhibit 2.1

The Ethical Domain in Public Accounting

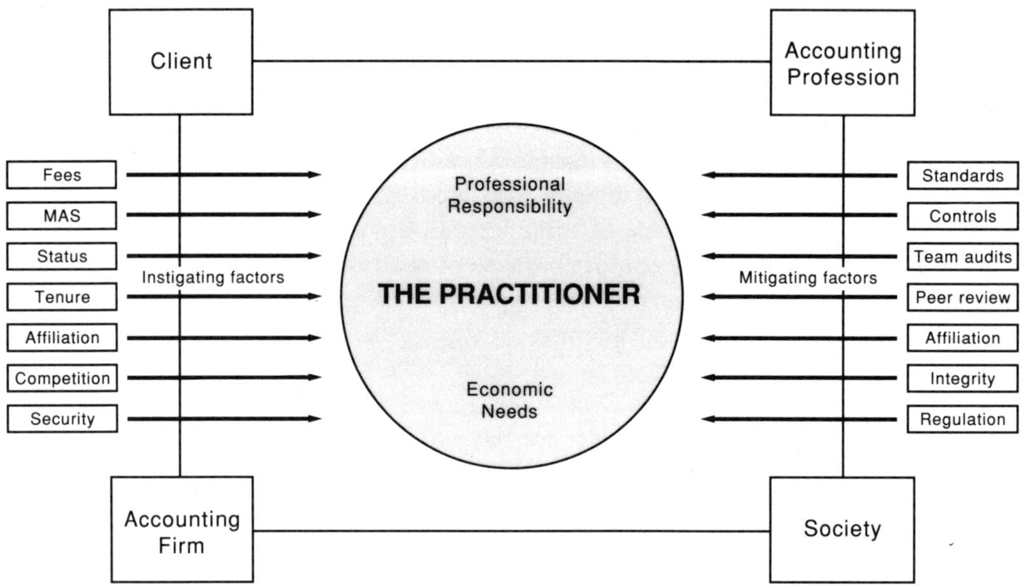

2.3 MITIGATING FACTORS

As discussed in the prior section, there are many factors that tend to cause the accounting practitioner to behave in a way that is deemed consistent or inconsistent with the rules and guidelines of the profession. Clearly, these factors work in conjunction with an individual's ethical capacity and various other situational and environmental variables. Thus, these factors alone are only a small part of the underlying thinking process used by the accountant or auditor when framing ethical judgment. A clear-cut picture of some behavioural variables may provide an insight into the very complex process of conflict resolution in the public accounting profession. Variables that potentially mitigate unethical behaviours for the accounting practitioner include:

1. professional standards and behavioural guidelines
2. internal controls to audit work
3. team auditing
4. peer reviews
5. affiliation with colleagues and associates
6. personal integrity and professionalism
7. federal laws, regulations and congressional oversight.

Professional Standards

A formal set of work and behavioural standards are used by professions to ensure compliance to a reasonable level of acceptable conduct when discharging one's professional duties or responsibilities to the public. Acceptable professional conduct is conditional upon many factors including the individual's personal beliefs and values, which are grounded in his or her ethical reasoning capacity. Although far from perfect, such standards serve as examples of how one should behave in a wide variety of situations and circumstances that may confront the professional in the course of practice.

To illustrate, assume for a moment that various professional and regulatory rules regarding auditor independence were suddenly revoked, and acceptable conduct regarding such matters was decided upon by each individual auditor. In some instances, chaos would emerge. For example, some practitioners might conclude that the limitations pertaining to common stock ownership of auditing clients were meaningless. Certain firms might actively invest in the clients that they are presently auditing. Yet other firms may strongly oppose stock ownership on the grounds that such activities would compromise their professional integrity and their responsibility to the public.

In another example, without rules on auditor independence, some auditors might choose to participate in their client organizations in terms of making managerial decisions or serving on the board of directors. Coupled with auditing services, such activity could generate significant profits for the public accounting firm as well as solidify the client-audit firm relationship. Despite potential benefits to the firm, some auditors still may choose to maintain independence to ensure a degree of professional skepticism and objectivity during the course of the engagement.

Obviously, each individual's perception regarding ethical responsibilities to colleagues, the firm, the client, or the public at large, can be quite different. Thus, not having an explicit code of conduct would cause some to reconsider their ethical obligations and responsibilities. On the other hand, many practitioners operate at standards far above those that are stated in the code. To these individuals, the existence of formal rules or guidelines that promote acceptable behaviour is irrelevant to their compliance. It is maintained, however, that for many practitioners, the code does serve as a useful benchmark for determining one's resolution of the various ethical conflicts confronted in the course of everyday professional practice. In this regard, professional standards serve as a mitigating factor to some practitioners' unethical behaviour.

Internal Controls over Audit Work

Ethical impropriety in many situations comes about when the accounting or auditing practitioner decides not to comply with the standards, norms or expectations of the profession. Even if such a decision is made by a single individual, there are many other factors that tend to mitigate his or her undesirable action (Mautz and Evers [1991]). In recognition of the possibility for fraud or negligence by any one individual, many public accounting firms have established a formal system of internal control that spot checks and attempts to assess the validity of all active audit engagements within the firm on an ongoing basis. Such controls often include a quality control review of selected workpapers to ensure consistency and completeness of all auditing work performed, an internal audit of detailed transactions carried out during fieldwork, and a detailed system of checks and balances conducted by various members of the auditing team to ensure that all the work stated in the workpapers were properly handled and recorded.

Working in concert, the above controls tend to mitigate the possible damages caused by one practitioner's carelessness, negligence or unethical deeds. Some argue that internal controls for the most part are corrective in nature, and thus do not prevent unethical behaviour from happening in the first place. Even with the best system of control, once an unethical act occurs, it is often very difficult, if not impossible, to find. This is especially so if the unscrupulous practitioner knows the detailed workings of the quality control system used to prevent such action by the firm. Others, however, argue that the mere existence of a quality control system discourages potential unethical behaviour. It is maintained that while such controls are far from perfect, they do, in fact, act as a deterrent to unethical behaviour for some members of the profession.

Team Auditing

An audit is typically conducted by more than one individual. Although not a formal mechanism for control, the mere existence of peer-to-peer collaboration over the course of the auditing engagement can substantially reduce the opportunity for one individual to engage in dysfunctional or nefarious work-related activities. In order to be an effective deterrent to an auditor's unethical behaviour, however, it is necessary to have competent supervision of all audit team members on an ongoing basis. Furthermore, strategic audit decisions, such as the determination of audit risk and planning materiality, should require at least one additional opinion. Finally, team auditing only serves as a control function when the opportunity for collusion between two or more auditors does not exist.

To illustrate how this might work, suppose that the corporate controller of the client's organization hoodwinks the audit senior into not reporting suspicious vendor records found in substantive tests of accounts payable transactions. To make matters worse, suppose that the audit senior is offered a large cash bribe to keep silent. While some individuals might be tempted by the offer, the fear of getting caught and the resulting public reprimand from firm management would discourage this unethical act. Clearly, the chances of getting caught increase substantially if other members of the audit team were involved in the vouching of accounts payable transactions and, thus, also could become aware of these questionable transactions. Because of such concerns, the audit senior may ultimately choose not to take the bribe and fulfill his professional responsibility by disclosing the problem to audit firm management. In other cases, the senior accountant would not take the cash or even be tempted by the offer, since his ethical perseverance (e.g., Component 4 in Rest's model) would not permit the acceptance of a bribe under any circumstances. For an individual who is motivated to behave ethically, the existence of an audit team neither contributes to nor hinders ethical action. Thus, personal beliefs, conviction and opportunity work hand-in-hand to guide the accountant's or auditor's resolution of ethical conflict. In this regard, team auditing lessens the opportunity for unethical acts.

Peer Reviews

Member firms of professional bodies such as the AICPA, CICA, CGA-Canada, and others have to undergo a peer review of attestation work (including audits and reviews) being provided to client organizations. A peer review is a detailed and independent investigation of a public accounting firm, including certain selected client engagements, by an independent body of accounting practitioners from other qualified firms and organizations. The purpose of the review is to ensure the member firm's compliance with the standards, rules and regulations required by the profession.

Very rarely does a peer review seek to uncover unethical actions of an individual practitioner or of an entire firm (Sullivan [1992]). However, if in the course of their investigation, some unethical activity is revealed, such a finding could possibly result in a very negative rating for the firm. In certain cases, very negative findings could lead to severe civil or criminal liability to the firm under investigation. Historically, this occurs only rarely, and in most cases the firm found to be in noncompliance will receive a public reprimand by the review team (Mautz and Evers [1991]). The consternation and embarrassment caused by a potentially negative peer review, however, serves to motivate the firm (and certain individuals within the firm) to comply with various professional and technical standards.

Affiliation

As discussed in the prior section of this chapter, group affiliation can often play an important role in the accounting practitioner's resolution of ethical conflict. Affiliation is an especially important control mechanism if the norms or conventions that are espoused by the work group are compatible with those of the firm and the profession. If the norms of the work group are consistent with those of the accounting firm, many individuals will embrace these rules in their attempt to "fit in". (See McNair [1991]; Ponemon [1990, 1992a]). In this respect, affiliation serves as an effective means for promoting compliance to standards of conduct as well as behavioural uniformity within a practice office, the firm or even the profession as a whole.

Suppose that the informal work group establishes a norm that suggests that in order to be successful in the firm, one must spend much of his or her free time (e.g., evenings and weekends) working on firm-related business. For an inexperienced accountant, such a norm might imply that he or she must put in the hours, no matter how much actual work needs to be accomplished. In certain instances, such a convention might cause some to slack off during normal business hours just to ensure enough work to complete later in the evening or weekend.

The firm's management is not merely concerned with hours worked by members of the organization, but with the efficiency of these hours. In fact, fewer hours and greater efficiency is almost always preferable to more inefficient hours. In this situation, the firm may wish to change the dysfunctional behaviour of the group. A reasonable first step is to dispel the myth regarding overtime activities. A second step might be to motivate group leaders to accept the particular goals of the firm. Assuming that group norms can be made consistent with the needs of management, this action would inevitably impact upon individual behaviour.

The group also plays an important role in the way the individual frames and deals with ethical conflict. If the group fosters unethical behaviour, group members who seek affiliation will be much more likely to behave improperly (Dirsmith and Covaleski [1985a]). If, on the other hand, the work group encourages a high ethical standard, the same individuals would be much less prone to unethical behaviours. Within the moral domain, affiliation often plays the pivotal role in the practitioner's ethical resolution to the many conflicts encountered in everyday practice. An individual's judgment and action surrounding a conflict, however, is typically a function of many other factors, including his or her cognitive capacity and self-chosen ethical beliefs.

Personal Integrity

Underlying all the many variables mentioned above is the individual's own personal ethic. Obviously, if all practitioners abide by a high ethical standard, detailed guidelines, ethical rulings and costly controls within the firm and the profession will be unnecessary. This is so because individuals with a high degree of integrity tend to form his or her ethical judgment free from the biases and pressures created both within and outside the public accounting firm.

For those with strong ethical values, affiliation and work-related pressures should play a minimal role in influencing ethical judgment and action.

On the surface, it would appear that a public accounting firm and the accounting profession as a whole would be much better off if somehow it could ensure that all accounting and auditing professionals were predisposed to the highest standards of ethical conduct in their everyday lives. Yet this would be a virtual impossibility, since the ethical character of each individual is a dynamic variable, always changing to the demands and requirements of a given situation. By upholding high ethical ideals, however, a firm and its management can create an atmosphere where principled reasoning and behaviour can flourish.

While this monograph deals with the practitioner's *ethical reasoning abilities* it does not directly address the issue of *personal integrity*. Integrity probably goes well beyond a person's reasoning level or obedience to rules, standards, or norms of professional conduct. Perhaps integrity is an outcome of a complex psychological process from which the individual gains the capability to withstand difficult ethical conflict in his or her professional and personal life. Integrity in this context may be somewhat akin to the four-component model defined by Rest [1986, pp. 3-4], wherein ethical behaviour is described as a function of ethical sensitivity, ethical reasoning, the balancing of ethical versus non-ethical values and persistence in making an ethical choice.

Regulation and Oversight

As mentioned in the Preface, the accounting profession has been under intense scrutiny by various subcommittees within the U.S. House of Representatives and Senate. The reason for such concern is the perception by various legislators that the accounting profession is unable to regulate and enforce the ethical compliance of member firms and practitioners. Over the past decade, Congressional Representatives John Dingell, Jr. (D. Michigan) and Ron Wyden (D. Oregon) have been leading a charge against the profession. Representative Dingell has been particularly sensitive to the fee arrangements between the largest accounting firms and their most significant auditing clients. As a result, Representative Dingell tentatively proposed that all accounting firms be assigned to auditing engagements in much the same manner as a public defender is assigned to a criminal case. By barring marketing and promotion activities within the profession, the various public accounting firms would be better able to render a fair and honest assessment of an auditee's financial condition.

To many, regulations such as those proposed by Congressmen Dingell would reduce much of the professionalism and autonomy that is presently enjoyed by most professionals. The AICPA has mandated new and more stringent measures to deal with members in noncompliance (Mautz and Evers [1991]; Sullivan [1992]). For those practitioners with high ethical standards and integrity, the existence of regulation, or new professional rules, would have an insignificant impact upon their professional and moral obligations to the public. Thus, regulation for these individuals would be unnecessary and perhaps even dysfunctional. For practitioners with less than high ethical standards, however, regulation might be imperative to constrain activities that could severely harm the general public as well as the reputation of the profession. Even in extreme circumstances of ethical impropriety, governmental regulation might be an unnecessary deterrent in light of other forces within the firm and the profession that prevent or correct problems in the workplace. For many accounting practitioners however, the threat of greater regulation by government legislators causes them to reconsider their professional responsibilities and ethical obligations to the general public. In this respect, mere rumor or conjecture regarding government intervention can have a socially useful purpose.

2.4 CHAPTER 2: CONCLUDING THOUGHTS

This chapter dealt with the many factors that mitigate or instigate the ethical impropriety of accountants or auditors in professional firms. The contribution of these factors to ethical behaviour within the accounting domain is a function of many other intervening variables including the individual's ethical reasoning skills when dealing with conflict. Exhibit 2.1 provides an overview of the factors that are believed to be associated with the accountant's ethical domain in professional practice.

In summary, to comprehend the various ethical or moral conflicts confronted by professional accountants or auditors, we believe that it is necessary to understand the cognitive processes that guide an individual's ethical sensitivity and cognitive (thinking) abilities. Based on the discussion of the psychology of ethical reasoning in the previous chapter, we maintain that this cognitive process can, in part, be represented by the stage-sequence models as proposed by Piaget (1932 [1966]), Kohlberg [1969] and Rest [1979a]. The next chapter will first illustrate how the psychology of ethical reasoning relates to ethical problem solving in accounting and auditing practice and then will discuss recently completed empirical studies, all employing the stage-sequence model of ethical reasoning, within the professional domain.

Chapter 3

Ethical Reasoning in Accounting and Auditing

The concept of professional ethics is more than an external measure by which the profession can maintain a virtuous image. For many practitioners, it is a concept that implies a reasoning capability that permits the individual to render judgment unaltered by self-interest that could impair his or her professional responsibility. The reasoning process is part of the individual's overall moral consciousness from which he or she deals with difficult ethical conflict or dilemmas in everyday practice. Ethical choice is just one of many types of decisions that the accountant or auditor must render in order to be an effective member of the profession. In this chapter, we relate the cognitive-developmental theory and ethical reasoning model to ethical judgment and behaviour extant in accounting and auditing practice.

In order to show how the psychology of ethical reasoning can be used to understand ethical behaviour in the professional domain, three hypothetical auditing cases are illustrated and analyzed according to the stage-sequence model posited by Kohlberg [1969] and Rest [1979a]. As a starting point, the first case is based on conflicts of interest caused by a firm's MAS endeavors. The second case involves the practitioner's independence strategy given a variety of situational factors. The third case involves client confidentiality. For each case, a series of standard responses according to the stage model of ethical cognition are given. It is important to note that the illustrated ethical resolutions to each auditing case represents only one of the many possible moral responses that could have been provided for an individual at a given stage according to the Kohlberg [1969] or Rest [1979a] models.

3.1 AUDITING ILLUSTRATIONS

Conflict of Interest[8]

Alice is a senior auditor for a national public accounting firm that provides auditing, tax and consulting services. The firm has developed a package called the "ACME Accounting System" that is sold to the general public as well as the firm's audit clients. Alice is the auditor in-charge of the ABC Company, Inc. engagement. During the course of this project, Alice is asked to evaluate the control structure of the client's internal accounting system, which is based on the ACME package. In the course of her evaluation, Alice uncovers several significant control weaknesses in the system. Before rendering her conclusions to ABC management, however, Alice is told by her boss to modify the negative comments in the management letter regarding the ACME system problems. What should Alice do?

Pre-conventional Level

Individuals at the pre-conventional level make the decision to do "right" to avoid punishment or to serve their own interest. Pre-conventional individuals are not cognizant of differences among individuals. They view their actions in physical terms and are not conscious of the psychological interests of others. Using the hypothetical dilemma as a measure of moral reasoning, the independent accountant at the pre-conventional level would make the judgement to inform ABC Company management or her superior partners only if it was deemed to be less harmful to her personally than if she concealed the facts. Conversely, if Alice could get away with not informing them, or if there is a low probability of getting caught, she would do so.

An independent accountant at Stage 1 (i.e., the first stage in the pre-conventional level) would decide to abide by the rules rather than seek personal gain, simply to avoid punishment or reprimand from a higher authority such as the partners in the firm, the accountancy board, or the general business community. At Stage 2 of the pre-conventional level, the reasons to do "right" are not only dictated by the threat of punishment, but by an overwhelming desire to serve one's own interest. Thus, if the accountant felt strongly enough about concealing the facts about the system, he or she would do so — even if the penalties were high.

To the auditor at the pre-conventional level, the ethical high road may not be pursued in a number of circumstances, which include the following:

1. if the risks of getting caught are relatively low
2. if the punishment from authorities is deemed to be minor or insignificant
3. if the personal gains are substantially greater than any of the perceived risks.

The pre-conventional accountant might go well beyond the selection decision; he or she might seek to profit (or make a commission) from the sale of additional software, assuming that the penalties for such action were perceived to be trivial or harmless.

Conventional Level

An individual at the conventional level has a need to be a good person and desires to maintain rules and authority that support stereotypical good behaviour. The individual feels obligated to keep the system of rules and conventions going, and seeks ways to avoid breakdown in the system. The conventional individual is aware of shared feelings, agreements and expectations that take primacy over individual interests. At Stage 3 (i.e., the first stage of the conventional level), the accountant's need to be a "good" person in the eyes of fellow accountants, the client and the profession as a whole is the primary motivator of moral action. The Stage 4 accountant is also aware of the needs of others, but has learned to differentiate the societal point of view from his or her personal motives. Thus at Stage 4, the rules of the profession tend to be upheld, except when they conflict with other social contracts that are believed to be more pressing or important (such as family issues or the church).

If Alice was at Stage 3, she might be motivated to keep silent on the software problems in order to win the approval of her colleagues within the firm as well as her boss. At Stage 4 however, because of a need to abide by the rules of the profession, Alice probably would feel morally obligated to provide her findings to the client as well as those individuals in the firm who are responsible for developing the ACME product. Alice would recognize that her own self-interest was at risk, but would conclude that the best interests of the client organization and the public accounting firm should always take precedence.

Post-conventional Level

The post-conventional individual follows self-chosen ethical principles, in which case particular laws or social agreements are usually valid because they rest on such principles. However, when laws or rules violate these principles, one acts in accordance with the principle rather than abiding by the rule. The individual's social perspective is that of a rational individual aware of values and rights prior to social attachments and contracts. At Stage 5 (i.e., the first stage in the post-conventional level), the independent accountant believes that the rules and laws governing moral action in the accounting profession are based on some rational calculation of overall utility or benefits to society. Here the individual recognizes that moral and legal points of view sometimes conflict — and often has difficulty integrating them. Stage 6 accountants have learned to balance moral principles and the rules and expectations of their profession and society. At Stage 6, the auditor makes a choice to "do right" if it is consistent with his or her self-chosen ethical principles.

The post-conventional practitioner also would recognize the client's interest; however, he or she might conclude that informing ABC Company management is more than abiding by a rule, it is also the morally sound position to take. Furthermore, the post-conventional accountant or auditor might have first considered if it was appropriate to audit the ABC Company system given the firm's involvement in the software selection project.

Post-conventional auditors might continue to advise the client to purchase a particular software package if they felt that the recommendation was given in the best interest of the client — even if it might compromise independence and objectivity. In summary, the post-conventional individual knows the rules, understands the underlying principle, and makes a decision that is guided by the principle rather than the rule. The objective of this hypothetical dilemma is to show that the behaviour of the independent accountant is a function of moral reasoning capabilities. The way in which Alice perceives the problem and resolves the conflict will result in some action consistent with her developmental stage or level of morality.

As can be seen from this very simple analysis of a very complex process of ethical reasoning, notions such as independence, objectivity, integrity, honesty and professionalism are all grounded in the individual's cognitive framework. Further, and perhaps more noticeably, these examples show that a person's ethical reasoning does not necessarily explain how the ethical conflict will be resolved.

Auditor Independence[9]

Bill is a staff auditor and CPA for a small firm that provides auditing services. The president of the DoGood Construction Corporation is searching for a chief financial officer (CFO), and has asked Bill to assist in the search and recruitment function. Bill is the "in-charge" auditor on the DoGood engagement which is among the largest and most profitable jobs for the firm. Bill truly believes that he can provide a valuable service to DoGood as well as his firm by performing the function. In addition, Bill already knows an individual, a personal friend, who is presently unemployed but has the right qualifications for this very important position. What should Bill do?

Pre-conventional Level

An individual at the pre-conventional level makes the decision to do right in order to avoid punishment and to serve one's immediate interest. The pre-conventional person is not cognizant of differences among individuals and will view his choices in physical rather than emotional terms. A pre-conventional Bill might gladly accept the new project even though it may jeopardize his professional independence. In addition, Bill might deliberately recommend his friend for the CFO position simply on the basis of greater control in future DoGood-Bill relationships. On the other hand, Bill might reject the client's offer if the potential penalties against him, by his firm or the accounting profession, for his misconduct were perceived to outweigh the potential gain.

At Stage 1 Bill might assist the client, without any regard to the code of ethics, because he may perceive the chances of getting caught and punished as being relatively low. At Stage 2, he is able to recognize the interests of others, but they count only to the extent that they can directly affect Bill. Hence, Bill's ethical actions are not only dictated by the threat of punishment, but by an overwhelming desire to maximize self-interest. In other words, if Bill believed that he could profit or gain stature within the firm by assisting DoGood, he probably would choose do so.

Conventional Level

The conventional Bill has a need to be a good person and desires to maintain rules, conventions and norms that support stereotypical good behaviour. At Stage 3, Bill would seek an ethical position that fulfilled his need to be socially accepted by his friend, or DoGood management or others in the accounting firm. Being a good person, Bill would justify a decision to assist DoGood in their CFO search on grounds that he felt obligated to his unemployed friend or he wanted to help the accounting firm by performing additional billable services.

At Stage 4, Bill feels obligated to firm policies or professional standards and would seek ways to avoid breakdown in the system. If Bill believed that assisting DoGood in the selection of a CFO candidate would violate audit independence, he would not work with the client in this capacity. In addition, even though Bill would feel an obligation to his unemployed friend, he would not disclose information about the position if he felt it could jeopardize his firm, harm the client or violate confidentiality rules. In this case, Bill would recognize that his own interests could be at stake, but would still be able to conclude that the best interests of his firm, the client or the profession must always take precedence to his own needs. Under conditions of conflicting interests between the firm's policies or professional standards, however, it is not at all clear whose interests Bill would uphold.

Post-conventional Level

The post-conventional Bill follows self-chosen ethical principles, in which case he regards particular laws or social agreements as being usually valid because they rest on such principles. When laws or rules violate these principles, Bill acts in accordance with the principle rather than strictly abiding by the rule. Bill would clearly recognize that the interests of DoGood, his firm and his friend were at risk, but would unequivocally choose the independence strategy that most conformed to the underlying principle at stake. Bill might conclude that working with DoGood and selecting his friend for the job is the morally correct position to take — even though the appearance of professional independence, and perhaps his position in the firm, is harmed. In this situation, Bill may know that his friend is in dire financial straits and would be a most competent CFO for DoGood. Bill might place the welfare of his friend (principle) above the independence rule. Another possible strategy available to Bill would be to refuse the project, but still recommend his friend to the client, assuming that his friend would ably fill this position.

If Bill was at Stage 5 in the Kohlberg model, he might choose a strategy that is not consistent with the mandate, rules, laws or guidelines of his immediate society. Even if Bill believed that the rules of the profession should be upheld, helping DoGood management and assisting his unemployed friend might be perceived as the more ethical resolution. Bill, however, might feel some ambivalence for this action. At Stage 6, ambivalence would no longer exist for Bill because he has the ability to resolve this dilemma by exercising fundamental ethical principles which do not rest on particular needs or social contracts.

As can be seen from this illustration, auditor independence is a complex phenomenon, wherein the individual's level of ethical reasoning plays an important role. However, the auditor's decision to abide by independence rules is guided by many other non-psychological factors as discussed in the previous chapter, including the benefits and penalties accruing from ethical behaviour, the various stakeholders involved, the existence of regulations and policies, and the nature of the client-audit firm relationship.

Client Confidentiality[10]

John is a CPA and the in-charge auditor on the Bolder Company and Colby Corporation engagements. While on the Bolder job, John learns that Colby is the only supplier of a product that is critical to the manufacturing of Bolder's final output. Colby is the only vendor in the marketplace. The next day, John learns from Colby's management that they are greatly increasing the price of their primary products — and the new pricing policy can bankrupt Bolder. John knows that Bolder recently considered the acquisition of a small company in Asia that, with some effort, can redirect its production to produce a product similar to the one made by Colby. However, the estimated unit cost was greater than the present (known and assumed stable) prices offered by Colby. Based on their limited information, Bolder did not seriously consider the purchase of this small company. What should John do?

Pre-conventional Level

For the pre-conventional practitioner, ethical behaviour equates to not getting caught doing something wrong, illegal or unethical. John makes his decision to do right to avoid punishment or to serve his immediate needs. In this instance, John might be unwilling to assist the Bolder Corporation because of a belief that there is nothing to gain from such action. On the other hand, John may see this situation as an opportunity to score points with the client or senior members of the firm. If the information was perceived to be very valuable, and the chances of getting caught were slim, John might actually play both sides and either withhold the information at a cost to Bolder, or sell the information to Bolder's management. If, however, the penalties for such action were perceived to be great, John would reconsider his unscrupulous plan.

Once again, we can further define John's behaviour according to his stage of ethical capacity. At Stage 1, John will simply seek ways to avoid harm and getting caught by his immediate authorities. At Stage 2, John might show concern for the possible loss of fees that may occur because of this dilemma. John might only seek solutions to his dilemma that have no impact upon his personal profit making with both Bolder and Colby.

Conventional Level

If John was at the conventional level, he would feel the need to be a good person and would deliberately seek and obey the rules that are supported by his reference group including, for example, other auditors in the firm, members of Bolder's or Colby's management, and management of the auditing firm. John might feel an obligation to inform Bolder, and perceive such an action as morally right given the circumstances of the situation. In contrast, John might believe that his first obligation is to the profession, and telling Bolder's management would be a violation of the rules regarding client confidentiality. John might still feel a need to help Bolder, but would believe that upholding the rules of the profession is far more important. In some cases, John might actually sacrifice personal gain if he truly believed that such action was in the best interests of his firm, the client or the accounting profession, all of which take precedence to his personal needs.

At Stage 3, John needs to maintain a social relationship with his fellow work associates, firm management and client personnel. At Stage 4, John is also concerned about social relations, but now can differentiate this point of view from those of his immediate reference group. At Stage 4, John might seek to maintain those rules that uphold the standards of his firm or the accounting profession.

Post-conventional Level

If John was at the post-conventional level, he would follow a set of ethical principles or beliefs that at times could be in conflict with the rules of the profession. In this example, John might inform Bolder even though it was a blatant violation of the code of conduct. One explanation for John's behaviour might be that his beliefs regarding the survival and welfare of the Bolder Corporation is considered by him to be far more important than client confidentiality. In contrast, John's ethical conviction might be consistent with the code, and in this situation informing Bolder would be a breach of such ethical principles. Perhaps John might feel compelled to inform Colby of the harmful consequences of the new pricing policy on Bolder, or recommend to Bolder's management that they reconsider alternative options. As a last resort, one strategy always available to John is to withdraw from both engagements because of the existing ethical conflict with both clients.

At Stage 5, John might start to believe that complying with a particular rule or standard of professional conduct, such as client confidentiality, is based on some rational calculation of the overall good for society. However, John might have difficulties integrating and accepting the utilitarian aspects of the rule that he is required to follow. At Stage 6, John follows only those rules that are consistent with his underlying ethical beliefs or moral values. At Stage 6, John makes a deliberate choice to "do right" if it is consistent with his self-chosen ethical principles.

These cases and corresponding discussion suggest that an auditing practitioner's resolution of difficult ethical conflicts is, at least in part, a function of his or her ethical reasoning level. As noted by Rest [1979a], this cognitive capacity is a fairly complex psychological system, from which the auditor or accountant frames a judgment in the wake of an ethical issue or problem. While the stage-sequence model may be a fair surrogate for an individual's ethical reasoning capacity, Rest's [1986] four-component model suggests that other intellectual capacities such as sensitivity, value systems and moral perseverance may well play an equally important part in determining ethical action. The next section briefly discusses the implications of using this cognitive-developmental model for studying the ethical judgments of professional accountants or auditors.

3.2 IMPLICATIONS TO ACCOUNTING AND AUDITING PRACTICE

In light of controls and quality checks that prevent and seemingly lessen instances of unethical behaviour within the profession, why should we be concerned about an individual practitioner's ethical reasoning levels? One answer to this question is very eloquently addressed by Ralph Walters, retired partner of Touche Ross and director of professional conduct for the California Society of CPAs [1986, p. 72]:

> We remind our members that the individual makes a difference. Our profession's image is largely the sum of our individual attitudes and actions. Each failure tarnishes the image of the profession. Each of us is a professional, and each responsible for maintaining high standards. We cannot rationalize questionable actions by hiding behind our firms. Each of us is accountable for his or her actions.

Assuming that an individual's ethical reasoning level is a determinant of ethical judgment in the accounting or auditing environment, then what value does this area of research provide? One way to answer this question is to discuss the potential use of such information, and that can be divided into three general areas as posited by Arnold and Ponemon [1987, p.25]:

- Gaining an insight into the underlying reasoning levels of practicing accountants or auditors in their resolution of ethical conflicts.
- Recognizing the differences in ethical judgment among professional accountants and auditors and the effect of these differences on practice.
- Identifying the means necessary to effect ethical propriety in the accounting and auditing professions.

Perhaps an integral understanding of the ethical reasoning process of accountants and auditors should be a prerequisite to the legislation of rules and regulations promoting desirable behaviour. Rules or guidelines that stress only one mode of ethical reasoning will do little to mitigate the unethical action of individuals whose reasoning is not consistent with this mode. For example, the primary motivator of ethical behaviour for an individual at the lowest ethical reasoning level in the Kohlberg [1969] stage model is to avoid punishment. In this case, rules that are not backed by punishment will normally not be adhered to by the individual at a lower stage of ethical cognition. Thus, behavioural norms that are consistent with the ethical frame of the intended population should certainly improve compliance. It is important to note, however, that rules in accounting may be seen as an institution for avoiding punishment. In this case, pre-conventional auditors may follow the rules only to defend themselves against allegations of wrongdoing or audit failure.

The suggested model of ethical cognition provides a framework that can be used to gauge those conflict areas that would have the most severe and damaging consequences to the profession. For example, if an overwhelming majority of partners are at a level where it is very likely that the quality and integrity of their firm's work product will come before marketing and promotion activities, then stringent rules limiting practice development would be unnecessary or perhaps dysfunctional to the desired behaviour. On the other hand, if most partners are at a level where profitability and personal economic gain are of primary concern, then rules on marketing activities that are not backed by authority would do little in mitigating behavioural impropriety.

While the theory of cognitive-development places an individual at an ethical reasoning stage, it is possible for individuals to move to higher stages. Thus, while these issues deal with fitting the rules of the profession to the stages at which we currently find the accountant, another possibility is to raise the level of the accounting practitioner such that he or she can better function in a dilemma-prone world. Here an understanding of the theory of ethical development is a necessary condition for effective training and education. The next section describes the results of several recently published research studies in the area of public accounting, auditing and accounting education — all drawing upon the psychology of ethical reasoning and Kohlberg's [1969] or Rest's [1986] stage-sequence model.

3.3 STUDIES IN ACCOUNTING AND AUDITING

Recently completed empirical studies have explored the underlying ethical reasoning processes of accountants and auditors in practice. Findings in this relatively new area of research are threefold. First, studies suggest that members of the public accounting profession are not reaching their potential for higher levels of ethical reasoning by virtue of selection-socialization in education (Ponemon and Glazer [1990]) and within public accounting firms (Ponemon [1990, 1992a]; Shaub [1991]). Second, findings show that ethical reasoning may be an important determinant of professional judgment in matters such as the disclosure of sensitive information (Arnold and Ponemon [1991]) and auditor independence (Ponemon and Gabhart [1990]). Third, results suggest that unethical and dysfunctional audit behaviour, such as the underreporting of time on an audit time budget, may systematically be related to the auditor's level of ethical reasoning (Ponemon [1992b]). In general, these works imply that ethical reasoning may be an important cognitive characteristic that may affect individual judgment and behaviour under a wide array of conditions and events in current professional practice. To show how the present work extends earlier research, brief synopses of recently completed studies in this area are provided below, and Exhibit 3.1 summarizes this literature.

Descriptive Studies

Mary Beth Armstrong [1987] studied accountants' ethical reasoning and moral development employing the Defining Issues Test for a sample of CPAs and accounting students in Southern California. Based on a mailed survey, she found that CPAs and accounting students tended to be at lower levels of ethical reasoning than comparable groups of college-educated adults or college-aged students as published in Rest [1979a]. Drawing from Rest's [1986] findings that a significant rate of ethical development can occur for many adults during their college years, she advanced the notion that accounting education may inhibit development to higher stages of ethical reasoning.

Lawrence Ponemon [1988, 1990] examined the ethical reasoning and ethical judgments of accounting practitioners in public firms. Fifty-two practicing public accountants from large and small CPA firms in the northeast region of the United States agreed to participate in a field study that required them to resolve the standardized Moral Judgment Interview (MJI) and

Exhibit 3.1

Review of Ethical Reasoning Studies in Accounting and Auditing

Author(s)	Description of the studies	Major research findings
Armstrong [1987]	DIT and ethical sensitivity survey completed by CPAs and accounting students from the southwestern region of the United States.	CPAs and accounting students have relatively low DIT P scores in comparison to other populations studied.
Ponemon [1990]	MJI and audit case completed by CPAs at various position levels in public firms in the northeast region of the United States.	MJI scores decrease for CPAs at higher positions in public accounting firms.
Ponemon and Gabhart [1990]	DIT survey and between-subject experiment on auditor independence completed by senior level auditors while attending a national firm's training program.	Auditor independence judgment and DIT P scores are related, wherein low DIT auditors were more sensitive to penalty than affiliation when framing judgment.
Ponemon and Glazer [1990]	DIT survey and comparative analysis of accounting students and alumni in public accounting practice from one state university and one liberal arts college, both in the eastern region of the United States.	Students and CPAs from the liberal arts college have higher DIT P scores than those from the conventional (AACSB) university program.
St. Pierre, Nelson and Gabbin [1990]	DIT survey and comparative analysis of accounting and non-accounting students in large university located in the southeastern region of the United States.	Accounting students have lower DIT P scores than other nonbusiness students, and female accounting majors have higher DITs than males.
Shaub [1991]	DIT survey of CPAs from the midwestern offices of one large public accounting firm and accounting students from one large midwestern university in the United States.	Students and CPAs have lower DIT P scores than the population of college-educated adults, and DITs are inversely related to CPAs' position level.
Arnold and Ponemon [1991]	DIT survey and between-subject experiment on internal auditors from public (state government) and private companies located in the northeastern region of the United States.	Auditors with higher DIT P scores are more likely to disclose sensitive audit findings, even under conditions of retaliation by management.
Holt and Jeffrey [1991]	DIT survey of accounting, business and liberal arts students from one large midwestern university in the United States.	Accounting students have higher DIT P scores than students in other programs at the same university.

Exhibit 3.1 (cont'd)

Author(s)	Description of the studies	Major research findings
Lampe and Finn [1993]	DIT survey, ethics questionnaire and comparative analysis of CPAs and accounting students from the midwestern region of the United States.	Accounting students and CPAs have relatively low DIT P scores and relatively high DIT Stage 4 percentage measures respectively.
Ponemon [1992a]	DIT survey of CPAs in nationwide cross-sectional sample and a two-year longitudinal study of auditors from one large public accounting firm in a large northeastern city in the United States.	DIT P scores increase from staff to senior levels and decrease, becoming more homogeneous, in the manager and partner ranks in two separate studies.
Ponemon [1992b]	DIT survey and experimental-lab study of underreporting on a simulated audit exercise for a sample of staff auditors from various practice offices in the United States who were attending a national training program.	Auditors with low DIT P scores are more likely to underreport time, under conditions of peer or time budget pressure, than auditors with high DIT P scores.
Ponemon [1993a]	Pre and Post DIT survey of ethical development and an economic choice experiment of undergraduate and graduate accounting students in one state university located in the northeastern region of the United States.	Students did not experience DIT P score increases over a one semester auditing course, even if they participated in a 10 week ethics program. A U-shaped relationship between students' DIT P score and free-riding behaviour was found.

an auditor role conflict based on a real life case study. Their stated responses were analyzed using a protocol analysis technique, resulting in an MJI stage score measure of ethical reasoning. Variables pertaining to the practice environment were also collected and examined to determine possible interactions with MJI scores. Findings revealed differences in subjects' ethical choice and stated resolution to the auditor role conflict according to their social position in the public accounting firm. That is, junior and senior level CPAs tended to acknowledge rules of conduct, while managers and partners tended to view profitability and litigation concerns as the most important antecedents to the resolution to the auditor-role conflict.

Ponemon [1990] also found a significant curvilinear association between MJI scores and years of public accounting experience, where ethical stage increased from the staff to supervisory levels and then sharply decreased in the manager and partner ranks. While findings are based on cross-sectional evidence from a relatively small, nonrandom sample of CPAs, Ponemon [1990] argues that the findings may have been brought about by socialization processes within accounting firms, thus causing individuals with too high or too low a level of ethical reasoning to leave the firm or profession.

Michael Shaub [1989, 1991] extended the work of Armstrong [1987] by attempting to measure the ethical sensitivity of CPA practitioners at all position levels from several offices of a Big-Six accounting firm (located in the midwest) and then related these ethical sensitivity measures to DIT P score results. While Shaub [1989] did not find a significant association between ethical reasoning (DIT P scores) and measured ethical sensitivity, his studies did provide three interesting findings. First, in his 1989 study, CPAs' DIT P scores also decreased in the manager and partner ranks, (similar to Ponemon's [1990] MJI results). Second, his 1991 study found significant differences between men and women, wherein female accounting students and CPAs tended to have higher DIT P scores than men at the same level or rank within the firm. Third, Shaub [1991] found a significant association between self-reported GPA and DIT P scores for both accounting students and practitioners, thus suggesting that ethical reasoning may be inextricably linked to other intellectual capacities as well as school achievement.

James Lampe and Don Finn [1993] also conducted a study of accounting students and CPAs in public firms (not including partners) using the DIT. This work built upon and extended Shaub's [1991] research by comparing subjects' DIT results to responses on a questionnaire containing seven short ethics scenarios. Their findings demonstrated that both accounting students and practitioners tend to have lower DIT P scores than college-aged students, college-educated adults and other professionals such as lawyers and doctors. They also found that DIT stage measures, rather than P scores, were a better predictor of ethical choice on the ethical scenarios. They also found that while DIT P scores were relatively low for most subjects, their percentage Stage 4 scores tended to be higher than those reported by Rest [1986]. Accordingly, Lampe and Finn [1993] conclude that, by virtue of the rule-oriented nature of accounting and auditing practice, the development of a Stage 4 moral orientation rather than principled reasoning (e.g., Stages 5 and 6) may be most important for professional accountants and auditors.

Most recently, Ponemon [1992a] attempted to study the influence of accounting firm socialization upon the individual CPA's level of ethical reasoning. Using the DIT, hypotheses concerning selection-socialization were explored. These hypotheses were tested using a triangulated research design based on a nation-wide, cross-sectional sample of 180 CPAs, a longitudinal sample of 221 auditors in one national firm over a two-year period, and an experimental study of 23 audit managers' promotion assessments of 54 senior level auditors in the same office. Findings of all three studies corroborate the existence of ethical socialization whereby those progressing to manager and partner positions within the firm tend to possess lower and more homogeneous levels of ethical reasoning. Experimental findings also suggest that firm managers' promotion decisions are biased in favor of individuals possessing ethical reasoning that is closer to their capacity. According to Ponemon [1992a], these findings imply that the ethical culture of the accounting firm stymies an individual's development to higher levels of ethical reasoning.

Ethical Judgment and Behaviour

Three recently published studies have sought to determine the existence of a relationship between ethical reasoning and ethical judgment or behaviour in the context of accounting and auditing. The first study, conducted by Ponemon and Gabhart [1990], was an experimental investigation of auditor independence judgments and employed 119 partners and managers in one national public accounting firm. Using the DIT P score to measure ethical reasoning, a hypothetical case study dealing with an independence dilemma framed in the third person to avoid potential self-reporting bias, and two between-subject manipulations, three significant findings were reported.

1. The authors found a systematic relationship between auditors' ethical reasoning and their resolution of the independence conflict, where auditors with relatively low DIT P scores were more likely to violate independence rules than those with higher DITs.
2. They found that the existence of penalty, or the likelihood of losing a job, has a much stronger effect on the independence judgment than the existence of affiliation, defined as the likelihood of hurting others. Further, interaction effects suggest that penalty is most salient for low DIT auditors.
3. DIT P scores explain a priority ranking of independence attributes, wherein auditors with lower DITs assigned greater importance to economic factors, such as client profitability and litigation, than auditors with higher DIT results.

In a related study, Arnold and Ponemon [1991] investigated the internal auditor's perceptions of whistle-blowing within the context of his or her level of ethical reasoning as measured by the DIT. Their experiment required 106 internal auditors to predict whether or not another person would engage in a whistle-blowing act under two different sets of conditions. The first set of conditions concerned the position of the individual discovering a fraud and the second dealt with the nature of the retaliation posed against the whistle-blower. Similar to Ponemon and Gabhart [1990], the task was presented in the third-person to minimize potential self-reporting bias that often accompanies studies of ethical issues. Findings revealed that internal auditors with relatively low levels of ethical reasoning were unlikely to predict whistle-blowing as a means for disclosing wrongdoing. This result is especially prominent when the probable retaliation meant job termination for the whistle-blower. Findings also indicated that the organizational position of the individual contemplating the whistle-blowing act influences internal auditors' predictions, with external auditors considered most likely to act, internal auditors next, and marketing analysts least likely to act.

Ponemon [1992b] examined the relationship between auditors' ethical reasoning and their underreporting tendencies by employing an experimental-lab design for a sample of 88 staff-level auditors from a national public accounting firm. The design of this experiment permitted the author to observe actual underreporting on a simulated audit task exercise during a firm training program. Findings revealed that underreporting was systematically related to the auditor's level of ethical reasoning — as measured by the Defining Issues Test (DIT) — where those with relatively low DIT scores were shown to underreport most severely. Results also showed that while an unattainable time budget affects behaviour, peer pressure has the most significant impact upon underreporting. In summary, this study makes three contributions to the auditing and psychology literature:

1. It is the first study to establish the significance of peer pressure as an antecedent to underreporting.
2. It suggests that an auditor's ethical reasoning may be an important determinant of underreporting behaviour under conditions of work-related pressure.
3. Perhaps most importantly, it indicates that ethical reasoning is in fact related to ethical behaviour.

Ethics Education

Several studies have attempted to investigate the role of college education on accounting students' ethical development. For example, Ponemon and Glazer [1990] examined accounting students and alumni from a small liberal arts college and large state university. Using the DIT, they found that only accounting seniors and alumni of the liberal arts college progressed to levels of ethical reasoning comparable to the DIT norms published by Rest [1986]. They conclude [1990, p. 204] that differences in students' moral development, ". . . may be caused, in part, by an educational process that inhibits students' abilities to develop an increasing sense of ethics, integrity or moral beliefs during the college years. These findings suggest that liberal learning in college may be an important factor in the development of students' and accounting practitioners' moral reasoning."

Other studies confirm Ponemon and Glazer's [1990] findings that students of traditional accounting programs may not be developing to higher levels of ethical reasoning (see, for example, Armstrong [1987]; Shaub [1991]; Lampe and Finn [1993]). However, Holt and Jeffrey [1991] found that accounting students from a large midwestern state university tended to have higher DIT scores than non-accounting students from the same school. They also found that students who choose accounting as their major have higher DITs than students choosing other business and nonbusiness disciplines. Hence, Ponemon and Glazer's [1990] finding may not be generalizable to all schools in all regions of the country.

While most accounting academics and practitioners readily agree that ethics should become a more significant part of the accounting curriculum, only three studies have attempted to assess the effectiveness of ethics education in accounting. Using the DIT, St. Pierre, Nelson and Gabbin [1990] and Shaub [1991] studied the influence of ethics courses on accounting students' ethical reasoning. While findings are mixed, neither study found that participation in a college ethics course consistently influenced students' ethical development as measured by the DIT. Ponemon [1992c] also studied the influence of ethics interventions, integrated into a one-semester introductory auditing course at both the undergraduate and graduate level, on the ethical development and ethical behaviour of accounting students. In this study, ethics interventions were based on the review and discussion of ethics cases following a well-known pedagogical framework over the first ten weeks of one academic semester. The effectiveness of these interventions was tested two ways. First, using the Defining Issues Test (DIT) and a pre/post-test research design, the ethical development of accounting seniors and graduate students in four separate auditing classes was assessed. Second, students' unethical behaviour, defined as excessive free-riding on an economic choice experiment based on the Prisoners' Dilemma, was observed by the researcher. In summary, results of this study revealed that ethics interventions did not cause accounting students' level of ethical reasoning to develop (increase) and did not curtail students' free-riding behaviour. Findings also provided evidence of an association between ethical reasoning and students' economic choices, where students with relatively low and high levels of ethical reasoning were most likely to engage in free-riding.

In summary, the psychology of ethical reasoning has been shown to be of consequence to the study of behaviour in accounting and auditing because many professional judgments are conditioned upon the beliefs and values of the individual practitioner. The current monograph builds upon and attempts to extend this area of study by seeking to fill three gaps in the aforementioned literature. These include:

1. the influence of cultural factors on auditors' ethical reasoning and moral development
2. the relationship between auditors' ethical reasoning and perceptions of dysfunctional or unethical behaviour in the audit setting
3. the effect of auditors' ethical reasoning on audit-task performance in current practice.

In the next chapter, the methods and results of a cross-cultural DIT study of auditing practitioners in two international accounting firms from offices located in Canada and the United States are reported. Chapter 5 extends the cross-cultural analysis by studying the influence of ethical reasoning on Canadian and U.S. auditors' perceptions of dysfunctional or unethical behaviour in the audit setting — including the underreporting of time, the shifting of time to another audit client, premature sign-off and shirking on audit tasks. In Chapter 6, the relationship between ethical reasoning and auditor task performance is examined. It reports findings from three separate studies that involve the assessment of audit risk, sensitivity to material accounting error and recognition of material distortions to financial statement information.

Chapter 4

Auditors' Ethical Reasoning: A Comparison of Firms in Canada and the United States

4.1 THE INFLUENCE OF PROFESSIONAL AND CULTURAL DIFFERENCES

As discussed in the previous chapter, recently completed empirical studies have explored the underlying ethical reasoning processes of accountants in professional practice. Findings of earlier works provide evidence to suggest that accountants may not be reaching their potential for higher levels of ethical judgment or behaviour. Ponemon's [1990, 1992a] studies of CPAs in U.S. firms, for example, showed that individuals at higher position levels within the public accounting firm environment had lower ethical reasoning skills (as measured by the MJI and DIT instruments). In his 1990 study, Ponemon concluded (p. 209), "This work suggests that differences in ethical behaviour are likely to reflect differences in socialization; thus different positions in a firm's hierarchy are likely to engender different ethical proclivities."

This chapter extends the analysis of auditing professionals by providing a comparative analysis of auditors from the public accounting professions in two different countries –– namely Canada and the United States. Relying upon cognitive-developmental theory, and using a well-known psychometric of ethical reasoning, it reports the results of cross-cultural studies of both chartered accountants (CAs) and CPAs from the practice offices of two international public accounting firms operating in Ontario and the Northeast region of the United States. Findings show marked differences in DIT P scores between CA and CPA professionals at the same position level within these firms. That is, while the present study shows once more that CPAs' DIT P scores tend to decrease at higher position levels, CAs' DIT P scores seem to increase — especially from the manager to partner ranks. Further,

CAs tend to have higher DITs than CPAs at comparable ranks within the public accounting firm. These findings suggest that the ethical socialization phenomenon shown in earlier works by Ponemon [1990, 1992a] and Shaub [1991] may not be a prevalent factor in the Canadian auditing profession.

The remainder of this chapter is organized as follows. In the next section the relevant literature on ethical socialization in public accounting firms is first reviewed and then the primary research question to be studied is presented. This is followed by a discussion of the empirical methods and results of a cross-sectional study of Canadian CAs and American CPAs from two international firms. Finally, the implications, limitations, and possible directions for future research are provided in the last section.

Socialization and Ethics in Accounting Firms

Researchers have long been concerned with explaining how individuals become successful in their chosen careers (Forbes [1987]; Hall [1976]; Lawrence [1990]; Rosenbaum [1979, 1984]; Whyte [1956]). Career success or individual attainment within organizations has been explained by psychological and sociological processes (Nystrom and McArthur [1989]). Much of this work suggests that promotion serves as an employee screening and signaling mechanism. That is, employees who get a promotion are likely to be perceived by management as having personal characteristics commensurate with the culture and philosophy of the organization. Several studies indicate the importance of symmetry in the perceptions of subordinates and superiors in terms of selection and promotion (Smircich [1983]; Weick [1979]). As a result, management is more likely to promote subordinates who share common views of the organization and its people. Other studies suggest that as employees assume greater managerial responsibilities within an organization, they tend to develop homogeneous cognitive traits, including their level of ethical reasoning (Avolio and Gibbons [1988]; Fisher, Merron and Torbet [1987]).

Studies of socialization in the accounting profession have typically focused upon the work-related behaviours, attitudes or perceptions of individuals employed by large public firms (cf. Dillard and Ferris [1989]). One common theme in this literature is the existence of an underlying and often deliberate process of socialization at work within the accounting firm, resulting in the acculturation and assimilation of all members entering and remaining in the profession (cf. Blank [1984]). Early studies revealed organizational conflict emerging from socialization pressures, resulting in systematic differences between the perceptions of newly hired versus highly experienced accounting practitioners (Rhode, Sorensen and Lawler [1976, 1977]; Sorensen [1967]; Sorensen and Sorensen [1974]). Other studies also found a widening gap between high-level and low-level accountants in terms of career goals and objectives (Sorensen, Rhode and Lawler [1973]; Sorensen and Sorensen [1972]). At the centre of such conflicts are often discordant values brought about by an individual's career aspirations versus the bureaucratic demands of the firm (such as general management, recruitment, administration or other mundane personnel matters). Those who maintain a low regard for bureaucratic details will typically become dissatisfied with their career and leave the firm.

Later studies examined determinants of an individual's career success and upward mobility in public firms. In general, these studies show that individuals who are able to adapt to the firm's culture or work ethic will more likely progress. Those unable to do so will quickly become disillusioned with their careers and leave the firm (Aranya and Ferris [1984]; Benke and Rhode [1980]; Blank [1984]; Bullen and Flamholtz [1985]; Dean, Ferris and

Konstans [1988]; Dillard and Ferris [1979]; Ferris [1977]). Other researchers have examined organizational processes or control mechanisms employed to motivate and convince employees to think and behave in the best interests of the firm (Dirsmith and Covaleski [1985a]; Hofstede [1968]; McNair [1991]; Merchant [1982]; Ouchi [1980]; Rockness and Shields [1984]; Wilkins and Ouchi [1983]). According to Ouchi [1980], two implicit mechanisms are clan control and selection-socialization. Davidson [1990] suggests that the selection-socialization process in accounting firms can occur in two ways. That is, the individual unable to fit into the culture of the firm may voluntarily choose to leave, or firm management may seek to hire and promote only certain types of individuals from the population of eligible personnel.

As in other organizations, the culture of an accounting firm can have a profound effect on the beliefs and values of its personnel (Dillard [1981]; Otley and Berry [1980]). Accounting firms may have self-perpetuating organizational cultures because their managements tend to select and promote individuals who are perceived to be similar to themselves (Benke and Rhode [1984]; Rhode, Sorensen and Lawler [1976]). An "up or out philosophy", and the lack of diversity among individuals in the partner ranks strengthens a firm's culture and its influence on the socialization of auditors at all position levels (Davidson [1988]; Dirsmith and Covaleski [1985a]). A strong culture may be beneficial to the accounting firm because it can reduce deviant (undesirable) behaviour (Neimark and Tinker [1986]). On the other hand, such a culture may demand too much social conformity _ reducing creative activities within the firm and ultimately weakening its competitive edge (Ouchi [1980]; Wilkins and Ouchi [1983]).

A strong organizational culture may cause those individuals who are unable to conform to the ethical norms or values espoused by accounting firm management to be weeded out of the firm. In support of this theory, studies of accountants' ethical behaviour show individuals at higher position levels having a stronger sense of commitment or obligation to the profession (Aranya and Ferris [1984]; Aranya, Lachman and Amernic [1982]; Armstrong [1984]; Loeb [1970]; Norris and Niebuhr [1983]; Schilit [1981]; Yerkes [1975]). Indeed, the ethical socialization process itself may serve as the principal catalyst for earlier findings (Ponemon [1990, 1992a]) of an inverse relationship between position within the firm and the individual accountant's ethical reasoning. As a result, individuals with too high a level of ethical reasoning may experience difficulty progressing to upper echelons in the accounting firm's formal hierarchy.

Research Question

The current monograph extends prior work by exploring the influence of professional and cultural differences on the auditor's level of ethical reasoning as he or she progresses to higher position levels within the auditing firm. While the ethical socialization process may explain why certain auditors assimilate into the ethical culture or moral atmosphere of the firm, the ethical reasoning of practitioners also may be influenced by a plethora of factors outside the purview of the firm and its management, including the extent of accounting standards, the level of professional entry requirements and the nature of professional education. For example, according to Lampe and Finn [1993], individuals with a strong rule-orientation may self-select into the accounting profession. This in turn leads to an accounting firm culture where pre- or post-conventional ethical reasoning may be dysfunctional to those who want to prosper within their organizations. However, this situation may not prevail for accounting professionals in other countries. For instance,

Benston [1975] notes that accounting standards in the United Kingdom are less restrictive than those in the United States. He goes on to explain these differences by comparing the professional, regulatory, economic and legal environments between the two nations and concludes that (p. 265) "The professional environment in the United Kingdom permits a greater degree of peer pressure on accountants than can be achieved in the United States and consequently the need for codified, explicit accounting standards to maintain the public image of accountants is greater in the United States." By virtue of this difference, one could speculate that individuals choosing to become accounting professionals in the United Kingdom may be less rule-oriented than their counterparts in the United States. This possibility may explain, at least in part, differences in the ethical reasoning capacities of individual accountants in the U.S. compared to the U.K.

The same may be true for the Canadian public accounting profession, which contains elements of both the U.S. and U.K. professions. Several studies have shown that the accounting profession in Canada differs from the United States in four major respects (see Bloom and Naciri [1989]; Bloom and Kantor [1991]; Dunmore and Falk [1992]; Johnston, Lemon and Neumann [1980]; Zind and Zéghal [1989]):

1. While the U.S. auditing profession is a regulated monopoly, three independent public accounting professions coexist in the Canada, including Certified General Accountants (CGAs), Certified Management Accountants (CMAs) and Chartered Accountants (CAs).
2. Though regulated by provincial law, professional bodies within each Canadian province have the primary authority in granting licences, setting practice standards and establishing educational requirements for members in public practice.
3. Examinations leading to professional certification (e.g., CGA, CMA, CA) seek to elicit professional rather than technical judgment from a broad range of essay-type questions. The CPA exam in the U.S., on the other hand, has become more objective and technically oriented in recent years.
4. As noted by Bloom [1984], accounting and auditing standards in Canada are less structured than those in the United States and, therefore, rely more heavily on the discretion of the professional accountant or auditor.

One could argue that these factors work together, making Canada less restrictive than the U.S. in terms of professional entrance and practice and, thus, allowing greater diversity in skills and intellectual abilities within the Canadian accounting and auditing community.

It is precisely these issues that may explain differences between auditing professionals in Canada and the United States in terms of their ethical reasoning and moral development. To this end, this study seeks to answer the following important research question:

> How do Canadian auditing professionals in CA firms compare to their counterparts in CPA firms within the United States?

Given that the auditing professions in Canada and the United States are relatively similar in terms of professional standards, business practices, historical underpinnings and socioeconomic characteristics, then findings of differences between these two groups would suggest that greater differences may exist for auditors from nations with a more diverse culture.

4.2 RESEARCH METHODS

Samples

The researchers contacted the managing partners of the offices of several international public accounting firms with practice offices located in the Northeastern region of the United States and Ontario, Canada during the summer and fall of 1990. The culmination of this effort was the agreement by the auditing departments of two accounting firms to participate in this study.[11] With the assistance of its management, all auditing personnel at the staff, senior, manager and partner levels were available for selection. All auditors were identified by firm management as having passed all parts of the uniform CPA or CA examinations. Auditing personnel were contacted by letter and a follow-up telephone call by a partner from auditing departments in the same offices. Information packages were sent to 251 CPAs from three offices of Firm 1 and two offices of Firm 2, and to 167 CAs from two offices of Firm 1 and one office of Firm 2. Because of a relatively high response rate, a second mailing was not employed. Still, non-response bias was estimated from late respondents (cf. Scheaffer, Mendenhall and Ott [1986, pp.35-36]).[12] Overall, this resulted in 235 usable returned responses collected over a seven-week period — or a 56.2 percent response rate.

Exhibit 4.1 (Panel A)

Response Rates and Sample Frequency of Participating
U.S. CPAs and Canadian CAs by Firm and Position Level

	CPAs in U.S. Firms			CAs in Canadian Firms			Overall Sample		
	Mailed	Returned	Rate	Mailed	Returned	Rate	Mailed	Returned	Rate
Firm 1:									
Staff	39	21	53.85%	25	16	64.00%	64	37	57.81%
Senior	50	31	62.00%	34	20	58.82%	84	51	60.71%
Manager	38	19	50.00%	19	10	52.63%	57	29	50.88%
Partner	20	9	45.00%	15	13	86.67%	35	22	62.86%
Subtotal	147	80	54.42%	93	59	63.44%	240	139	57.92%
Firm 2:									
Staff	25	13	52.00%	15	9	60.00%	40	22	55.00%
Senior	30	18	60.00%	23	13	56.52%	53	31	58.49%
Manager	31	14	45.16%	20	11	55.00%	51	25	49.02%
Partner	18	8	44.44%	16	10	62.50%	34	18	52.94%
Subtotal	104	53	50.96%	74	43	58.11%	178	96	53.93%
Overall:									
Staff	64	34	53.85%	40	25	64.00%	104	59	56.73%
Senior	80	49	62.00%	57	33	58.82%	137	82	59.85%
Manager	69	33	50.00%	39	21	52.63%	108	54	50.00%
Partner	38	17	45.00%	31	23	86.67%	69	40	57.97%
Total	251	133	52.99%	167	102	61.08%	418	235	56.22%

Exhibit 4.1 (Panel B)

Description of Sample by Gender, Average Age, Average Years of Auditing Experience and Position Level by Firm for U.S. CPAs and Canadian CAs

	CPAs in U.S. Firms						CAs in Canadian Firms					
	Men			Women			Men			Women		
	No.	Age	Exp.	No.	Age	Exp.	No.	Age	Exp.	No.	Age	Exp.
Firm 1:												
Staff	10	23.0	1.8	11	23.6	1.3	10	23.2	1.5	6	23.8	1.1
Senior	17	25.2	3.9	14	26.7	5.5	12	26.0	3.9	8	24.5	3.7
Manager	11	28.2	6.7	8	27.8	6.3	7	29.1	6.8	3	28.1	7.0
Partner	6	41.3	19.5	3	43.9	19.0	11	38.3	17.2	2	43.2	21.8
Total/Avg.	44	27.6	6.3	36	27.4	5.5	40	29.2	7.5	19	26.8	5.3
Firm 2:												
Staff	6	23.6	1.8	7	23.0	1.1	5	22.7	1.2	4	22.9	1.3
Senior	10	25.4	4.4	8	26.2	4.9	8	24.4	3.6	5	26.2	4.3
Manager	7	27.0	5.9	7	30.4	7.1	8	28.1	6.3	3	29.1	6.4
Partner	6	42.2	21.2	2	40.7	19.1	8	37.5	16.2	2	36.4	15.5
Total/Avg.	29	28.9	7.7	24	27.7	5.6	29	28.7	7.4	14	27.3	5.5
Overall:												
Staff	16	23.2	1.8	18	23.4	1.2	15	23.0	1.4	10	23.4	1.2
Senior	27	25.2	4.1	22	26.5	5.3	20	25.4	3.8	13	25.2	3.9
Manager	18	27.7	6.4	15	29.0	6.7	15	28.5	6.5	6	28.6	6.2
Partner	12	41.8	20.3	5	42.6	19.0	19	37.9	16.7	4	39.8	18.6
Total/Avg.	73	28.1	6.8	60	27.5	5.6	69	29.0	7.4	33	27.0	5.3

Each packet of information contained the full (six story) version of the DIT, an instruction booklet, a personal history data sheet, an ethics questionnaire, and a covering letter from the researchers (all materials are provided in the Appendices). Of the returned DITs, 29 were unusable because of completion error. The remaining DITs were submitted to the Centre for the Study of Ethical Development at the University of Minnesota for independent scoring and tabulation. Panel A of Exhibit 4.1 provides the response rates and sample frequency of participating CPAs and CAs by firm and position level. Panel B of Exhibit 4.1 provides a description of the samples by gender, age and auditing experience by position level and firm for both CPAs and CAs. As can be seen, the sample is well balanced in terms of gender, age, experience and position level within each firm in both countries.

Measurement of Ethical Reasoning

The Defining Issues Test [Rest 1979b] was used to measure each CPA's and CA's level of ethical reasoning. As noted in Chapter 1, it is a widely used and reliable psychometric instrument and provides a measure of an individual's level of ethical reasoning according to the cognitive developmental theories posited by Piaget (1932 [1966]), Kohlberg [1969] and Rest [1979a]. The DIT is a self-administered questionnaire that includes a series of six hypothetical conflicts (see Appendix A). For each conflict or dilemma, subjects are required to select and rank order those issues that have, in their opinion, the most significant influence on its resolution.

The DIT provides several responses representing the most typical modes of thinking in terms of the underlying cognitive-developmental theory. In scoring the questionnaire, points are assigned to each subject's responses using a scale of four points for the most important to one point for the least important. The points corresponding to the highest modes of ethical cognition are used to construct a single measure known as the "P" (principled) score, computed for each subject. Rest [1986, p. 5] describes it as ". . . the relative importance a subject gives to principled considerations in making a decision about ethical dilemmas."

More specifically, the P score measures the percentage of Stages 5 and 6 (post-conventional) responses made by an individual subject to the entire instrument. Results, therefore, are expressed as a continuum from 0.0 to 1.0. In addition to the P score, the DIT results are also reported (in percentage form) as stages of ethical reasoning. Thus, since the stage-sequence model is developmental and sequential, a higher P score indicates a lower percentage of Stages 1 through 4 responses.

4.3 RESEARCH FINDINGS

Comparative Analysis

As reported in Exhibit 4.2, Spearman Correlations (Hollander and Wolfe [1973, pp. 191-192] between DIT P scores and various demographic attributes were compiled for CPA and CA samples, yielding a different pattern of association for DITs in each sample. For CPAs, DIT P scores were negatively associated with chronological age ($\rho = -0.378$), experience ($\rho = -0.403$), and position level ($\rho = -0.560$) at the $p < 0.01$ level. Although insignificant, age, experience and position level are all positively correlated to CAs' DIT P scores. Because age, experience and position level are themselves highly correlated in both samples, a stepwise (backward) canonical analysis was undertaken to determine the root correlation (Thompson [1984 p. 47]). This test revealed that position level ($R_c = 0.58$), and not experience ($R_c = 0.11$) or age ($R_c = 0.05$), explained the relationship to DIT P scores for CPAs. For CAs, however, the same canonical test did not reveal a dominant root correlation. Finally, using the binomial and sign tests, gender and DIT P scores were seemingly unrelated at all position levels.

Exhibit 4.3 reports DIT P score means, medians, standard deviations, ranges and percentage ethical stages (Stages 2 through 4) by the position level of CPAs and CAs.[13] The pattern of DIT P score mean and medians for CPAs are similar to those reported by Ponemon [1992a] and Shaub [1991]. That is, DIT P scores increase at the senior level and then decrease in the manager and partner ranks. As a result, partners of U.S. accounting firms have DIT P scores that are over 20 percent lower than staff level auditors. Looking at percentage DIT stage scores, the majority of CPAs are within the conventional level of ethical reasoning. That is, Stages 3 and 4 represent (on average) about 46.3 percent [22.53% + 23.73%] of CPAs' ethical reasoning as compared to an average DIT P score of 42.1 percent [18.19% + 23.91%] of CAs' ethical reasoning. Further, the percentage of Stage 3 reasoning for CPAs consistently increases from the staff to partner ranks. Thus, CPA partners are predominantly at Stage 3.

Exhibit 4.2

Spearman Correlations for DIT P Scores and Age, Experience, Rank and Education by U.S. CPAs and Canadian CAs

	DIT P score	Age	Experience	Position Level	Education
CPAs in U.S. Firms (n = 133)					
DIT P score	1.000				
Age	– 0.378*	1.000			
Experience	– 0.403*	0.616*	1.000		
Position	– 0.560*	0.454*	0.716*	1.000	
Education	0.021	– 0.010	– 0.001	0.030	1.000
CAs in Canadian Firms (n = 102)					
DIT P score	1.000				
Age	0.092	1.000			
Experience	0.140	0.581*	1.000		
Position	0.116	0.510*	0.656*	1.000	
Education	0.071	– 0.021	– 0.030	0.011	1.000

* Denotes that Spearman Correlation (Hollander and Wolfe [1973, pp. 191-192]) is significant at or beyond the $p < 0.01$ level.

Notes

Age, experience and education are measured in years as continuous variables. Position is a 4-point categorical variable from 1, denoting staff, through 4, denoting partners.

Spearman correlation analysis was inappropriate for gender because it is a dichotomous [0,1] variable. Binomial and sign tests were performed. However, no statistically significant relationship was found between gender and other demographic variables.

The pattern of mean and median DIT P scores shows that CAs differ from CPAs at all position levels. For instance, the overall sample suggests that Canadian practitioners have significantly higher DITs than their U.S. counterparts (e.g., DIT P score mean of 44.16 versus 40.03). CAs' DIT P scores also consistently increase from the staff to partner levels within both accounting firms. While overall increases seem to be relatively small, this pattern is quite different from CPAs in U.S. firms and may suggest that the process of firm socialization for CPAs may be very different from CAs in the two participating accounting firms.

The Wilcoxon Signed Rank test (Hollander and Wolfe [1973, p. 68]) was used to test the significance of differences between DIT medians for CPAs and CAs at adjacent position levels.[14] Results for CPAs show that seniors have higher DIT P scores than managers at $p < 0.01$, and managers have higher DIT P scores than partners at $p < 0.05$. For CAs, partners have higher DIT P scores than managers at $p < 0.05$. The Kruskal-Wallis and Jonckheere procedures (Hollander and

Exhibit 4.3

DIT P Score Means, Medians, Standard Deviations, Ranges, and Percentage Stages

			CPAs in U.S. Firms		
DIT Measures	Staff (n=34)	Senior (n=49)	Manager (n=33)	Partner (n=17)	Overall (n=133)
P Score Means	40.16	42.40	38.67	35.57	40.03
P Score Medians	41.50	43.00 –	37.90*,–	35.75*	40.50*
P Score S.D.	11.11	10.94	9.50	6.08	10.06
P Score Range	43.90	50.00	40.10	38.80	50.00
P% Stage 2	9.93	9.55	7.62	8.04	8.98
P% Stage 3	18.10	19.12	27.50	31.59	22.53
P% Stage 4	26.16	23.44	22.01	23.07	23.73
			CAs in Canadian Firms		
DIT Measures	**Staff** (n=25)	**Senior** (n=33)	**Manager** (n=21)	**Partner** (n=23)	**Overall** (n=102)
P Score Means	43.17	43.61	45.93	46.67	44.16
P Score Medians	43.33	43.00	45.33*,+	48.00*	45.33*
P Score S.D.	13.16	11.08	12.53	9.01	11.32
P Score Range	44.15	47.00	53.00	44.90	53.00
P% Stage 2	9.17	8.07	6.76	7.41	7.94
P% Stage 3	19.11	20.12	14.50	17.93	18.19
P% Stage 4	21.76	23.95	25.66	24.73	23.91

Notes

The Wilcoxon Signed Rank test (Hollander and Wolfe [1973, p. 68]) was used to test the significance of differences between DIT P score medians at adjacent position levels. A minus sign (–) denotes that DIT P score decreases at next higher position level at or beyond the $p < 0.05$ level. A plus sign (+) denotes that DIT P score increases at next higher position level at or beyond the $p < 0.05$ level.

The Mann-Whitney U test (Hollander and Wolfe [1973, p. 71]) was used to test the significance of differences between DIT P score medians for American CPA and Canadian CA samples at each position level. Asterisks (*) denote significant differences between CPA and CA samples within a given position level at or beyond the $p < 0.05$ level.

Wolfe [1973, pp. 120-124]) were also used to test the order of DIT P scores by CPAs' or CAs' position level. Results show that the following order is significant at the 0.01 level for CPAs: senior ≥ staff ≥ managers ≥ partners, where at least one inequality is strict.[15] A marginally significant order ($p < 0.10$) was found for participating CAs as follows: partners ≥ managers ≥ staff ≥ senior.

The Mann-Whitney U test (Hollander and Wolfe [1973, p. 71]) was employed to test the significance of DIT P score differences between CPA and CA samples at each position level.

Exhibit 4.4

DIT P Score Differences between Canadian and U.S. Auditors by Firm Position Level*

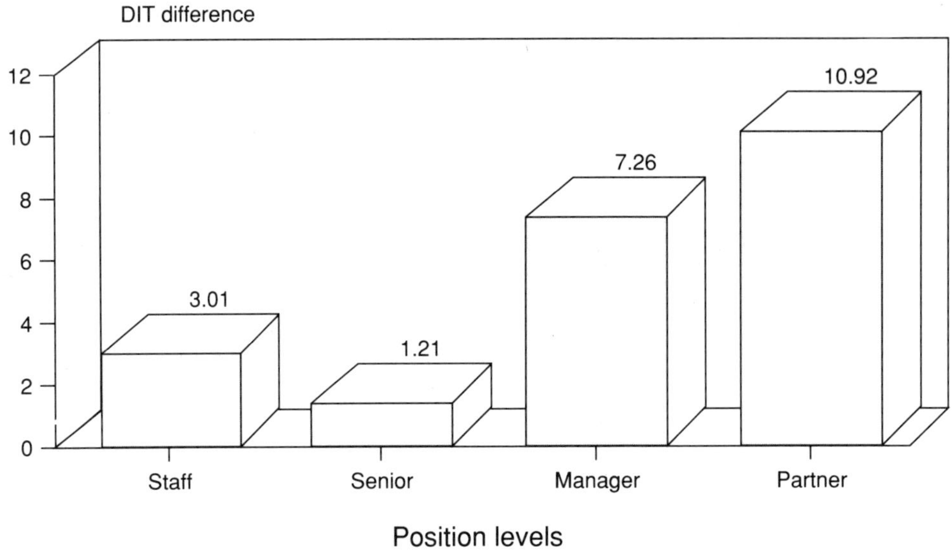

* Difference – Canadian DIT minus U.S. DIT at each position level (see Exhibit 4.3).

As indicated in Exhibit 4.3, Canadian audit managers have significantly higher DITs than American managers. In addition, Canadian audit partners have significantly higher DITs than American partners. These DIT P score differences between Canadian CAs and American CPAs by position level are illustrated using a bar chart format in Exhibit 4.4.

As suggested by Ponemon [1990, 1992a], selection-socialization processes would cause CPAs' DIT P scores to become more homogeneous at higher position levels. Looking at Exhibit 4.3, CPAs' DIT standard deviations and ranges provide partial support for this process. That is, the standard deviation is highest for seniors and is lowest for partners in both participating firms. DIT P score ranges are also lower for partners and managers in U.S. firms. Hence, decreases in both DIT P score means and variation in the manager and partner ranks provides evidence of a weeding-out effect for CPAs with too high a level of ethical reasoning before reaching upper management positions within the firm's hierarchy. In contrast, the DIT P score standard deviations and ranges for the CA sample provide no discernible pattern. In addition, standard deviations and ranges are higher for CAs compared to CPAs at corresponding position levels.

Exhibit 4.5 provides a comparison of the present findings to previous studies of accounting professionals as well as to the DIT P score norms published by Rest [1979a, 1986]. As can be seen, the present study yields three interesting findings. First, as shown in Panel A of Exhibit 4.5, the DIT P score mean for the sample of American CPAs is not significantly different from earlier DIT studies of accounting professionals (cf. Armstrong [1987], Lampe and Finn [1992], Ponemon [1988], Ponemon and Glazer [1990], Shaub [1989]). Second, Canadian CAs have a DIT P score mean that is significantly higher than all previous studies of U.S. accounting practitioners. Third, while DIT P scores for CPAs are

Exhibit 4.5

Comparisons to DIT P Score Norms

Panel A: Comparison to previous studies of CPAs.

Prior studies of accounting professionals in U.S. firms	Sample Size	DIT P score
Armstrong [1987]	119	38.5
Ponemon [1988]	180	38.1
Shaub [1989]	207	41.3
Lampe and Finn [1993]	207	40.0
Weighted average of four studies	713	39.6
Present study — U.S. CPAs	133	40.3
Significance of difference (p-value)		0.6832
Present study — Canadian CAs	102	44.2
Significance of difference (p-value)		0.0038

Panel B: Comparison to DIT P score norms published by Rest [1979a, 1986].

			Significance levels	
Norm group	Sample Size	DIT P Score	CPAs (p-value)	CAs (p-value)
Seminarians in church	27	57.8	0.0000	0.0000
Practicing physicians	157	49.5	0.0003	0.0810
Practicing attorneys	102	47.3	0.0091	0.1432
College graduates	856	45.8	0.0398	0.7595
College students	885	44.9	0.0613	0.8192

The p-values shown above were computed using an aggregate two-tailed t statistic derived from meta analysis.

significantly lower than standard DIT norms, CAs (and not U.S. CPAs) tend to have DITs that approximate the norms published by Rest [1986] for college educated adults and other professional groups.[16]

Summary of Findings

In summary, cross-sectional results suggest that the CPAs' position within the accounting firm is strongly associated with DIT results, wherein DIT P scores first increase from the staff to senior levels and then decrease in the manager and partner ranks. A less discernible relationship seems to exist for CAs, wherein DIT P scores tend to increase slightly from the staff to partner levels. Because the stage-sequence model is developmental, one would expect individuals' DIT measures to increase or stay the same over time, but never decrease. If this were true, however, then why does the pattern of results reflect *decreasing* DIT P scores in the manager and partner ranks for U.S. but not Canadian auditors? Three reasons can be advanced. First, individual managers and partners in U.S. firms may retrogress to lower ethical stages as they progress in their careers. However, this would be a clear contravention of the stage model. Second, as noted by Sorensen, Rhode and Lawler [1973], a generation gap may still exist between CPAs at higher and lower ranks within the U.S. accounting profession, but not in Canada. As a result, in comparison to staff and seniors or their Canadian counterparts, those in the manager and partner ranks in U.S. firms may not have been exposed to a socially or culturally diverse environment, thus inhibiting their development. As noted by Ponemon and Glazer [1990] in their study of two markedly different educational institutions in the United States, one such factor is the nature and quality of accounting education. Thus, by virtue of different entry, curricular and professional examination requirements (Bloom and Kantor [1991]), the extent of ethical development of accounting students in Canadian universities may be high when compared to students in American schools. Along these lines, Rest [1986, pp. 110-111] suggests individuals experiencing university and graduate school education can achieve DIT P scores that are, on average, ten points higher than those who do not have this background.

A third reason is that socialization within U.S. accounting firms — and not Canadian firms — may have resulted in the selection and promotion of those managers and partners at lower levels of ethical reasoning. This process may be formal or informal. For example, the CPA's ethical reasoning level might well affect social discourse with peers, superiors, and clients. In this situation, someone who is different in some way might be perceived by firm management as less credible or competent than others who are similar to themselves. Further, the incentive structure of the U.S. firm might motivate employees to participate in certain work-related rituals, such as underreporting time or underestimating an audit budget, to prove their credibility (Dirsmith and Covaleski [1985a]; McNair [1991]). Perhaps individuals with a higher capacity for ethical reasoning may be unwilling to participate in such rituals, thus failing to prove their worthiness to the firm. Finally, public accounting firms in the U.S. may operate in a more competitive business environment than Canadian firms, and success may necessitate management of accounting firms to accede to the demands of clients. Being less willing to do so, CPAs with higher capacities for post-conventional ethical reasoning may find it difficult to advance or may be more likely to voluntarily leave the firm.

The pattern of DIT P score increases and decreases for CPAs, but not for CAs, may suggest that ethical socialization is a dynamic process, wherein the auditor's ethical reasoning capacity is influenced by the culture of the accounting firm as well as the nature of the accounting profession. Consider, for example, the slight increases in DIT P score means for both CPAs and CAs at lower echelons in the two participating public accounting firms. Perhaps this is due in part to the technical or "craft" aspects of accounting. Those with higher ethical reasoning capacities may be better able to perform audit work under conditions of work-related pressure. On the other hand, auditors with lower ethical reasoning capacities may attempt to resolve pressure by engaging in dysfunctional behaviours such as premature sign-off or slacking on assigned tasks. As a result, they fail to master the craft aspects of their job, receive negative appraisals by their superiors, and are denied promotion.

At higher echelons, the business aspects of auditing may dominate individual evaluations and promotion decisions in U.S. firms, but not in Canada. By virtue of firm profitability and "deep pocket" legal liability concerns in the United States, individuals with lower ethical reasoning capacities may be better able to deal with business issues — thus achieving promotion to the partnership ranks. In Canada, by virtue of fewer rigid standards of accounting and auditing and different legal liability rules than in the U.S., CAs who progress to the partner level in public accounting firms may be those who are better able to render professional judgment and resolve ethical conflict under a wide range of circumstances in everyday practice. The implications and limitations of these findings are discussed in the last chapter of this monograph.

Chapter 5

Ethical Reasoning and the Perception of Dysfunctional Behaviour in the Audit Setting

This chapter explores the influence of ethical reasoning on auditors' perceptions of unethical or dysfunctional behaviour in the audit setting. Employing an experimental instrument for a sample of actual auditors at various position levels from Canadian and U.S. offices of two international public accounting firms, four behaviours related to audit budget distortion or audit quality reduction are examined — namely, the underreporting of chargeable time, slacking on audit work, prematurely signing off on audit work and shifting time between two or more auditing engagements. As discussed in an earlier chapter, these behaviours are of interest because they are thought to be ways of coping with work-related pressure and ethical conflict in the audit setting. Hence, while distortion of an audit budget or quality reduction acts violate the official policies of most auditing firms [Rhode 1978], empirical evidence suggests that they may not be viewed as unethical or even dysfunctional by some auditors (see, for example, Dirsmith and Covaleski [1985a, 1985b]; McNair [1991]; Ponemon [1992b]).

This chapter shows that auditors' perceptions of these behaviours are systematically related to their level of ethical reasoning as measured by the Defining Issues Test (DIT). In particular, auditors with relatively high DIT scores were shown to perceive underreporting, slacking and premature sign-off in a more negative light than auditors with lower DITs. Also found were differences between Canadian and U.S. auditors, where CPAs — especially those at the staff and senior levels — were more likely than CAs to believe underreporting, shifting time or premature sign-off is a pervasive response to budget pressure in the audit setting.

The remainder of this chapter is organized as follows: the relevant literature on budget pressure and dysfunctional behaviour in auditing are provided, and then a conceptual framework and research question are advanced. Next, the methods of an experimental study are explained and results are reported. Probable reasons for the reported findings are provided in the final section.

5.1 BACKGROUND AND THEORY

In response to competitive (Marxen [1990]) and stressful (Kelley and Margheim [1990]) conditions within the firm, auditors may engage in certain work-related behaviour that may be dysfunctional to audit firms, the accounting profession and the general public who are the beneficiaries of audit quality, because they ultimately lead to a reduction in the quality and credibility of the independent audit (cf. Rhode [1978]). Perhaps the most commonly studied behaviour, underreporting of chargeable time (wherein auditors report fewer hours than were actually utilized to complete a specific task), may actually be undertaken to mitigate other dysfunctional acts that could substantially reduce the quality and perceived credibility of an auditing engagement (McNair [1991]). Alternatively, reporting actual time and exceeding the audit budget may signal poor performance, or even incompetence, to firm management. Hence, some auditors may believe that misrepresentation, such as underreporting, premature sign-off, slacking on audit work or shifting time to another audit engagement is the only workable solution to an unattainable work budget.

Dysfunctional behaviour, however, may cause ethical tension for the auditor because it may be viewed as a violation of firm policy and written standards. Further, it may breach the norms of co-workers or go against the auditor's personally held beliefs or values. Some auditors will choose to report honestly and diligently complete all assigned work, even if time budget overruns will negatively affect their reputation. In contrast, other auditors will choose to engage in questionable time-reporting practices because they are believed to be an audit-related ritual proving their loyalty to the firm (Dirsmith and Covaleski [1985a]).

The following section provides a summary of the literature that is relevant to the present study. It includes a discussion of time budgets and their influence on individual behaviour in the context of job performance and appraisal within an organization such as the public accounting firm.

Time Budgets and Behaviour

Time budgets have been closely linked to dysfunctional behaviour in many different types of organizational settings (see, for example, Holstrum [1971]; Hopwood [1972]; Merchant [1985]; Stedry [1960]; Swieringa and Moncur [1972]). The key factors underlying these undesirable consequences are the perceived attainability of the budget, its acceptance by those affected by the budget, and feedback utilization. Feedback utilization provides an incentive structure from which the individual can evaluate the tradeoffs inherent in attainability versus acceptance concepts. In the presence of adequate incentives, an individual agent might be motivated to accept a more rigorous budget target than he or she would in a similar situation with less compelling incentives (Chow [1983]; Holstrum [1971]; Marxen [1990]; Stedry [1960]). Accepting a rigorous target, and working toward it, are two separate events for the individual. When true effort cannot be directly observed, and the only means of monitoring performance is outcome-related, there is potential for misrepresentation of effort by an agent.

The key aspect of this phenomenon is the information asymmetry that exists between the budget and true performance. That is, complete information regarding an agent's true performance is often an economic infeasibility to a firm due to the costliness of observing actual effort. The existence of this form of information asymmetry is the key characteristic of reputation theory models (Carmichael [1984]; Holmstrom [1984]; Kreps and Wilson [1982]; Milgrom and Roberts [1982]). Kreps and Wilson [1982] find that only a small amount of imperfect information about the true value of an individual's work ability is necessary to generate a reputational effect in a multiperiod setting. Milgrom and Roberts [1982] also note that asymmetric information plays a crucial role in their analysis, since it provides the rationale for factoring past actions into expectations of a firm's future actions. Information asymmetry, combined with a setting involving repeated actions in which prior outcomes are observable, provides the necessary and sufficient conditions for a reputational effect to emerge in the audit setting. As a result, the auditing environment itself may cause individuals to become motivated to distort a time budget or limit actual work effort in order to signal competence to the management of the firm.

Early research on budgeting has shown that individuals respond in a seemingly undesirable manner when faced with time pressure (Argyris [1953]; Hofstede [1968]; Stedry [1960]). These works suggest that the management control structure of a firm might inadvertently contribute to certain dysfunctional behaviours such as accepting and attempting to attain an unrealistic budget standard by distorting productivity measures, slacking off on work, or underreporting time. While distorting audit time budgets is prohibited by the formal policies of many firms (Rhode [1978]) and the auditing profession (e.g., Commission on Auditors' Responsibilities [1978]; National Commission on Fraudulent Financial Reporting [1987]), research has shown that it is often not penalized within the formal incentive structure unless it reaches extreme levels (McNair [1991]; Swieringa and Moncur [1972]). Taking this one step further, Dirsmith and Covaleski [1985a] suggest budget distortion may be part of the firm's informal communication structure and is viewed as a way to signal devotion to peers or the management of the firm. While these studies provide different explanations of this phenomenon, they all indicate that it may serve a unique purpose within the audit setting where cost and quality tradeoffs are a fact of life.

Studies of auditor behaviour under conditions of time budget pressure focus on the motivation of the individual rather than the structure of the firm itself. Underreporting (Lightner, Adams and Lightner [1982]; Lightner, Leisenring and Winters [1983]) and premature sign-off (Fleming [1979]), for example, have been the focus of much examination. More recent studies have examined the interaction between underreporting and other dysfunctional behaviours that directly reduce audit quality (Kelley and Margheim [1987]; Kelley and Margheim [1990]; Margheim and Pany [1986]).

Budget Distortion and Audit Quality Reduction

Underreporting and shifting time to another budget are two manipulations to an outcome signal. Since actual effort, and competence, are predominantly unobservable in the audit setting, auditors can alter the time report to meet preset standards. These one-period irrational acts may represent an investment strategy for the auditor who wishes to obtain a promotion based on perceived competence. As McNair [1991] observes, underreporting or shifting time to another client engagement may not be perceived as unethical or dysfunctional by the management of an audit firm because such acts do not necessarily result in a reduction of audit quality. In contrast, auditors also can alter an outcome signal by doing less audit work (Rhode [1978], McNair [1991]). In light of the difficulty in effectively monitoring job performance, auditors can slack off or shirk by expending less effort on an assigned task. At extreme levels, auditors can avoid work altogether by prematurely signing off on the audit program. Clearly, by having a negative impact on audit quality, slacking and premature sign-off can be very costly to auditors through increased exposure to litigation and a commensurate reduction in the firm's reputation.

Underreporting, premature sign-off, slacking, and shifting time have been attributed to many causes. For example, researchers have shown that unattainable time budgets, explicit peer pressure, the auditor's personally held beliefs and ethical values, fee arrangements, the auditor's perceptions of performance appraisals, firm size, the auditor's position level within the firm and stress have all been found to influence such behaviour. Most of these research findings are empirically derived, based on survey results from large cross-sections of public accounting professionals.

Rhode [1978], Kelley and Seiler [1982], and Kelley and Margheim [1990] all found that the frequency of auditors' dysfunctional behaviour increased as time budgets became more difficult to meet. Kelley and Seiler [1982] also found that auditors at the staff and senior level, compared to managers and partners, were more willing to engage in underreporting or shifting time between audit clients. Further, Lightner, Adams and Lightner [1982] found that explicit peer pressure, such as a supervisor's request to underreport or shift time, as well as the auditor's own ethical beliefs and values, influenced negative behaviour.

Auditors believing that time budget compliance would lead to a positive performance evaluation were shown to be more likely to underreport (Lightner, Leisenring and Winters [1983]). Further, auditors from smaller accounting firms perceived a higher frequency of dysfunctional audit behaviour than those from Big Eight firms (Margheim and Pany [1986]). Also, the structure of the client billing arrangement was shown to influence negative behaviours such as underreporting (Kelley and Margheim [1987]). That is, auditors working on a fixed-fee basis were more likely to underreport or engage in other audit quality reduction acts such as premature sign-off or slacking. Kelley and Margheim [1990] also studied the influence of certain personality traits on auditors' underreporting under stressful conditions caused by time budget pressure. Findings revealed engagements that were highly structured and managed by seniors with a Type A personality had fewer incidents of underreporting by audit staff. Further, they write [1990, p.22], "The descriptive results of this study suggest that an alarming number of underreporting and audit quality reduction acts are occurring in practice."

While these studies make important contributions to the auditing literature, they are limited in two respects. First, results have been based on self-reported (survey) responses. Thus, given the sensitive nature of questions asked, subjects may have an incentive to distort time reports or misrepresent work activities (Buchman and Tracy [1982]). Second, the research does not provide a cognitive construct for explaining auditor behaviour. The present study extends these works by utilizing an experimental design using the third person construct. Accordingly, as noted by Ponemon and Gabhart [1990], such a design is particularly useful when attempting to elicit the true (unbiased) ethical orientation of subjects. In addition, it extends Ponemon's [1992b] work by showing that ethical reasoning is a cognitive determinant of dysfunctional behaviour in the audit setting.

Framework and Research Question

Prior research has shown that work-related pressure in the audit setting influences behaviour (Choo [1986]; Gaertner and Ruhe [1981]; Haskins, Baglioni and Cooper [1990]; Kelley and

Margheim [1990]; Lord [1990]). Such pressure has typically been defined in terms of unattainable time budget standards (Chow [1983]; Fleming [1979]). That is, the more difficult the time budget, the greater the pressure and the more likely that underreporting or audit quality reduction acts will occur. According to Lightner, Adams and Lightner [1982], Dirsmith and Covaleski [1985a], and McNair [1991], informal peer pressure also can influence underreporting and audit quality reduction. For example, the auditor may be told to do something unethical by a superior, may perceive other members of the same audit firm underreporting, may view their own performance as insufficient or may perceive other members of the audit team as being more skilled in performing assigned tasks. The present study advances the idea that the auditor's level of ethical reasoning will lessen the effect of time budget pressure on dysfunctional audit behaviour because the capacity to resist such pressure may be motivated by the ethical values that the individual brings to the task.

The relationship between time budget pressure, ethical reasoning and four dysfunctional audit behaviours (e.g., underreporting, slacking, premature sign-off, and shifting time) is illustrated in Exhibit 5.1. The mediating variable or catalyst in this framework is the moral conflict emerging from an unattainable audit budget that, in turn, will be used to evaluate the auditor's job performance. Also of importance is the underlying ethical reasoning level of the individual auditor assigned to the audit engagement. The auditor's reasoning can be broadly defined in terms of three developmental levels and six stages (see Exhibit 1.1).[17]

Exhibit 5.1

Mediated Relationship between Audit Pressure, Ethical Reasoning and Dysfunctional Behaviours

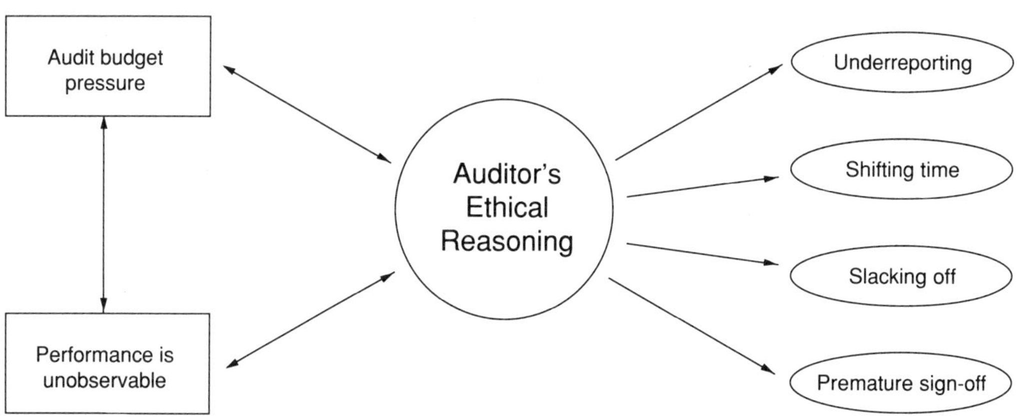

According to Kohlberg [1984, pp. 624-628], an individual at the pre-conventional level (Stages 1 and 2) makes the decision to do "right" to avoid punishment or to serve one's own interest. The pre-conventional person is not cognizant of differences among individuals. He or she views moral action in physical terms and is not conscious of the psychological interests of others. The auditor at the pre-conventional level would make the judgment to underreport or engage in other audit quality reduction acts if it were deemed more beneficial than reporting honestly. Similarly, if the auditor believed that the same outcome could be achieved by prematurely signing-off, and there was a low probability of getting caught, he or she might choose to do so rather than underreport. Thus, under conditions of audit work pressure and without sanctions being imposed by the firm, the pre-conventional auditor is likely to engage in underreporting, shifting time or other acts that could reduce audit quality.

The conventional (Stages 3 and 4) individual is aware of shared feelings, agreements and expectations that take primacy over individual interests and has a need to be a "good" person in the eyes of co-workers, management and the profession as a whole (Kohlberg [1984, pp. 628-633]). At Stage 3, the individual desires to maintain rules and authority that support stereotypical good behaviour. At Stage 4, the individual feels obligated to keep the system of rules and conventions going, and seeks ways to avoid breakdown in the system. The Stage 3 auditor would be greatly influenced by the existence of peer pressure (social conformity) or the unwritten rules of a peer group in framing a decision. He or she would justify dysfunctional behaviour, such as underreporting or shifting time, on the basis of what others do. In contrast, the Stage 4 auditor, depending upon his or her sense of obligation to the firm, may feel a need to report honestly despite pressure from peers to do otherwise.

The post-conventional (Stages 5 and 6) individual follows self-chosen ethical principles, in which case particular laws or social agreements are usually valid because they rest on such principles. However, when laws or rules violate these principles, one acts in accordance with the principle rather than abiding by the rule (Kohlberg [1984, pp. 634-639]). The individual recognizes that moral and legal points of view sometimes conflict, but has learned to balance moral principles with the rules and expectations of the profession and society. Hence, the auditor makes a choice to engage in some form of behaviour only if it is consistent with his or her self-chosen ethical principles. However, because the post-conventional auditor would most likely perceive the dysfunctional consequences of underreporting, slacking, shifting time and premature sign-off, he or she would see the rules as too important to break. Thus, auditors at the post-conventional level understand firm policies, know the informal (unwritten) rules of peers, and are influenced by their ethical principles (such as fairness, honesty and justice).[18]

In summary, the way in which an auditor perceives the problem and resolves the conflict will result in judgment consistent with his or her level of ethical reasoning.[19] Auditors at lower levels of ethical reasoning will be more sensitive to work-related pressure, and will be more likely to engage in dysfunctional behaviour. Those at higher levels will show greater resilience to work-related pressure under identical conditions, and will be less likely to engage in questionable time reporting practices or audit quality reduction acts. The primary research question explored in the present study is:

> Are auditors' perceptions of underreporting, premature sign-off, slacking and shifting time within the audit setting related to their level of ethical reasoning?

5.2 METHODS

As discussed in Chapter 4, a study of 235 auditors from two international public accounting firms in Canada and the United States was conducted. All subjects were members of an auditing department in large practice offices located in Ontario and the Northeast region of the U.S. In all cases, the unit of analysis was the individual auditor and data were collected on a subject-by-subject basis. See Exhibit 4.1 for details concerning sample frequency and demographics for U.S. CPAs and Canadian CAs in the two firms.

Experimental Task

Experimental materials included a biographical information sheet, an experimental instrument based on a case involving an auditor completing an audit task and an ethics questionnaire (see Appendix B). Similar to the methodology used by Ponemon and Gabhart [1990] and recommended by Rest [1986], the case was posed in the third person and was specified as being based on an actual event. The case involving an auditor conflict, about an individual who is assigned audit work that cannot be completed within the preset budget constraints, was mailed to all subjects along with the Defining Issues Test.

> Jane is an auditor for a large international public accounting firm located in the eastern region of the country. She has recently been assigned to the XYZ Corporation to assume in-charge responsibility for the completion of its year ending 19X1 financial statement audit. The XYZ Corporation is a large, public and somewhat complex organization that has engaged Jane's firm for many years. Even though Jane is a well trained and highly competent individual, she is having extreme difficulty in meeting the preset audit time budget completed by her superiors. To date, she has exceeded the audit time budget by over 35 percent.
>
> Jane knows that she is being evaluated by her superiors for promotion in the very near future and also believes that meeting one's time budget is an important factor for consideration in the performance appraisal and promotion process.
>
> Based on the audit evidence collected to date and the history of clean (unqualified) audit opinions rendered in the past, Jane is certain that the remaining substantive audit procedures to be completed by her and her staff will not yield material audit findings. Jane also believes that much of her remaining work on this job, such as filing and reviewing workpapers, can be performed away from the client's premises.

A delphi group of five auditors (one partner and four managers) and two auditing professors was employed to develop the experimental case and treatments for purposes of external validity. All members of the group reached consensus within three iterations on three major facts, all incorporated into the audit scenario provided above. First, the expert panel believed that auditors functioning at the senior level within the auditing firm are most susceptible to time budget pressure. This finding has been corroborated by earlier research (see Kelley and Margheim [1987]; Kelley and Margheim [1990]; Margheim and Pany [1986]). Second, the panel believed that extreme work-related pressure is caused by time budget overruns in excess of one third of the overall engagement (defined as a 35 percent overrun in the present case). Third, and perhaps most importantly, panel members believed that under certain conditions, many auditors would engage in some type of dysfunctional behaviour (especially underreporting) if the chances of getting caught were deemed to be very low.

Auditors were asked to rate their beliefs regarding the likelihood of each of the four separate dysfunctional auditor behaviours using a 100 point continuous bipolar adjective scale, where 0 denotes "no", 100 defines "yes", and 50 means "indifference" or complete uncertainty. To reduce possible demand characteristics within the instrument, each of the following four questions (e.g., dependent variables) were randomized for all subjects.

1. **Underreporting**: Assuming that Jane has the opportunity to underreport (eat) time without getting caught, will she do so?
2. **Shifting:** Assuming that Jane has the opportunity to shift her time to another chargeable engagement in the audit firm without getting caught, will she do so?

3. **Slacking:** Assuming that Jane has the opportunity to do the remaining work more quickly, but less carefully, without getting caught, will she do so?

4. **Premature sign-off:** Assuming that Jane has the opportunity to prematurely sign-off on much of the remaining work without getting caught, will she do so?

Treatments

In addition, auditors were randomly mailed one of two experimental conditions resulting in two between-subject groups of sizes 122 and 113, respectively.[20] The facts provided to all auditors were held constant except for two treatments concerning penalty (e.g., avoiding personal harm) and affiliation (e.g, doing as you perceive what others do) that were operationalized as follows:

- **Penalty:** Jane is told by the audit partner in-charge of the XYZ engagement that he is disappointed in her performance on the XYZ engagement so far and that if budget overruns continued he would be forced to give her a negative performance appraisal.

- **Affiliation:** Jane believes that from time to time most people in her firm have distorted their time budgets by eating time or shifting chargeable hours to another client engagement. She also believes that many auditors in her firm slack-off or prematurely sign-off on audit work in order to report that they got the job done within the prespecified audit time budget.

Given the findings reported by Ponemon and Gabhart [1990] and by Arnold and Ponemon [1991] in related studies of auditors' ethical judgment, subjects' self-assessed likelihoods of dysfunctional behaviour in the given case are expected to be higher under conditions of penalty than affiliation. In addition, the threshold anticipation of this study is that auditors with relatively low DIT P scores should be most affected by penalty and auditors with relatively high DIT P scores will be most affected by affiliation when framing their judgment. This is so because the pre-conventional individual resolves moral conflict by minimizing harm to self while the conventional individual explicitly considers the consequences of his or her moral action upon others (cf. Colby and Kohlberg [1987]; Kohlberg [1984]).

5.3 RESULTS

As reported in Exhibit 5.2, Spearman correlations (Hollander and Wolfe [1973, pp. 191-192]) were computed to explore associations between DITs, the four dysfunctional behaviours, and various demographic variables such as position level (rank), firm, gender (sex) and nation.[21] Underreporting and shifting are negatively correlated to DIT P scores at the $p < 0.10$ level. In addition, underreporting is positively correlated to shifting and is negatively correlated to premature sign-off at the $p < 0.10$ level. Also, rank is negatively correlated to underreporting, shifting time and DITs at or beyond the $p < 0.05$ level. None of the remaining Spearman correlations are statistically significant.

In general, the pattern of Spearman correlations is consistent with earlier work (Dirsmith and Covaleski [1985a, 1985b]; McNair [1991]) in that underreporting or shifting time may be perceived as a way to reduce audit quality reduction acts such as premature sign-off or slacking. The inverse relationship between position level and the two time-reporting behaviours also may reflect a differential effect where staff and senior level auditors are more likely to view underreporting or shifting time as a means to enhance promotion prospects within the firm than are managers and partners. Again, this is consistent with McNair's

Exhibit 5.2

Spearman Correlations for Four Dysfunctional Behaviours by DIT P Scores, Position Level, Firm, Sex and Nation

	UR	ST	SL	PS	DIT	Rank	Firm	Sex	Nation
UR	1.00								
ST	0.16*	1.00							
SL	0.04	0.01	1.00						
PS	– 0.17*	– 0.03	0.09	1.00					
DIT P Score	– 0.18*	– 0.16*	0.04	– 0.01	1.00				
Rank	– 0.29**	– 0.25**	0.11	– 0.06	– 0.21**	1.00			
Firm	0.00	0.01	0.07	– 0.01	– 0.04	0.00	1.00		
Sex	0.01	– 0.02	0.03	– 0.04	0.08	– 0.12	– 0.01	1.00	
Nation	– 0.11	– 0.09	0.01	0.00	0.10	0.00	– 0.02	0.07	1.00

Legend

UR denotes underreporting, ST denotes shifting time, SL denotes slacking and PS denotes premature sign-off. DIT refers to the P score (measured in percentage form).

Notes

Rank, firm, nation and sex are qualitative variables. Rank pertains to the auditor's position level in the firm, where 1 denotes staff, 2 denotes senior, 3 denotes manager and 4 denotes partner. Firm pertains to the two auditing firms that participated in this study, where 0 denotes Firm 1 and 1 denotes Firm 2. Nation pertains to the U.S. and Canada, denoted by 0 and 1, respectively. Sex is defined as 0 for men and 1 for women.

*Spearman correlation is marginally significant at the $p < 0.10$ level.

**Spearman correlation is significant at or beyond the $p < 0.05$ level.

[1991] finding that audit seniors are more likely than audit managers to perceive underreporting as an acceptable alternative to audit quality reducing acts.

Exhibit 5.3 reports the sample sizes (n) and mean values for underreporting (UR), shifting time (ST), slacking (SL) and premature sign-off (PS) by treatment, position level and DIT P score group. CPA and CA samples are separately shown, each post-stratified into high or low DIT groups based on their respective DIT P score median (see Exhibit 4.3 for a description of DIT results for both samples).[22] The Tukey pairwise and multiple comparison procedures (Neter, Wasserman and Kutner [1985, pp. 754-758]) were used to determine the significance of mean differences using a 95 percent confidence interval.

Differences in the mean values between low and high DIT groups for CPAs in U.S. firms reveal that DIT P scores influence auditor ratings in all four behaviour categories. Tukey's pairwise comparison procedure revealed that UR, ST, SL and PS are all significantly ($p < 0.01$) higher for low DIT auditors than for high DIT auditors. An examination of mean values also shows possible differences by auditors' position level, where staff and senior level auditors provide higher ratings to all behaviour categories than audit managers and audit partners. Employing the Tukey multiple comparison procedure, the following order is significant for UR, ST and PS at or beyond the $p < 0.05$ level: seniors ≥ staff ≥ managers ≥ partners (where at least one inequality is strict).

Experimental treatments also yield interesting findings. Auditors experiencing a penalty provide slightly higher overall mean ratings to all four dysfunctional behaviour categories than auditors experiencing the affiliation treatment. Between-group differences are especially salient for low DIT auditors. Using Tukey's pairwise comparison procedure, low DIT auditors

Exhibit 5.3

Means and Sample Sizes for Underreporting, Shifting, Slacking and Premature Sign-off by Low and High DIT, Treatment and Position for CPA and CA Samples

		CPAs in U.S. firms					CAs in Canadian firms				
Treatment		**Stf**	**Snr**	**Mgr**	**Ptr**	**Total**	**Stf**	**Snr**	**Mgr**	**Ptr**	**Total**
				Low DIT P score group							
Penalty	n	10	10	7	5	32	8	8	5	6	27
	UR	0.69	0.87	0.35	0.35	0.62	0.43	0.44	0.45	0.40	0.43
	ST	0.63	0.75	0.32	0.27	0.54	0.30	0.33	0.34	0.33	0.32
	SL	0.21	0.46	0.38	0.26	0.33	0.21	0.24	0.23	0.22	0.22
	PS	0.32	0.42	0.07	0.08	0.26	0.13	0.13	0.11	0.10	0.12
	Avg.	0.46	0.63	0.28	0.24	0.44	0.27	0.29	0.28	0.26	0.27
Affil.	n	8	12	10	5	35	7	7	6	4	24
	UR	0.53	0.61	0.37	0.23	0.47	0.35	0.32	0.34	0.36	0.34
	ST	0.52	0.59	0.17	0.13	0.39	0.24	0.25	0.21	0.20	0.23
	SL	0.25	0.43	0.29	0.22	0.32	0.12	0.13	0.09	0.11	0.11
	PS	0.15	0.26	0.11	0.05	0.16	0.13	0.12	0.11	0.15	0.12
	Avg.	0.36	0.47	0.23	0.15	0.33	0.21	0.21	0.19	0.20	0.20
				High DIT P score group							
Penalty	n	6	15	7	4	32	5	8	6	6	25
	UR	0.44	0.57	0.22	0.33	0.44	0.30	0.35	0.32	0.33	0.32
	ST	0.46	0.52	0.26	0.15	0.40	0.19	0.25	0.22	0.20	0.21
	SL	0.21	0.32	0.05	0.17	0.22	0.15	0.08	0.12	0.13	0.12
	PS	0.17	0.06	0.07	0.06	0.08	0.11	0.08	0.09	0.11	0.10
	Avg.	0.32	0.37	0.15	0.17	0.29	0.19	0.19	0.19	0.19	0.19
Affil.	n	10	12	9	3	34	5	10	4	7	26
	UR	0.57	0.63	0.25	0.23	0.48	0.36	0.38	0.39	0.39	0.38
	ST	0.56	0.62	0.21	0.09	0.45	0.35	0.31	0.32	0.30	0.32
	SL	0.25	0.24	0.20	0.22	0.23	0.09	0.10	0.14	0.12	0.11
	PS	0.13	0.07	0.06	0.10	0.08	0.10	0.08	0.12	0.11	0.10
	Avg.	0.38	0.39	0.18	0.16	0.31	0.23	0.22	0.24	0.23	0.23

Exhibit 5.3 (cont'd)

Treatment		CPAs in U.S. firms					CAs in Canadian firms				
		Stf	Snr	Mgr	Ptr	Total	Stf	Snr	Mgr	Ptr	Total
		Combined DIT groups									
Penalty	n	16	25	14	9	64	13	16	11	12	52
	UR	0.57	0.72	0.29	0.34	0.48	0.36	0.40	0.38	0.36	0.38
	ST	0.54	0.63	0.29	0.21	0.42	0.24	0.29	0.28	0.27	0.27
	SL	0.21	0.39	0.22	0.22	0.26	0.18	0.16	0.17	0.17	0.17
	PS	0.25	0.24	0.07	0.07	0.16	0.12	0.11	0.10	0.11	0.11
	Avg.	0.39	0.50	0.22	0.21	0.33	0.23	0.24	0.23	0.23	0.23
Affil.	n	18	24	19	8	69	12	17	10	11	50
	UR	0.55	0.62	0.31	0.23	0.44	0.36	0.35	0.37	0.37	0.36
	ST	0.54	0.60	0.19	0.11	0.36	0.30	0.28	0.26	0.25	0.27
	SL	0.25	0.34	0.24	0.22	0.31	0.10	0.12	0.11	0.11	0.11
	PS	0.14	0.16	0.08	0.07	0.10	0.12	0.10	0.12	0.13	0.11
	Avg.	0.37	0.43	0.21	0.16	0.30	0.22	0.21	0.21	0.22	0.22

Legend

n denotes sample size for each cell, UR denotes underreporting, ST denotes shifting time, SL denotes slacking on audit work, PS denotes premature sign-off.

in the penalty treatment group provide significantly ($p < 0.001$) higher mean ratings to UR, ST and PS than low DIT auditors in the affiliation treatment group. In addition, high DIT staff and senior auditors experiencing affiliation provide significantly ($p < 0.05$) higher ratings to UR and ST than high DIT auditors experiencing penalty. These findings suggest that even though penalty has a more profound impact on auditor ratings in the context of the present experiment, both treatments seem to be connected to auditors' ethical reasoning in a fashion that is consistent with Kohlberg's [1984] theory.

Examining the means for CAs in Canadian firms shows that low DIT auditors provide significantly ($p < 0.05$) higher ratings for UR, ST and SL under conditions of penalty. On the other hand, high DIT auditors provide significantly ($p < 0.05$) higher rating to UR and ST under conditions of affiliation. In sharp contrast to CPAs, the means for UR, ST, SL and PS are nearly identical across position levels for CAs in Canadian firms. Further, and perhaps most noticeably, CAs provide significantly lower ratings to UR, ST and SL than CPAs at comparable position levels. Using Tukey's pairwise comparison, these differences are significant at or beyond the $p < 0.01$ level. Similar to CPAs, however, the pattern of means by treatment groups suggest that low DIT CAs are more sensitive to penalty than affiliation.

In summary, these findings suggest that auditors with lower DIT P scores may perceive underreporting, shifting time, slacking, and premature sign-off in a different way than auditors with higher DITs — especially under conditions of penalty accruing from a poor performance appraisal. Findings also show marked differences between CPA and CA samples, where CPAs seem to be more likely than CAs to provide higher ratings to three of the four dysfunctional behaviour categories. These differences are particularly pronounced for CPAs at the staff and senior levels compared to their counterparts in CA firms.

Analysis of covariance (ANCOVA) was employed to refine the examination of possible relationships among the four dysfunctional behaviours, DIT P scores (the covariate), auditor's position level and two treatment groups.[23] A three-way fixed effect model was employed on each form of the dependent variable.[24] Because of differences in the distribution of DIT P scores between Canadian and U.S. auditors as illustrated in Exhibit 4.3, separate ANCOVA models were computed for CPA and CA samples. To control for unequal sample sizes between treatment groups, the method of unweighted means (Neter, Wasserman and Kutner [1985, p. 753]) was employed. Exhibit 5.4 reports the four ANCOVA models for auditors in U.S. firms in panel A and the four ANCOVA models for Canadian auditors in panel B.

The models shown in panel A for underreporting $F_{(7,133)} = 4.12$, $p < 0.0001$) and shifting time $F_{(7,133)} = 3.19$, $p < 0.001$) provide a relatively good overall fit, as reflected by highly significant F-statistics. Also, the main effects in both models are statistically significant for DIT P scores ($p < 0.001$), position levels ($p < 0.001$) and treatment (UR, $p < 0.02$; ST, $p < 0.01$), as well as the interactions for DIT by position (UR, $p < 0.05$; ST, $p < 0.02$) and DIT by treatment (UR, $p < 0.02$; ST, $p < 0.05$). Although the overall model for premature sign-off is only marginal $F_{(7,133)} = 1.70$, $p < 0.08$), its main effects for position ($p<0.09$) and the interaction for DIT by position ($p < 0.05$) are statistically significant. Finally, the model for slacking is not significant with respect to its main effects, interactions and overall fit $F_{(7,133)} = 1.21$, $p < 0.33$). These results show that for CPAs in the two participating firms, perceptions of underreporting, shifting time and premature sign-off are related to ethical reasoning as measured by the DIT. In addition, such perceptions seem to be related to the auditor's position level within the firm as well as the interaction of position and DIT P score. In short, these results corroborate the pattern of means reported in Exhibit 5.3, showing that CPAs' DIT P score levels, position level and treatment all seem to influence beliefs about unethical behaviour on the experimental task (especially those pertaining to underreporting and shifting time).

Even though all ANCOVA models summarized in panel B are less significant than those in panel A, underreporting ($F_{(7,102)} = 2.48$, $p < 0.01$) and shifting time ($F_{(7,102)} = 2.13$, $p < 0.02$) still provide a relatively good overall fit. The main effects in both models are statistically significant for treatment (UR, $p < 0.02$; ST, $p < 0.09$) and especially for the interaction of DIT by treatment (UR, $p < 0.01$; ST, $p < 0.02$). While the overall models for premature sign-off ($F_{(7,102)} = 1.39$, $p < 0.35$) and slacking ($F_{(7,102)} = 1.14$, $p < 0.57$) are not significant, the main effect for position is marginally significant ($p < 0.08$) for premature sign-off. Like the ANCOVA results in panel A, these models provide some evidence that auditors' DIT P scores may be an important determinant of perceptions about underreporting and shifting time in the audit setting. In comparison to CPAs, however, the ANCOVA results for CAs, in conjunction with the mean values reported in Exhibit 5.3, indicate salient differences in the way auditors in Canadian firms perceive unethical or dysfunctional behaviours as studied by this research. The reasons for these findings are posited in the next section.

5.4 DISCUSSION

The objective of this chapter was to explore the role of ethical reasoning on auditors' perceptions of four unethical behaviours dealing with time reporting and work-quality reduction in the audit setting. Experimental findings suggest that perceptions of under-

Exhibit 5.4

Three-Way Analysis of Covariance on Dysfunctional Behaviour Predictions for DITs (Covariate), Position and Treatment

Panel A: Models for CPAs in U.S. Firms (n = 133)

	Underreporting		Shifting		Slacking		Premature Sign-off	
Effects	**F-stat**	**p-val**	**F-stat**	**p-val**	**F-stat**	**p-val**	**F-stat**	**p-val**
A = DIT	4.54	0.00	3.87	0.00	1.45	0.23	1.17	0.42
B = Position	4.01	0.00	4.13	0.00	1.17	0.65	1.74	0.09
C = Treatment	2.37	0.02	3.01	0.01	1.03	0.51	1.32	0.19
A * B	1.99	0.05	2.18	0.02	0.99	0.63	1.95	0.05
A * C	2.23	0.02	1.98	0.05	1.56	0.13	1.59	0.11
B * C	0.85	0.77	1.01	0.49	0.92	0.64	0.76	0.82
A * B * C	1.02	0.55	1.22	0.38	1.18	0.39	1.11	0.56
Overall	4.12	0.00	3.19	0.00	1.21	0.33	1.70	0.08

Panel B: Models for CAs in Canadian Firms (n = 102)

	Underreporting		Shifting		Slacking		Premature Sign-off	
Effects	**F-stat**	**p-val**	**F-stat**	**p-val**	**F-stat**	**p-val**	**F-stat**	**p-val**
A = DIT	1.54	0.24	1.47	0.24	1.03	0.55	1.46	0.42
B = Position	1.01	0.83	0.93	0.70	0.97	0.72	1.89	0.08
C = Treatment	2.58	0.02	1.71	0.09	1.45	0.28	1.51	0.19
A * B	1.49	0.19	0.92	0.71	1.09	0.59	1.03	0.62
A * C	3.23	0.01	2.38	0.02	1.34	0.19	1.66	0.12
B * C	0.95	0.42	1.01	0.63	1.52	0.13	0.87	0.75
A * B * C	1.02	0.53	1.46	0.22	1.21	0.38	1.46	0.26
Overall	2.48	0.01	2.13	0.02	1.14	0.57	1.39	0.35

Notes

CPA and CA samples could not be combined for purposes of ANCOVA computations due to differences in the underlying distribution of DIT P scores, which served as the covariate in these models.

The method of unweighted means was used to adjust for unequal cell sizes in ANCOVA computations (Neter, Wasserman and Kutner [1985, p. 753]).

reporting, shifting time and premature sign-off in the audit setting are related to the auditor's DIT P score. Findings also indicate that influence of DITs is especially salient under conditions of audit budget pressure and the associated penalty caused by a poor performance appraisal due to a significant time budget overrun. Specifically, results suggest that low DIT auditors are more likely than high DIT auditors to believe that individuals resolve budget pressure by engaging in budget distortions or misrepresenting actual performance. Evidence of a differential effect was also found in U.S. firms, where auditors at the staff and senior levels were more likely than managers and partners to view underreporting and shifting time as a more pervasive activity within the audit firm. Finally, experimental findings reveal the existence of two significant differences between Canadian and American auditors. First, CAs were less likely than CPAs to perceive shifting time, slacking and premature sign-off as a way to resolve budget pressure in the audit setting. Second, Canadian auditors at various position levels did not differ in terms of their perceptions of the four behaviours examined in this study.

Several reasons can be brought forward to explain the differential effect among auditor perceptions at different position levels in U.S. firms but not in Canadian firms. As a starting point, consider the works of auditing researchers who have attempted to study the socialization process in major public accounting firms. For example, McNair [1987] observed that senior auditors in U.S. firms perceive the strongest link between "meeting budget" and promotion. The present findings also support the notion that the need to meet budget (e.g., underreporting and shifting time), are believed to be a more dominant factor for audit seniors than for managers or partners. As studied in earlier works (Blank [1984]; Dirsmith and Covaleski [1985a, 1985b]; McNair [1987, 1991]), differences in auditor perceptions may be caused by a differential screening process in large CPA firms, where junior level auditors are judged basically on technical skills for promotion to senior. On the other hand, seniors are judged on learning the business aspects of auditing for promotion to manager, while promotion to partner is based on a manager's ability to bring new clients and increased billings to the firm. This business aspect relates to the ability to maximize billable hours for an audit — or hours a client is willing to pay for. Thus, if hours cannot be billed to the client, there may be little incentive to charge them to the job or show a cost (time) overrun. Yet underreporting or shifting time, if hours could be billed, could be an equally poor decision in a business sense, as it reduces the firm's profits.

Perhaps the differential screening process alluded to by auditing researchers is not as widespread, or may not even exist, in Canadian audit firms. For example, as posited in Chapter 4, differences in the nature and structure of the Canadian accounting and auditing professions may result in a more diverse group of individuals achieving upward mobility within large audit firms. Drawing from the findings presented in Chapter 4, CAs may be better able to render professional and ethical judgments in the auditing domain by virtue of higher ethical reasoning levels. Taking this possibility one step further, the ability to render professional judgment, in addition to a general business competence, may be a more significant factor for promotion to the management ranks within Canadian CA firms than U.S. CPA firms.

Three additional explanations for Canadian and American differences can be posited. First, firm policies in Canadian firms may be more stringent that comparable policies in U.S. firms, thus influencing auditors' motivation to engage in audit budget distortion or quality reduction acts. Second, differences in client billing practices between Canadian and American firms also may affect the nature and extent of work-related pressure that can give rise to dysfunctional behaviour in the audit setting. Third, the informal norms of individuals within auditing firms might differ by national boundary. In this regard, Canadian auditors who are thought to have distorted their time budget or engaged in a quality reduction act may be cast away by others in the firm. Knowing this possibility, Canadian auditors with relatively low

(Stages 2 and 3) and relatively high (Stages 4 and 5) levels of ethical reasoning may be more negatively disposed to such behaviour.

In summary, the results of this chapter, in conjunction with the findings presented in Chapter 4, provide a foundation for future work in the cross-cultural ethics area in auditing. However, much work is still required to validate the research framework proposed in Exhibit 5.1. Questions that could be explored include researching the nature and extent of work-related pressure in the audit setting to gain a better understanding of the ways auditors at different position levels within the firm's formal hierarchy react to, or learn to cope with, difficult conflicts such as those caused by an unattainable audit budget. Research is also needed to more rigorously examine the association between ethical reasoning and unethical behaviour in the audit setting, such as time budget distortions or audit quality reduction acts.[25] Finally, much additional research is needed to examine the role of professional and cultural orientation on the ethical reasoning, moral development and ethical judgment-making abilities of accountants and auditors by studying practitioners in different nations on a global basis.

Several limitations can be identified in this research. First, the samples of auditors from only two accounting firms with offices in the northeast region of the United States and Ontario, Canada, limit our ability to generalize results to the population of all auditors in both countries. Second, participating auditors were all volunteers. While the response rates were generally high, the degree to which these individuals differed from those who did not participate could not be evaluated. Third, the DIT P score was used as a surrogate for each subject's level of ethical reasoning. The DIT is based upon a model which suggests that an individual's moral reasoning is subject to measurement. The extent to which the DIT P score errs in measuring an individual's moral reasoning has been discussed by Rest [1986]. A fourth limitation pertains to the use of the third-person construct and whether or not the auditor's prediction of what another person would do is in fact what he or she actually believes. Fifth, the unanticipated significant differences between U.S. and Canadian auditors indicates that the relationships among the experimental variables may be even more complex than posited in Exhibit 5.1. This finding suggests further study might be useful.

Despite caveats and limitations, however, experimental findings are consistent with the posited interrelationships between the auditor's level of ethical reasoning and his or her perceptions of dysfunctional behaviour in the audit setting. The implications of the present study for the practice and theory of auditing, as well as possible future research extensions, are discussed in the final chapter of this monograph.

Chapter 6

The Role of Ethical Reasoning in Audit Judgment

This chapter provides a theoretical and empirical explanation of the individual auditor's capacity to reason within the ethical domain.[26] It demonstrates how such reasoning influences the auditor's recognition of potentially important attributes of client management and, hence, affects judgment and decision making during the audit engagement. Its theory is based upon the cognitive-developmental theories advanced by Kohlberg [1969] and Rest [1979a]. As noted earlier, the psychology of ethical reasoning is described as a mode of intelligence permitting the individual to perceive moral conflict and judge its resolution.

The development to higher stages of ethical reasoning results in a heightened sensitivity to conflict and an increased ability to judge the ethical motivations of others in more precise and objective terms (cf. Rest [1986]). To illustrate its importance, consider the planning phase of the audit. Here, the auditor attempts to assess the ethical motivations of client management in terms of their potential distortion of financial information (Antle [1982, 1984]; Noreen [1988]). As a result, audit planning typically involves the evaluation of qualitative characteristics of the client organization including the competence and integrity of its management (Anderson and Marchant [1989]).[27] Proper evaluation requires the auditor to sense potential trouble signs (i.e., "red flags") such as incompetent and/or unethical management. Thus, the auditor's sensitivity or *gut feel* regarding these characteristics could possibly be linked to a more developed level of ethical reasoning as defined by Kohlberg [1969] and Rest [1979a].

To test this theory, three empirical studies were undertaken employing experienced auditors from the U.S. practices of two international accounting firms. The first experiment examined the relationships among auditors' ethical reasoning, their perceptions of the competence and integrity of management from actual client organizations and firm-assigned audit risk. Findings revealed that auditors' ethical reasoning moderates the relationship of perceived competence and perceived integrity upon audit risk. Specifically, client management believed to possess high competence and low integrity resulted in the highest assigned audit risk for only those clients audited by managers with relatively high levels of ethical reasoning. Hence, these auditors were configural in the processing of competence and integrity (Brown and Solomon [1990, 1991]), while auditors at lower levels of ethical reasoning were not. The second study experimentally tested the influence of ethical reasoning upon these auditors' predictive judgments regarding undetected material error to financial statements. The third study investigated the relationship between auditors' ethical reasoning and their sensitivity to both positive and negative contextual information regarding the client organization and its management when evaluating the materiality of a given accounting error.

In summary, all results corroborate the importance of ethical reasoning as a determinant of audit judgments that rely on qualitative impressions of the client or its key managers. Auditors with more highly developed levels of ethical reasoning show greater sensitivity to potentially important signals of the client organization and its management when judging audit risk or the possibility of material accounting error. These findings are of consequence to auditing researchers and practitioners because they suggest that the examination of auditor task performance would be incomplete without considering the ethical reasoning of the individual auditor. Thus, the present research may explain salient performance differences, heretofore not explained by experience or expertise, on tasks requiring the auditor to evaluate qualitative characteristics of the client organization and its management.

The remainder of this chapter is organized as follows: in the next section, a theoretical framework is developed and three research questions are advanced. In the sections thereafter, methods and results of three separate empirical studies are reported. Finally, the implications and limitations of the present research are discussed.

6.1 THEORY DEVELOPMENT

Auditor Impressions of Client Management

The fundamental role of external auditing is to ascertain the reliability of financial information represented by the management of the client organization (Committee of Sponsoring Organizations of the Treadway Commission (COSO) [1992]; National Commission on Fraudulent Financial Reporting (NCFFR) [1987]). The value of the auditing function to the client, its stakeholders and society as a whole is based upon the auditor's ability to detect *moral hazard* resulting from misrepresented financial information (Antle [1982, 1984]; Noreen [1988]). Thus, auditing standards enacted in 1988 require the auditor to base his or her examination on the extent of possible material financial distortions believed to exist within the client organization (SAS Nos. 53 and 55, AICPA [1988]). If the auditor believes that key managers are willing to *juggle the books*, then audit procedures will include detailed examinations of account balances and will rely more heavily on external sources of audit evidence such as observation and independent confirmation. If the auditor believes that managers are fair and honest in their reporting, then he or she can rely more heavily on internal sources of audit evidence such as managers' representations of operations and substantive analytic reviews.

One reason for audit inefficiency is when auditors incorrectly perceive the financial reporting strategy of client management. Such inefficiency is especially troublesome for auditors when they are unable to recognize unethical management and detect subsequent distortions to financial reports. For example, recent events in the U.S. savings and loan industry show that auditors are likely to be held culpable for failing to identify the fraudulent acts of client management, thus resulting in severe and costly litigation and a probable loss of reputation for the auditing profession.

To mitigate error in judgment, auditors attempt to carefully validate propositions about the reporting strategy of client management during the planning phase of the audit engagement. These propositions are typically framed in terms of the competence and integrity of client management (Anderson and Marchant [1989]; Willingham and Wright [1985]). From these judgments, the auditor assesses the likelihood of material distortions, determines the appropriate level of audit risk and sets a level for planning materiality in accordance with generally accepted auditing standards (cf. SAS No. 47, AICPA [1983]; Section 5130, Canadian Institute of Chartered Accountants *Handbook*).

To illustrate the auditor's judgment, consider the relationship among competence (**C**), integrity (**I**) and the probability of material distortion (Φ) by managers within the client organization. That is, the auditor assesses **C** and **I** to determine Φ. Holding all else constant, when **I** is judged to be high, Φ will be low. Similarly, when **C** is judged to be high, Φ will be low. However, the combination of **C** and **I** are configurally related to Φ. For example, consider the worst case of Φ; that is, when managers are believed to be highly competent and dishonest or, namely, *competent crooks*. Here, by virtue of the crafty and unscrupulous manager, material accounting error is well hidden and its discovery is beyond the scope of normal auditing procedures. Exhibit 6.1 illustrates the configuration of **I** and **C** with respect to four levels of Φ.

Following this simple example, assuming that auditors are risk-averse individuals, their preference ordering to the likelihood of material distortions to a client's financial statement information can be simply defined as:

$\Phi_{hl} > \Phi_{ll}$ or (Equation 6.1a)

$\Phi_{lh} > \Phi_{hh}$ (Equation 6.1b)

Auditors operationalize their risk preferences for Φ by assigning high audit risk (or a low materiality threshold) to Φ_{hl} and low audit risk (or a high materiality threshold) to Φ_{hh}. Because auditors must rely upon their beliefs about client management in their assessments of Φ, audit risk and planning materiality, it is important to understand how perceptions of **I** and **C** are framed. As a starting point, consider the psychology of ethical reasoning. As noted previously, this area of psychology provides a theory that explains the human decision making process prior to behaviour. It is concerned with the process which individuals follow to recognize, reason and resolve ethical conflict.

Ethical Reasoning and the Recognition of Client Ethics

The current monograph extends the purview of ethical reasoning to the domain of audit practice because, in addition to behaviour, progression to higher stages of ethical reasoning fosters an individual's sensitivity to critical events, issues and conflicts (Colby and Kohlberg [1987]; Kohlberg [1969]; Rest [1979a, 1986]). This deepened sensitivity and cognitive skill (e.g., Components 1 and 2, respectively, in Rest's four-component model) permits the individual to

Exhibit 6.1

The Likelihoods of Undetected Management Distortions (Φ) to Financial Statements by Low or High Competence and Integrity Levels

	Low integrity	**High integrity**
Low competence	$\Phi_{ll} \rightarrow$ Moderate risk While distortion is possible, auditor is able to detect it. Audit risk is moderate to high.to detect.	$\Phi_{lh} \rightarrow$ Moderate risk Distortion is unlikely, but management is likely to make material error that the auditor is able Audit risk is moderate.
High competence	$\Phi_{hl} \rightarrow$ High risk Distortion is possible and the auditor may be unable to detect error. Audit risk is extremely high.	$\Phi_{hh} \rightarrow$ Low risk Distortion is unlikely and management is not likely to make material error. Audit risk is low.

Where Φ_{ij} denotes the likelihood for undetected material distortions to a client's financial statements.

role play, gain empathy and, in colloquial terms, place oneself in another person's shoes. As a result, individuals at higher stages are better able to gauge the ethical motivations of other people (Reeder and Coovert [1986]). For example, at lower stages, the individual is unable to gauge differences in the way other people respond to and resolve ethical conflict. At moderate stages, the individual is able to detect differences; however, they are only understood with respect to his or her normative preferences or values. Here the individual will fail to discriminate potentially important differences in ethical motivations because of an inability to judge others beyond stereotypical labels such as good, bad, right or wrong. At higher stages, the individual expects that another's ethical motivation will differ and such differences, as long as they are perceived to be rational and just, are accepted.

According to Kohlberg [1969], stages of ethical reasoning can be viewed as cognitive equilibria. Within each stage is defined an individual's intellectual capacity to recognize moral conflict and conceive its resolution. This stage-sequence model is based upon four fundamental propositions:

1. Each stage implies a qualitative difference in the individual's thinking structure.
2. Each thinking structure is part of an invariant sequence of an individual's intellectual and moral development.
3. Each stage in the sequence forms a structural whole in terms of the individual's organization of thought.

4. The stages combine to form a hierarchial order of increasingly complex, separated and integrated cognitive structures.

Thus, a higher stage builds upon the cognitive structures found at the adjacent lower stage of development.

To illustrate ethical reasoning within the context of an audit, consider the auditor's recognition of the ethical characteristics of client management resulting in a prediction of their financial reporting strategy. Since the management's distortion strategy (Φ) to financial information is never revealed to the auditor *ex ante*, the auditor must rely on individual experiences, instincts and internalized ethical sensibilities to frame his or her judgment about the quality of the financial statements. Based on these intellectual capacities, the auditor is only able to predict **I**, an unbiased estimator of Φ. Because the task of predicting **I** requires the auditor to make normative inferences about management (e.g., such as their honesty, trustworthiness, integrity), **I** will depend on the individual auditor's stage of ethical reasoning. Thus, $(\mathbf{I}|S_j)$ will denote a prediction of Φ made by an auditor at the jth stage of reasoning according to the Kohlberg [1984] model, where S_j is defined as the jth stage of development for all $j = 1, \ldots, n$. Letting a_j represent one of many cognitive structures[28] that collectively form the ethical reasoning capacity known as S_j, the following properties are assumed to hold:

1. If $a_j \in S_j$ and a_j is $> a_i$, then $a_i \in S_j$ (i.e., monotonicity from above). Thus, if one's cognition is capable of producing $a_i \in S_j$, he or she can certainly produce $a_i \in S_{j+1}$ (i.e., monotonicity from below).

2. $S_i \neq S_j$, for all $i \neq j$. Hence, stages contain qualitative differences in intellectual structures serving the same basic functions at various points in an individual's development. Taking this one step further, Rest [1979a] would suggest that S_i is a distribution rather than a single point in the developmental process.

3. $S_1 < S_2 \ldots < S_n$. This means that higher stages form an invariant sequence, order or succession in individual development. Kohlberg states [1984, p. 6] "Cultural factors may speed up, slow down or stop development, but they do not change in sequence."

4. $S_j = ß[S_{j-1}, S_{j-2}, S_{j-3} \ldots S_1]$ for all $j > 1$. This means that each stage of cognition is cumulative, consisting of the cognitive structures found in all lower order stages of development (ß denotes the integrating coefficient for stages $j > 1$). Kohlberg describes this property of the model as the hierarchical integration of lower order stages. Kohlberg writes [1984, p. 7] "Stages form an order of increasingly differentiated and integrated structures for fulfilling a common function."

Because higher stages of ethical reasoning result in greater skills for identifying and resolving ethical issues, this research advances the notion that auditors at higher stages will be better able to recognize the ethical characteristics of client management and, hence, are more likely to predict correctly their distortion strategies. With proper assessment of Φ, the auditor will be better able to frame strategic judgments concerning the audit engagement (Fellingham and Newman [1985]). Thus, by virtue of cognitive (ethical) development, auditors at higher stages perceive the ethical characteristics of client management more precisely. Letting $(\sigma^2|S_j)$ denote the variance (difference) between Φ and **I** for an individual at S_j, by deduction the following inequality is posited:

$$(\sigma^2|S_1) \geq (\sigma^2|S_2) \geq \ldots (\sigma^2|S_k), \text{ where } k > 2 \qquad \text{(Equation 6.2)}$$

In summary, the auditor's ability to frame reliable predictions of Φ will depend, in part, on his or her stage of reasoning. Auditors at lower stages are less able to frame the ethical characteristics of the client management and, therefore, are more likely to render unreliable predictions of Φ. Taking this connection one step further, high-stage auditors are more likely to recognize the importance of their obligations to others within the firm or the standards of the profession. As a consequence, they will be motivated to look for material distortions to financial information during the audit, and if found, will act ethically on their discoveries. The implications of poor audit judgment and insufficient auditor action are manifold, including inappropriate specifications of audit risk, planning materiality, and the scope of substantive auditing procedures.

To illustrate the consequences of Equation 6.2, consider the audit risk assessment process. During the planning phase of the engagement, the auditor is required to evaluate qualitative characteristics of the client organization and its management (cf. SAS No. 55, AICPA [1988]; Sections 5200 to 5220, Canadian Institute of Chartered Accountants *Handbook*). To determine the potential distortion strategy (Φ) of management, the auditor evaluates the competence (**C**) and integrity (**I**) of client management. In this context, competence is defined as management's technical or bureaucratic proficiency when fulfilling their job, whereas integrity is defined as management's ability to follow an ethical course of action, especially under conditions of economic, social or political pressure within the organization. Assuming that the parameters **C** and **I** are configural with respect to Φ, the following relationship is advanced:

$$\Phi = C + I + C \star I \qquad \text{(Equation 6.3)}$$

However, since **C, I,** and Φ are never observable to the auditor during the planning phase, he or she predicts c, i, **I**, respectively, such that E(c) = C, E(i) = I, and E(**I**) = Φ. Given that c and i are conditioned upon the auditor's stage of ethical reasoning, S_j will again denote the auditor's cognitive stage (j=1,. . .,k). Accordingly, the following prediction of management's distortion strategy is advanced:

$$\mathbf{I} = (c|S_j) + (i|S_j) + (c \star i|S_j) + (u|S_j) \qquad \text{(Equation 6.4)}$$

where $(u|S_j)$ is defined as random error such that E(u) = 0. Given the variance inequality defined in Equation 6.2, $\sigma^2(u|S_j) \geq \sigma^2(u|S_{j+1})$. Also, as a result of Equation 6.4, three sources of variation can be attributed to $\sigma^2(u)$.

$$\sigma^2(u|S_j) = [(\sigma^2(c) + \sigma^2(i) + cov(c,i))|S_j]. \qquad \text{(Equation 6.5)}$$

Therefore, in the process of framing **I**, the auditor has three sources of judgment error. The first lies in the assessment of management's competence, the second concerns management's integrity, and the third involves the configuration of competence and integrity. Assuming that audit risk (AR) is the outcome variable of the auditor's prediction of Φ, and following Equation 6.4, AR can be defined as a simple additive transformation:

$$AR = AR(\mathbf{I}, \underline{x}) = [(c + i + c \star i + u)|\, S_j] + \underline{x} + \underline{e} \qquad \text{(Equation 6.6)}$$

Here, $\underline{x}$ is a vector containing all other state variables considered by the auditor when assessing AR, and is assumed to be orthogonal and stationary to c and i. Thus, $\underline{e}$ is an error vector resulting from the inclusion of random variables found in $\underline{x}$ such that $E(\underline{e}) = \underline{0}$. Based on Equations 6.5 and 6.6, and holding all $\underline{x}$ constant, the auditor's assessment of AR will be more reliable at $S_j > S_{j-1}$. The dynamics of this result imply that auditors at lower stages will be more likely to under-audit $[AR(\Phi) > AR(I)]$. As a result, the auditor may fail to recognize, or sufficiently act upon his or her discovery of material distortions to financial statement information.

Research Questions

The theoretical framework to be tested by this research is illustrated in Exhibit 6.2. It advances a relationship between the auditors' perceptions of the ethical characteristics of client management and certain critical judgments regarding the audit such as materiality and audit risk. As posited above, the auditor attempts to judge the reliability of client management by assessing their competence and integrity, and these assessments are affected by ethical reasoning. Thus, auditors at higher stages of ethical reasoning are better able to recognize ethical issues and are more motivated to render reliable judgments of the client organization and its management (such as audit risk).

Within the context of critical audit judgments, such as audit risk, planning materiality and fraud detection, the following three research questions are sought by this research:

1. Does ethical reasoning influence auditors' perceptions of the competence and integrity of client management?

2. Does ethical reasoning influence auditors' sensitivity to the likelihood of material error to financial statements?

3. Does ethical reasoning influence auditors' ability to frame audit evidence concerning the materiality of accounting error?

Regarding the first two questions, the lower the perceived competence or integrity, the more skeptical the auditor should be about the reliability of management and, therefore, the higher the assigned audit risk or the lower planning materiality will be for a given client engagement. The most risky situation occurs, however, when members of client management are believed to be smart and dishonest. As a result, competence and integrity perceptions should be configurally related to audit judgments. The first study explores the influence of auditors' ethical reasoning on perceptions of client management in the context of actual firm-assigned audit risk. The second study provides an experimental test of auditor sensitivity to competence and integrity cues when judging the likelihood of financial statement distortion by the management of the client organization. The third study examines auditors' perceptions of material accounting error under conditions of positive or negative contextual information about the client. In essence, all three studies attempt to test one fundamental proposition; that is, by virtue of "moral expertise" (see Gaa [1992]), auditors at higher stages of ethical reasoning should be better able to render judgment in the professional domain.

Exhibit 6.2

Research Framework and Hypothesized Relationships

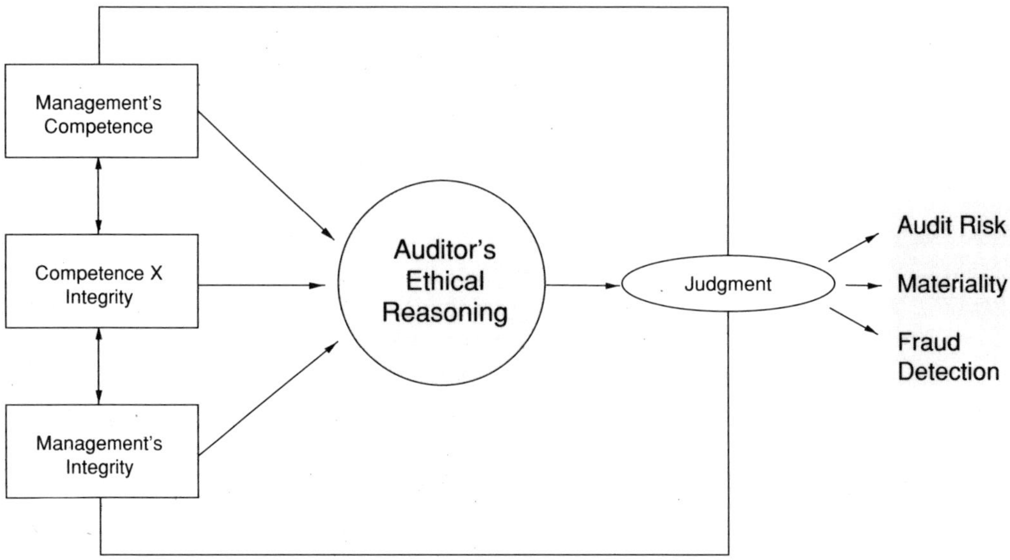

6.2 STUDY ONE: AUDITORS' PERCEPTIONS OF THE COMPETENCE AND INTEGRITY OF CLIENT MANAGEMENT AND AUDIT RISK

Sample

Sixty-one audit managers from one international accounting firm participated in this study by completing a survey under the supervision of the researchers. The sample was gathered as follows. First, the researchers contacted the partners-in-charge of the offices of various international public accounting firms located in a large city in the northeastern United States. The culmination of this effort was the agreement by one accounting firm to participate in this study. With the assistance of their managers, a stratified random sampling plan to select clients was adopted. This plan was based upon the audit risks assigned to each of the selected clients by the offices of the accounting firm during the planning of the clients' audits. The sampling procedure allowed audit clients to be selected randomly from the population of all active (nonbankrupt) clients within the firm and ensured sufficient representation of client organizations with respect to all risk levels.

The sampling unit was the audit manager assigned to the selected audit client because he or she was responsible for determining the relative scope of audit work based upon the firm's predetermined audit risk for the client. The audit manager also approved the plan and programs prepared by the supervisor or senior, thereby assuring that the work performed properly reflected the audit risk. Because each audit manager could have audit responsibility for several clients, it would be possible to receive several perceptual responses (one response for each client) from one or more of the managers. The inclusion in the data of several responses by the same individual can lead to potential error in data analyses (Scheaffer, Mendenhall and Ott [1986]). Thus, the sampling plan ensured that managers could only be selected once.

Seventy audit managers representing the audit engagements of 70 client organizations were selected. Each auditor was contacted directly by an audit partner from the same office, resulting in the participation of 61 managers. At the time of this study, all 61 managers were actively involved in the management of several engagements on an ongoing basis. On average, audit managers held 6.7 years of experience, were 30.1 years of age and had 16.5 years of education (36 males and 25 females). DIT P score results for the sample were as follows: mean of 36.21, median of 36.70, standard deviation of 9.56 and range of 63.30. Tests of DIT P scores by demographic variables revealed no significant differences.

Survey Instrument

Auditors' perceptions of the competence and integrity of managers of the selected sample of client organizations were surveyed (see Appendix C). The independent variables in this study are the auditor's ratings or attributions regarding the integrity and competence of the management of selected audit clients (Kelley and Michela [1980]; Weiner [1986]). These ratings were captured using two bipolar adjective scales collected from structured interviews conducted by one researcher over a three-week period. Managers were independently required to provide their perceptions of the selected clients in terms of a 1 to 5 point scale where "1" represented high competence (or high integrity) and "5" represented low competence (or low integrity). The anchor point to both adjective scales was "3" representing the "medium".

The reliabilities for competence (r_c) and integrity (r_i) ratings used in the present study were assessed two ways: cross-sectional analysis ($r_c = 0.81$; $r_i = 0.84$) and a split-half (randomized block) design ($r_c = 0.79$; $r_i = 0.86$). To validate the adjective ratings, relative ratios for competence and integrity were compiled for each client in terms of all other clients managed by these audit managers. Because auditors may specialize in specific industries, they may not work on clients in all ranges of competence and integrity. For example, using the 5-point scale, a manager with seven clients could perceive them all as being highly competent. The ratio measure converts this response to a relative measure by ranking the auditor's perceptions of each client with respect to his or her other clients. If a correlation exists between these two measures, then the adjective scale captures the managers' experiences with their actual clients.[29] Using Spearman correlates (ρ), a comparison was made between ordinal and ratio measures, proving significant for competence ($\rho = 0.63$ $p < 0.005$) and integrity ($\rho = 0.55$ $p < 0.01$), and this suggests that adjective scale responses are internally consistent measures.

Measure of Audit Risk

Firm-assigned audit risk used to plan the scope and extent of the audit field work was provided by the firm and is the dependent variable. Here, audit risk denotes the possibility that unresolved material error in the financial information under examination will be sufficient to distort the financial statements taken as a whole.[30] Audit risk computations and risk assignments were performed by an independent quality control department within the office for all new and continuing audit clients. The final assessment of a client's audit risk, however, typically reflected the auditor's beliefs. Thus, auditors on the engagement held veto power if the firm-assigned audit risk did not adequately reflect their perceptions of the client organization and its management. Audit risk assignments for all selected clients were categorized by the firm according to a five-point ordinal scale, where "1" represented the lowest risk level and "5" represented the highest risk level for active (nonbankrupt) audit clients.

Research Findings

Spearman correlates (ρ) were computed for all survey and demographic variables. This resulted in three significant ($p < 0.01$) correlations for:

1. competence and audit risk ($\rho = 0.479$),
2. integrity and audit risk ($\rho = 0.441$) and
3. competence and integrity ($\rho = 0.514$).

Multivariate and moderated regressions were employed to test the effect of auditors' DIT on their estimation of competence, integrity and audit risk. Here, audit risk (dependent variable) was regressed on competence and integrity perceptions (independent variables), and one moderating variable (DIT P score). The moderated relationship was tested by the interaction or cross-product between the moderator and each independent variable. If the interaction is statistically significant, the moderator can be viewed as influencing various levels of the dependent and independent variables (cf. Arnold [1982]; Baron and Kenny [1986]; Cohen and Cohen [1983]; Jaccard, Turrisi and Wan [1990]).

Exhibit 6.3 reports the results of multivariate (Model 1) and moderated regressions (Models 2 through 4).[31] As shown in Model 1, coefficients for competence ($\hat{\beta} = 0.905$, $p < 0.001$), integrity ($\hat{\beta} = 1.05$, $p < 0.001$) and the interaction between competence and integrity ($\hat{\beta} = -0.159$, $p < 0.01$) are significant. Using a one-tailed t-test, competence and integrity are significantly related to audit risk. Further, the interaction of competence and integrity is negatively related to audit risk, suggesting that discordant perceptions (e.g., high competence and low integrity) rather than concordant perceptions (e.g., low competence and low integrity) are significantly related to audit risk. In short, these significant findings corroborate the model illustrated in Exhibit 6.3.

The influence of DIT P scores upon auditor perceptions and audit risk is revealed by the significant cross-product terms in Model 2 and Model 4. The DIT is negatively related to competence ($\hat{\beta} = -0.0232$, $p < 0.01$) in Model 2 and to the interaction of competence and integrity ($\hat{\beta} = -0.00447$, $p < 0.05$) in Model 4. However, the insignificant cross-product in Model 3 suggests that the DIT does not moderate integrity and audit risk. Further, the negative cross-product in Model 2 indicates that the DIT may actually weaken the relationship at higher levels. In other words, perceptions of competence and not integrity become more salient for audit managers with lower DIT P scores.

To further explore this relationship, audit risks were predicted using Model 2 for low ("5") and high ("1") competence by low ("5") integrity. Separate regressions were computed by substituting representative DIT P scores and treating competence and integrity levels as constants, resulting in two reduced models for low ($AR = 7.45 - 0.0767 * DIT$) and high ($AR = 3.81 + 0.0161 * DIT$) competence.[32] Two interesting relationships are revealed in Exhibit 6.4. First, perceived audit risk *decreases* with increasing DIT P scores when both competence and integrity are judged to be low. Second, and perhaps more importantly, when competence is high and integrity is low, audit risk *increases* with increasing DIT P scores. These relationships suggest that in the context of audit risk assessment, auditors with lower DIT results place greater reliance on incompetent management and auditors with higher DIT results are more sensitive to competent, low integrity management — or the so-called "competent crook" phenomenon as previously described. Hence, these findings suggest that the appropriate answer to the first research question (page 87) is positive.

Exhibit 6.3

Multivariate and Moderated Regression Analyses for Audit Risk and Perceptions of Competence (**C**) and Integrity (**I**) by Auditors' DIT P Scores

	Models			
Variables	**(1)**	**(2)**	**(3)**	**(4)**
1. DIT P Score (DIT)	– 0.0076 (– 0.870)	0.0393 (2.20)	0.0151 (0.82)	0.0116 (0.94)
2. Competence (**C**)	0.905 (3.31)**	1.63 (3.77)**	0.894 (3.11)**	0.891 (3.41)**
3. Integrity (**I**)	1.05 (5.60)**	0.992 (5.40)**	0.886 (4.36)**	1.09 (5.14)**
4. **C** x **I**	– 0.159 (– 3.95)**	– 0.144 (– 3.81)**	– 0.149 (– 3.27)**	– 0.0154 (– 0.20)
5. DIT x **C**		– 0.0232 (– 2.91)**		
6. DIT x **I**			0.00367 (0.46)	
7. DIT x **C** x **I**				– 0.00447 (– 2.14)*
Constant term	0.535	– 2.06	– 0.223	– 1.23
Adjusted R^2	0.404	0.481	0.402	0.452

* and ** denote $p < 0.05$, $p < 0.01$ levels, respectively.

Coefficients are the estimated parameters from OLS regression. In parentheses are the t statistics. Significance levels were determined as a one-tailed test.

Exhibit 6.4

Predicted Audit Risk from Model 2*

(see Exhibit 6.3)

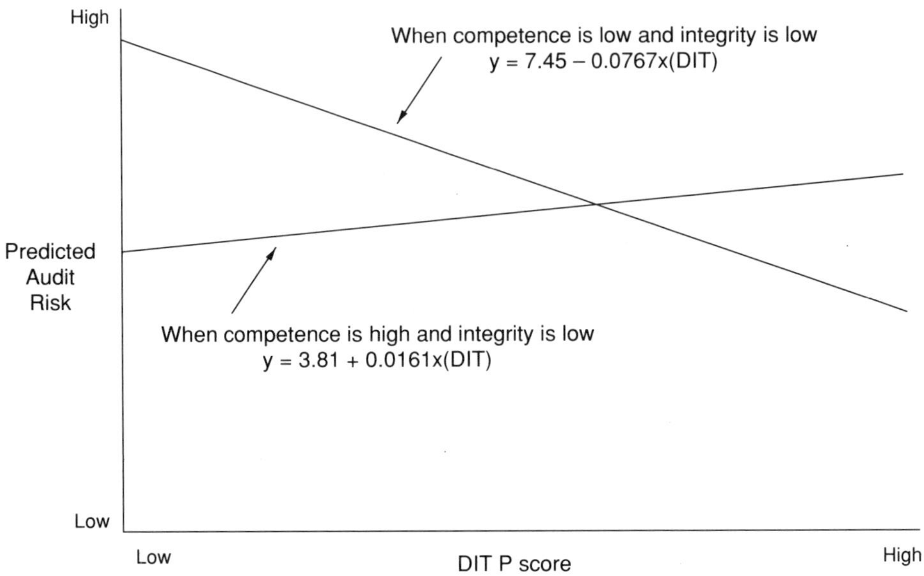

*Integrity is a constant in both moderated models, where **I** = 5 (low).

6.3 STUDY TWO: AUDITORS' RECOGNITION OF DISTORTIONS TO FINANCIAL STATEMENT INFORMATION

Experimental Task

An experiment involving the probabilistic prediction judgments of the same 61 audit managers was conducted (see the previous section for a description of this sample). Audit managers were required to predict whether or not an auditor failed to detect a material accounting error during the course of an audit. Each audit manager read the scenario providing descriptive information about the client organization and its management (Appendix D). A Bayesian design (Libby [1981]) was used to measure the informativeness of four within-subject treatments regarding the competence and integrity of client management. Here, a completely uninformative treatment would result in a prediction equivalent to priors, which were set (to 50 percent) in the instructions to the case.

The case was posed in the hypothetical third person.[33] Rest [1979a, Ch. 4] describes the strategy of test construction and emphasizes that moral judgment issues must be framed in terms of the third person, or as is done in this study, by using a hypothetical auditor. To paraphrase Rest, cognitive-developmental research never seeks to predict what a person would do, but rather what they believe ought to be done. Hence, the narrative to the case is as follows:

> John is an experienced audit manager with a large national public accounting firm. He is responsible for the 198X audit of XYZ Corp; the company has been an audit

> client of the accounting firm for five years. Unqualified audit opinions have been issued in all previous audits.
>
> The XYZ Corporation is a minicomputer manufacturer with sales offices and plants throughout North America. Its common stock is publicly traded on a major securities exchange. XYZ also plans to issue more common stock in the first quarter of the next fiscal year to finance a major expansion. During the past five years, normal economic conditions have prevailed in XYZ's industry. Further, XYZ revenues and income have steadily increased in all prior years.
>
> Because of technological changes in the microchip industry, a significant amount of the XYZ inventory is obsolete. Further, key managers of the XYZ Corporation are aware of this problem. An inventory write-down, however, will decrease net income this year by over 10 percent.

The resolution of the case hinges on the perceived *reliability* of XYZ management. While reliable management would likely disclose the inventory problem to the auditor, unreliable management may evade the issue, distort the facts, or even inhibit the auditor's examination. It is important to note that the case does not define the materiality threshold for the XYZ audit. However, the net income effect of the write-down was above the 10 percent level that is typically considered material for most firms (cf. Chewning, Pany and Wheeler [1989]; Holstrum and Messier [1982]).

The information given to all subjects was held constant except for four factual manipulations dealing with the competence and integrity of client management.[34] Competence and integrity levels were defined in terms of 0 to 100 percent as illustrated by a continuous scale. The case also stated that the audit senior assessed these characteristics during the planning phase of the engagement. Hence, a 2^2 factorial design was employed with treatments defined as:

1. high competence and high integrity
2. high competence and low integrity
3. low competence and high integrity
4. low competence and low integrity.

Competence and integrity ratings were placed at the 20 percent level to denote a low scale (negative) response and the 80 percent level to denote a high scale (positive) response.

After reading the scenario, each subject was asked to provide a prediction (subjective posterior probability) that John (a) detected or (b) failed to detect XYZ's obsolete inventory. Predictions were made by assigning 0 to 100 points to one of two dichotomous categories. A point allocation of 50 points to either category would denote complete indifference, thus reflecting no revision from priors.

Experimental Results

Nonparametric and ANOVA tests were employed to examine the influence of ethical reasoning upon auditor predictions. The Kruskal-Wallis and Jonckheere procedures (Hollander and Wolfe [1973 pp. 120-124]) were used to test differences in the order of median predictions for four treatments by low and high DIT P score groups.[35] Exhibit 6.5 provides experimental means, medians, standard deviations and ranges by DIT groups. Looking across DIT groups, three of the four medians (and means) are almost identical. However, a marked difference does exist between DIT groups for the treatment high competence and low integrity. Letting Ω_{ij} denote the treatment, i the competence level (l = low, h = high) and j the integrity level (l = low, h = high), median predictions can be ordered at the $p < 0.05$ level as follows for auditors in the low DIT group:

$$\Omega_{ll} \geq \Omega_{hl} \geq \Omega_{lh} \geq \Omega_{hh}$$

Exhibit 6.5

Prediction Medians, Means, Standard Deviations and Ranges by Four Experimental Groups for Low and High DIT Auditors

Panel A: Low DIT Auditor Group:

	Low integrity	High integrity	Overall
Low competence			
Median	71.00	50.00	65.00
Mean	70.67	50.80	62.11
Standard deviation	15.53	13.16	15.83
Range	60.00	55.00	61.00
High competence			
Median	52.50	22.00	45.00
Mean	54.17	26.03	34.56
Standard deviation	14.09	16.73	15.48
Range	70.00	60.00	70.00

Using the Kruskal-Wallis and Jonckheere procedures, cell medians were significantly different and could be ordered as: 71 ≥ 52.5 ≥ 50 ≥ 22 at the 0.05 level of significance. The mean and median DIT P score for the low DIT group were 28.3 and 29.9, respectively.

Panel B: High DIT Auditor Group:

	Low integrity	High integrity	Overall
Low competence			
Median	70.00	50.00	60.00
Mean	69.58	46.52	54.52
Standard deviation	14.31	14.46	14.96
Range	60.00	65.00	65.00
High competence			
Median	80.00	20.00	50.00
Mean	82.17	22.55	53.16
Standard deviation	14.37	14.82	16.01
Range	55.00	60.00	60.00

Using the Kruskal-Wallis and Jonckheere procedures, cell medians were significantly different and could be ordered as: 80 ≥ 70 ≥ 50 ≥ 20 at the 0.01 level of significance. The mean and median DIT P score for the high DIT group were 43.9 and 43.5, respectively.

In contrast, for auditors in the high DIT group, the median predictions can be ordered at the $p < 0.01$ level, as follows:

$$\Omega_{hl} \geq \Omega_{ll} \geq \Omega_{lh} \geq \Omega_{hh}$$

The difference between the order of median predictions is caused by the treatment Ω_{hl}. That is, auditors with higher DIT P scores, on average, assign a much higher probability of *undetected material accounting error* when managers possess high competence and low integrity. Further, it is interesting to note the general equivalence between the theoretical ordering suggested in an earlier section (see Equation 6.1) regarding management's distortion strategy (Φ_{ij}) and the order of treatment medians (Ω_{ij}) for auditors in the high DIT group. Hence, by virtue of Equation 6.1, auditors with higher DIT results seem to be more rational in their prediction of material accounting error.

To complete the analysis, individual (one-way) ANOVA tests were used to contrast the significance of each experimental treatment by DIT P score level. These tests did not show significant differences between DIT levels for Ω_{ll} ($F_{(1,60)} = 0.08$), Ω_{lh} ($F_{(1,60)} = 1.46$) and Ω_{hh} ($F_{(1,60)} = 0.74$). However, a highly significant ($F_{(1,60)} = 59.4$, $p < 0.001$) difference was again revealed for Ω_{hl}. Because a Bayesian design was employed, the informativeness of each Ω_{ij} could be assessed by subtracting priors from each prediction. Using a one sample t test, Ω_{ll} and Ω_{hh} were significantly ($p < 0.01$) different from priors for both DIT groups, but Ω_{hl} was only significant ($p < 0.001$) for auditors in the high DIT group.

In summary, this experimental finding confirms the results shown in Exhibit 6.4. That is, auditors' ethical reasoning influences both audit risk and predictions regarding the detection of material accounting error under conditions where client management is judged to have high competence and low integrity. The implications of these results for the practice and theory of auditing are discussed in the last section of this chapter.

6.4 STUDY THREE: AUDITORS' MATERIALITY JUDGMENT AND THEIR SENSITIVITY TO CONTEXTUAL CLIENT INFORMATION

Sample

An experiment involving the prediction task judgments of 131 auditors from U.S. offices of one international public accounting firm was conducted. All subjects completed the experiment in a classroom setting while attending the firm's senior training program held in a large Southwestern city. Subjects from seventeen audit practice offices located throughout the United States participated. In the present research, the unit of analysis was the individual auditor. On average, auditors held 2.4 years of experience, were 24.3 years of age and had 16.31 years of education (79 males and 52 females). DIT P score results for the sample were as follows: mean of 38.2, median of 38.7, standard deviation of 11.6 and range of 60.3.

Experimental Task

An experimental task adopted from Krogstad, Ettenson and Shanteau [1984, p. 58] involving a proposed adjustment by an auditor to a client's year-end allowance for doubtful accounts was provided to all subjects. Each subject read a scenario that gave descriptive information about an audit client. Instructions to the case explicitly set experimental priors (base rate) to

50 percent. Each subject was required to predict, given the facts provided, whether or not the adjustment proposed by the auditor was material. The narrative to the case is as follows:

> John is the auditor-in-charge of the XYZ Corporation. John is a senior auditor in a national public accounting firm, ABC & Co. The financial statements of XYZ were audited by ABC for the past four consecutive years. Net income after taxes (per company books) is $6,226,000 for the current year. During this audit, normal economic conditions prevailed; that is, real GNP at four percent, inflation rate at eight percent, prime interest rate at ten percent. Dow Jones Industrial Average at 1950 and New York Stock Exchange price-earnings ratio at 14.
>
> Normal audit procedures lead John to believe that the year-end allowance for doubtful accounts should be increased. The proposed adjustment will decrease current income after taxes by 2.7 percent.

All subjects were provided with the same instructions and case except for contextual information regarding the client organization and its management (Appendix E). The experiment attempted to test auditors' sensitivity to both positive and negative contextual factors that is reflected in their probabilistic prediction of materiality. For those in one experimental group, the following negative contextual audit evidence was included with the above narrative:

> The XYZ Company management has been less than completely cooperative and open in all dealings with John's firm and in connection with the current audit. The company's management follows unconservative accounting policies in areas of income determination and asset valuation, and its reported earnings are generally viewed as of low quality.

To those in another experimental group, the following positive contextual information was included with the above case.

> The XYZ Company management has been completely cooperative and open in all dealings with John's firm and in connection with the current audit. The company's management follows conservative accounting policies in areas of income determination and asset valuation, and its reported earnings are generally viewed as of high quality.

As can be seen, the net income effect of the proposed entry is 2.7 percent, representing the lower bound in the Krogstad, Ettenson and Shanteau [1984] experiment. This value was chosen because it is very close to (immediately below) the tolerable error limits recommended by the audit firm participating in this study. Consequently, the accounting error should be perceived as relatively immaterial.

Subjects were randomly assigned to two experimental and one control group (of sizes 43, 44 and 44 respectively) and given the experimental instrument, the Defining Issues Test and the debriefing questionnaire. Auditors in the control group were given the case without positive or negative contextual audit evidence. Therefore, only non-normative information, such as the income effect of the accounting error, could influence their judgments. In the present study, sensitivity to contextual factors is measured by comparing between-subject groups' average probabilistic judgment for the manipulations provided. After reading the scenarios, each subject was asked to predict whether the adjustment being proposed by the auditor would in fact be material. The relative materiality of the accounting error was captured using a 1,000-point continuous measure where "1,000" denoted absolute certainty regarding the materiality, and "0" denoted absolute certainty regarding the immateriality, of the accounting error. Such measures have been commonly used in probabilistic prediction studies (see, for example, Ashton [1982]; Kahneman and Tversky [1973], Libby [1981]).

The subjective probability $P_j(i)$ assessed by subjects, regarding the materiality of the proposed adjustment given the jth contextual message for an auditor defined in the ith DIT P score subgroup, was analyzed in the present study. In addition, the odds-likelihood ratio $L_j(i)$ was computed for each between-subject group. According to Libby [1981, p. 55], "The likelihood ratio determines the amount by which these prior expectations should be revised in light of new data and is considered a measure of 'informativeness' or diagnostic value of the data." Thus, when contextual factors are positive, auditors are expected to be more likely to perceive an accounting error as immaterial and when contextual factors are negative, auditors will be more likely to perceive the accounting error as material. Also, by virtue of ethical reasoning, high DIT auditors should be more sensitive to both positive and negative contextual information about the client and its management than low DIT auditors when judging the materiality of a given accounting error.

Research Findings

To determine the extent of associations among DITs and demographic data, Spearman correlations on experience, age and education were computed. In general, findings are consistent to those reported in Chapter 4, showing that DIT P scores are negatively correlated ($\rho = -0.154$, $p < 0.05$) to the auditor's experience within the public accounting firm. Exhibit 6.6 provides the sample frequencies, DIT means and standard deviations for subjects randomly assigned to each between-subject experimental group and post-stratified using the median DIT P score for the sample. A nonparametric χ^2 (Feinberg [1983, p. 40]) revealed no violation of independence due to the random assignment of subjects into experimental and control groups.

Exhibit 6.7 reports mean and median posterior probabilities and likelihood ratios by subjects post-stratified by DIT level. The first column in the exhibit reflects the priors set for the experiment. The second column provides mean and median responses for the experimental group receiving positive contextual information. The third column, for negative contextual information, and the fourth column displays responses for the control group. As can be seen, differences across experimental groups are evident. That is, using the Wilcoxon rank sum test and the Hodges-Lehmann estimator (Hollander and Wolfe [1973, pp. 75-78]), medians are significantly greater than priors under conditions of negative information for both high ($p < 0.001$) and low ($p < 0.01$) DIT subgroups. In the positive condition, however, only the high DIT auditors differ significantly ($p < 0.01$) below priors. In other words, the high DIT auditors are more sensitive to negative and positive contextual factors in this experiment than are the low DIT auditors. It is also interesting to see that medians for auditors in the control group are almost exactly equal to priors. This suggests that auditors perceived the information contained in the narrative as neutral.

Exhibit 6.6

Sample Frequency, DIT Means and Standard Deviations
by Auditors Assigned to Experimental or Control groups

	Contextual Evidence			
	Positive	**Negative**	**Control**	**Overall**
Low DIT group				
Sample size	23.0	21.0	21.0	65.0
DIT P score mean	26.7	26.3	27.1	26.8
DIT Standard deviation	4.5	5.2	5.0	4.9
High DIT group				
Sample size	20.0	23.0	23.0	65.0
DIT P score mean	48.2	48.7	48.8	48.5
DIT Standard deviation	6.7	6.5	7.3	6.8
Overall				
Sample size	43.0	44.0	44.0	131.0
DIT P score mean	38.4	37.9	38.1	38.2
DIT Standard deviation	11.2	12.5	11.5	11.6

Exhibit 6.7

Mean and Median Subjective Probabilities and Likelihood Ratios for Materiality Judgment by DIT and Treatment Groups

	Priors	Contextual Evidence Positive	Contextual Evidence Negative	Control
Low DIT group				
Probability				
Mean	50.0	47.7	62.1	52.3
Median	50.0	46.0	64.5*	51.0
Likelihood				
Mean	1.00	0.88	1.73	1.01
Median	1.00	0.85	1.82*	1.04
High DIT group				
Probability				
Mean	50.0	42.1	73.6	51.7
Median	50.0	36.0**	78.5**	52.0
Likelihood				
Mean	1.00	0.54	4.03	1.05
Median	1.00	0.57**	3.65**	1.08
Overall				
Probability				
Mean	50.0	45.1	68.1	52.0
Median	50.0	40.0*	70.0*	52.0
Likelihood				
Mean	1.00	0.72	2.93	1.03
Median	1.00	0.67*	2.33	1.08

*Using the Wilcoxon rank sum test (Hollander and Wolfe [1973, p. 68]) the reported median value differs from priors at the 0.01 level of significance.

** The reported median value differs from priors at the 0.001 level of significance.

Exhibit 6.8 depicts the interaction between treatment and DIT P score level. As can be seen, negative contextual evidence yields average predictions that exceed priors (50.00) for both high and low DIT auditors. In the case of positive contextual evidence, prediction means are significantly below priors for high DIT auditors only. These findings corroborate the theory specified earlier (see Exhibit 6.2), in which ethical reasoning was predicted to influence auditors' sensitivity to qualitative (normative) factors about the client organization and its management.

Exhibit 6.8

ANOVA Interactions for Materiality
Judgment by Treatment and DIT Groups

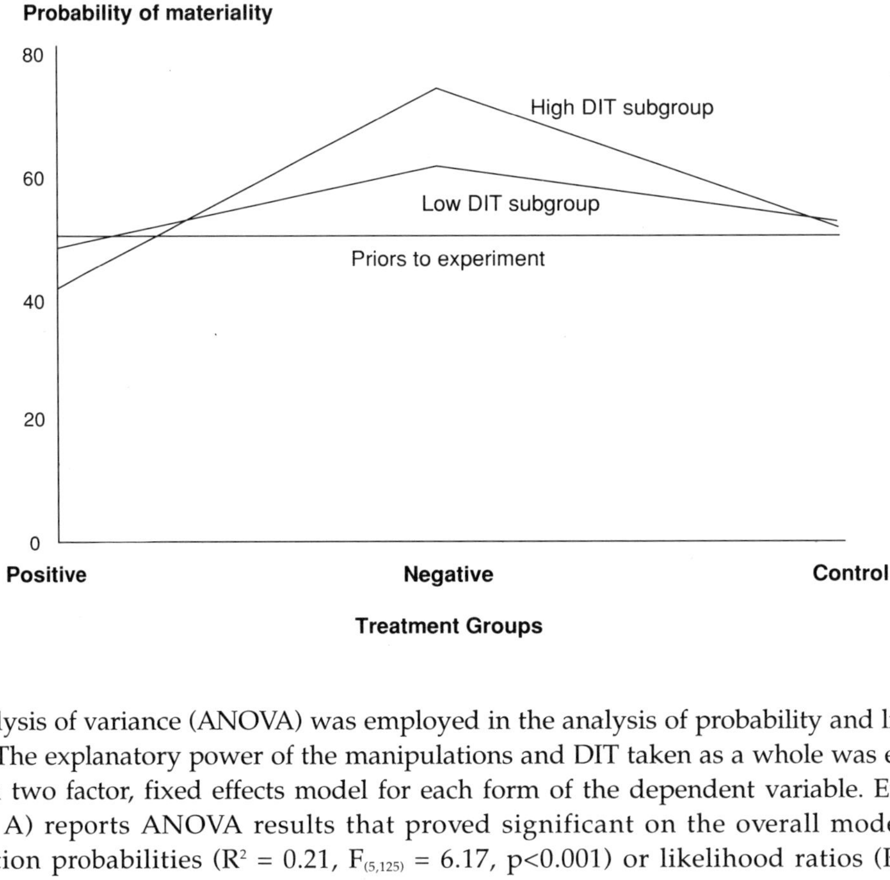

Analysis of variance (ANOVA) was employed in the analysis of probability and likelihood ratios. The explanatory power of the manipulations and DIT taken as a whole was evaluated using a two factor, fixed effects model for each form of the dependent variable. Exhibit 6.9 (Panel A) reports ANOVA results that proved significant on the overall models using prediction probabilities ($R^2 = 0.21$, $F_{(5,125)} = 6.17$, $p<0.001$) or likelihood ratios ($R^2 = 0.19$, $F_{(5,125)} = 5.22$, $p < 0.01$) as dependent variables. The interaction between experimental treatments and DIT level is also highly significant for both probability ($p < 0.005$) and likelihood ($p < 0.025$) models.[36]

To assess the significance of DIT P scores in relation to experimental treatments, separate regression models on auditor materiality judgments were employed on the two between-subject experimental groups. Exhibit 6.9 (Panel B) illustrates the estimated univariate regressions for both subsamples. As can be seen, materiality predictions are negatively related ($t = -1.48$, $p < 0.065$) to DIT when contextual information is positive, and are positively related

Exhibit 6.9

Analysis of Variance and Regression Tests for Materiality Judgment by DIT, Treatment Group and Their Interaction

Panel A: Two-way analysis of variance

Dependent variable = subjective posterior probability

Source	DF	SS	MS	F-value	p-value
DIT level	1	92	92	0.016	n.s.
Treatment	2	8,168	4,084	7.362	0.001
Interaction	2	7,044	3,522	6.346	0.005
Error	125	69,295	554		
Total	130	84,599			

Dependent variable = likelihood ratio

Source	DF	SS	MS	F-value	p-value
DIT level	1	278	278	0.413	n.s.
Treatment	2	7,214	3,607	5.435	0.009
Interaction	2	5,807	2,903	4.381	0.025
Error	125	82,770	662		
Total	130	96,069			

Panel B: Regression models

Experimental group	Estimated equation	t-ratio	p-value
Positive (n=43)	48.0 – 0.189 * (DIT)	–1.48	0.0646
Negative (n=44)	44.7+ 0.542 * (DIT)	2.32	0.0254

For purposes of OLS regression, materiality judgments were expressed as a subjective posterior probability. Using a two sample t-test, differences between regression coefficients are significant at $p < 0.001$ level.

($t = 2.32$, $p < 0.0254$) when contextual information is negative. This confirms earlier findings showing that as the auditor's level of ethical reasoning increases, so does his or her sensitivity to both positive and negative qualitative cues regarding the audit client when judging the materiality of an accounting error. The implications and limitations of these findings, as well as those presented earlier in this chapter, are discussed in the next section.

6.5 IMPLICATIONS OF THE THREE STUDIES

Discussion

This research set out to explore the influence of ethical reasoning upon the audit judgment based on a theory that suggests that an auditor's ability and motivation to judge the characteristics of client management are enhanced by the ethical reasoning level of the individual. Survey results provide only partial support for this theory by showing that perceptions of management competence and auditors' ethical reasoning are inversely related, while perceptions of management integrity and ethical reasoning are not related. However, another important relationship was found. That is, findings reveal that as the auditor's ethical reasoning increases, so does his or her sensitivity to competent, low integrity management. Further, results show that auditors at lower levels of ethical reasoning are more sensitive to management with low competence and low integrity. Thus, they may fail to discriminate properly critical audit conditions where managers are believed to be competent and unethical. Finally, the third study shows that individual cognitive differences may explain why some auditors are more sensitive to certain kinds of contextual information than others.

These results imply that, by virtue of their cognitive capacity, certain auditors may be unable to frame reliable judgments regarding the ethical characteristics of client management. Hence, *inability* rather than *gullibility* may explain why certain auditors fail to detect obvious warning signs of the client organization and its management. This finding is even more disconcerting given the results from several earlier studies (Armstrong [1984, 1987]; Ponemon [1990, 1992a]; Ponemon and Gabhart [1990]; Ponemon and Glazer [1990]; Shaub [1991]), all showing that the ethical reasoning of professional accountants and auditors tends to be significantly lower than comparable norms for college-educated adults (see Rest [1979a, 1986]). Hence, improper assessments of client management, erroneous audit judgments and poor audit quality may be a pervasive problem in the audit setting. Consequently, allegations of audit failure and litigation problems may continue to plague the public accounting profession.

In light of the national U.S. savings and loan crisis, recessions in world financial markets and the demise of the seventh largest public accounting firm in the United States (Laventhol and Horwath), audit firm management should be wary of future events that can soil the reputation of their firm and the auditing profession as a whole. Obviously, a soiled reputation reduces the value of an independent audit. As a result, clients and financial statement users alike will place less faith in audit opinions and place greater reliance on legal or contractual arrangements. As the demand for audit services declines, government authorities may become more actively involved in the regulation of the profession. Loss of the public trust and resulting governmental interventions could cause the demise of the profession. Beyond litigation and regulatory concerns is the quality of professional practice which, according to this research, may improve considerably if auditing firms became more concerned about the ethical reasoning and judgment-making capacities of individual auditors.

There are remedies available, however. For example, the audit firm can develop specific tests, decision aids or expert systems that help the auditor evaluate the ethical characteristics of client management and properly incorporate this assessment in critical judgments concerning the auditing engagement. However, this approach is problematic for three reasons. First, the management of the client organization may view it as demeaning and thus will be unwilling to participate. Second, specific tests to evaluate client ethics also would imply that the audit firm has broadened its responsibility to detect fraud. Since tests are seldom perfect indicators of reality, this will lead to greater exposure and legal liability for the auditor. Third, decision aids (expert systems) that can generate reliable predictions of human (value laden) judgments are in only their technological infancy.

Perhaps a more practical strategy is to further the moral development of individual auditors within the firm, thus increasing their sensitivity to ethical conflict and improving their ability to recognize unethical client management. A feasible method of moral development is effective educational interventions at both the university and the firm level. As indicated by Rest [1988], development to higher levels of ethical reasoning can occur at all ages and in all environments under certain, well defined conditions. Because empirical evidence suggests that traditional ethics education does not influence moral development (cf. Kohlberg [1984]; Rest [1986]; Ponemon and Glazer [1990]), these programs should be replaced by new interventions that foster the highest order of ethical reasoning.

Limitations and Conclusion

Three limitations in the three research studies can also be identified. First, a sample of auditors from two large U.S. audit firms limits the ability to generalize results to the population of auditors in all firms from all countries. Second, while the research utilized different empirical methods and instruments, auditor judgment in real situations was never observed or captured. Thus, the results of all three studies may be caused by artifacts of the experimental context itself and not by the auditor's cognitive ability to deal with normatively important information about the client organization and its management.[37] Third, the DIT P score was used as a surrogate of each auditor's level of ethical reasoning. The DIT is based upon a model that suggests that an individual's reasoning is subject to measurement. The degree to which the DIT errs in measuring an individual's reasoning capacity has been discussed by Rest [1986].

Despite these limitations, the results of this research suggest that ethical reasoning is a determinant of judgment in the audit setting. Additional research should be pursued to test the generalizability of these findings to other areas of auditing and accounting, or by employing other empirical methods. For example, experimental markets can be effectively used to test relationships between individual (ethical) cognitions and auditor judgments. In summary, the present research has shed some light on one possibly important dimension of auditing — namely, the auditor's ability to attend to and process the ethical characteristics of the client organization and its management. To this end, we hope that these studies will pave the way to many important projects in the future. The consequences of these findings to auditing practice will be discussed in the last chapter.

Chapter 7

Research Implications, Extensions and Concluding Thoughts

7.1 IMPLICATIONS OF THE RESEARCH

This research set out to explore the influence of ethical reasoning upon professional judgment in accounting and auditing. It advanced a theory that a person's capacity to frame and resolve ethical issues should be positively related to his or her sensitivity to contextual audit evidence as well as to the possibility of unethical behaviour in the audit setting. Empirical findings from Chapter 6 corroborate this theory by showing that an auditor's recognition of qualitative audit evidence regarding the client organization and its management, in the context of assessing audit risk, financial statement distortions, and the materiality of an accounting error, is enhanced by his or her level of ethical reasoning. In particular, auditors with higher DIT P scores were found to more effectively process competence and integrity cues regarding client management than auditors with lower DIT P scores — especially when managers were judged to have low integrity. This finding implies that auditors with low DIT P scores may fail to discriminate critical audit conditions where a client's managers are not believed to be completely ethical or trustworthy.

Along similar lines, the results in Chapter 5 suggest that auditors with low DIT P scores are less likely than auditors with high DIT P scores to view questionable behaviours in the audit setting — such as the underreporting of chargeable time, shifting time to another billable engagement and premature sign-off on an audit program — as a negative and dysfunctional reaction to audit budget pressure. To the extent that the experimental prediction of what another will do is a fair surrogate for what an individual really believes (see Ponemon and Gabhart [1990]; Arnold and Ponemon [1991]), these findings are somewhat disturbing. They suggest that low DIT auditors, especially those at the staff and senior levels in U.S. firms, may be willing to engage in dubious time-reporting activities and certain audit quality reduction acts when faced with work-related pressure.

The findings reported in Chapters 5 through 6 are even more disconcerting given the results of several earlier empirical studies (summarized in Exhibit 3.1), all showing that the ethical reasoning of professional accountants and auditors tends to be significantly lower than comparable norms for college-educated adults. Hence, improper assessments of client management, erroneous audit judgments and unethical work-related behaviours may be pervasive problems in the audit setting. As a consequence, audit firms and their client organizations may be exposed to audit quality problems as well as the most costly and severe forms of litigation.

The results provided in Chapter 4 also show a convergence of ethical reasoning levels below comparable norms for college-educated adults as individuals progress to higher positions within public accounting firms in the United States. This does not seem to be the case for CAs in the two participating Canadian firms, where auditors at all position levels tend to possess higher DIT results than their U.S. counterparts. In other words, cross-sectional empirical findings provide *prima facie* evidence that the ethical reasoning capacities of firm management (i.e., partners and managers) in the United States differ from their Canadian counterparts. Taking this one step further, perhaps the process of ethical socialization alluded to by Ponemon [1990, 1992a] for individuals entering and remaining in the U.S. public accounting profession may not exist, or may be different, in Canada.

It is important to note that the findings of this research do not necessarily mean that the ethical motivation or action of audit firm management in the United States should be seriously questioned; according to Rest [1986, p. 60], ethical reasoning is only part of an individual's overall capacity to frame and resolve ethical issues. Many other variables may play an equally important role in ethical behaviour. What these findings do suggest, however, is that partners in U.S. firms tend to think at the conventional level (Stage 3), while partners in Canadian firms are more likely to reason at higher levels (Stages 4 and 5). This implies that the ethical reasoning of partners in U.S. firms is primarily influenced by their need to affiliate with peers or a referent group (e.g., the client, office colleagues, or the accounting firm) when judging or attempting to resolve ethical conflict. Assuming that the referent group is the accounting firm, adherence to the rules of the profession will result as long as such rules are consistent with the norms of the firm. If, on the other hand, rules of the profession are not consistent with the norms of the firm, then firm norms will take precedence.

By virtue of higher DIT P scores, partners in Canadian CA firms may be better able to independently frame ethical judgments separate and apart from the values and needs of clients, colleagues within the firm, or the accounting firm as a whole. In addition, in comparison to U.S. partners, these individuals may have a greater sensitivity to ethical conflict not well defined by the firm or the profession. Because the practice of accounting is dynamic, many conflicts are not resolved by simply adhering to codes of conduct or professional standards (Gaa [1992]). This is especially true for partners who, by virtue of their position, are typically exposed to the most difficult and pressing problems within the organization. While those at higher ethical reasoning levels would be expected to be better able to resolve difficult ethical conflicts, this research, as well as earlier studies by Ponemon [1990, 1992a] and Shaub [1991], suggest that relatively few of these individuals rise to upper management positions in U.S. firms. If this is true, then CPAs making it to the top of the auditing firm hierarchy may be ill-equipped to deal with and resolve the multitude of ethical conflicts that abound in everyday practice.

There are at least two remedies available. First, managers of firms in the United States can adopt new and detailed rules of conduct that attempt to specify, in concise and clear language, a single correct ethical strategy to any particular ethical conflict. It is important to note, however, that the rule-makers themselves should possess high ethical reasoning since they must deal with many new and uncharted conflicts that are likely to arise. Second, managers of U.S. firms can develop to higher levels of ethical reasoning. As a result of their ethical development, partners also will develop greater understanding of subordinates with differing ethical capacities. This, of course, would discourage selection-socialization as evidenced by Ponemon [1990, 1992a] in his research.

As noted previously, effective pedagogical interventions at both the university and the firm level may foster the moral development of individual accountants and auditors. Further, Rest [1988] suggests that development to higher levels of ethical reasoning can occur at all ages and in all learning environments. The findings of this research may suggest that education in Canada may be more conducive than in the United States for developing the ethical reasoning skills of students choosing to pursue a career in public accounting. As a starting point, perhaps accounting educators in the United States should seriously consider the effectiveness of traditional ethics interventions in accounting and, when necessary, replace these with formal courses and programs that are designed to foster the highest order of ethical reasoning (cf. Ponemon and Glazer [1990]).

Some might doubt the need for change on the grounds that the market for public accounting services dictates the level and value of ethical standards within the accounting profession (Noreen [1988]). Thus, as long as firms in the United States are profitable, ethical standards must be acceptable to the public at large. However, this justification is inappropriate for two reasons. First, if selection-socialization in U.S. firms effectively weeds out those individuals with high ethical reasoning, it will be difficult to attract and retain such employees. That is, many of the best and brightest accounting students will choose alternative career paths. The lack of diversity among those progressing to partnership will cause the ethical culture or moral atmosphere of U.S. public accounting firms to become stagnant. Perhaps stagnation and an inability to adapt to new cultures will cause accounting firms in the United States to find it increasingly difficult to compete and survive in the global business community. This may not be the case for Canadian firms, where the ethical reasoning of public accounting professionals may not diminish at higher position levels.

Second, as discussed in the previous chapter, the U.S. savings and loan debacle and downward economic trends in the United States may have caused the public to view the public accounting profession in a more negative light. As a consequence of negative perceptions, client organizations and financial statement users in the future may depend less on the attestations provided by independent auditors, thus reducing the demand for public accounting services. Such declines might prompt governmental authorities such as the Securities and Exchange Commission, General Accounting Office and Congress to become more actively involved in the regulation of the profession. This in turn may cause firms in the United States to lose their professional autonomy and incentive to provide high quality auditing services. In the end, this would be most detrimental to the general public who are the beneficiaries of audit quality.

It is precisely these problems and concerns that have generated much interest in ethics within the public accounting profession in the United States, leading to revised codes of conduct, an independent public accounting oversight board, proposed governmental regulatory action and a continuing stream of academic research in the applied professional ethics area (as reviewed in Chapters 2 and 3). Assuming that this research can be extended to the general population of practicing auditors in the United States and Canada, then the presented findings may have significant implications to auditing practitioners and auditing researchers alike, because they show that the auditor's ethical reasoning is inextricably linked to his or her capacity to form both ethical and technical judgments in the professional domain. Further, and perhaps more importantly, the trend of decreasing DIT P scores brought about by firm socialization may not extend to audit firms operating in other countries. Hence, the management of U.S. public accounting firms should look to practice offices in other countries (such as Canada) to model a firm-wide moral atmosphere than permits an individual's development to the highest levels of ethical reasoning.

7.2 RESEARCH EXTENSIONS

As mentioned in earlier chapters, several limitations and weaknesses in the present research can be identified. Despite these limitations, however, the results of this research suggest that ethical reasoning is an important determinant of professional judgment in the audit setting. Additional studies should be pursued to test the generalizability of these findings to other areas of auditing and accounting, or by employing other empirical methods. For example, more rigorous experimental-lab designs can be effectively used to test relationships between specific cognitions and auditor judgments (see, for example, Dopuch, King and Wallin [1989]; Ponemon [1992b]).

In addition, given the highly specialized and somewhat technical nature of ethical conflict in accounting and auditing practice, the use of a domain-specific psychometric instrument may make an important contribution to this area of study. For instance, researchers may wish to develop an internally reliable and externally valid measure of ethical reasoning that directly relates to ethical choice in auditing. Perhaps measures from a domain-specific instrument for auditors, in conjunction with corroborating measures from other generic instruments such as the DIT or MJI, would provide a better overall diagnostic of the individual auditor's ethical reasoning level and ethical judgment in professional practice.

The results reported in this monograph support the findings of several previous studies that have found an association between auditors' ethical reasoning and their sensitivity to ethical issues in the audit setting (see Exhibit 3.1). Unlike earlier works, however, this study was the first to examine cross-cultural differences between practitioners in the United States and Canada. As reported in Chapter 4, marked differences between American and Canadian practitioners seem to exist in terms of ethical reasoning as measured by DIT P scores. Despite statistically significant findings, however, this study does not provide irrefutable evidence of differences in the ethical socialization process among Canadian and U.S. public accounting firms. That is, by virtue of a cross-sectional research design, the process of selection-socialization in U.S. and Canadian audit firms was never really observed and can only be inferred from the pattern of DIT P scores. To this end, longitudinal research studies are needed to examine auditing or accounting practitioners over their career path to determine whether certain types of individuals are "weeded out" of the firm because of ethical, social or intellectual orientations that differ from firm management. Other studies are needed to provide a greater understanding of the social dynamics present in both U.S. and Canadian audit firms in order to determine its effect upon an employee's ethical development over time.

Another interesting extension to the present research would be to compare members of different professional accounting organizations in the same country. For example, researchers could examine both CAs and CGAs in Canadian provinces where both professional groups have auditing rights. A similar study can be conducted in the United States that compares CPAs with other non-competing professional accounting or auditing groups such as Certified Management Accountants (CMAs) and Certified Internal Auditors (CIAs). Further research is necessary to examine the influence of cultural variation brought about by religious, social and economic differences on the development of ethical reasoning and judgment in accounting or auditing. For example, studies of practitioner groups from a diverse sample of nations, including countries in Asia, Europe and South America, may produce even more striking differences than that presented for CAs in Canada and CPAs in the United States.

Beyond cross-cultural studies, researchers could explore the influence of ethical reasoning in other accounting domains. Consider, for example, the practice of taxation in public accounting firms, where rules of practice may often be ambiguous. As a consequence, resolution of ethical conflict is not accomplished by following a clear-cut rule such as independence, but instead is attained by exercising professional discretion and judgment. Two additional areas that also require future research are management accounting and internal auditing. Ethical reasoning may be especially salient for these professional groups given their dual and often conflicting allegiance to their professions as well as to the management of their organization. Along these lines, Arnold and Ponemon [1991] found that ethical reasoning was an important determinant of an internal auditor's ethical behaviour when communicating sensitive issues (e.g., fraud) in the organizational setting.

The individual differences in ethical reasoning by position level and by country as reported in this monograph only hints at the true complexity of the ethical socialization phenomenon that may exist in large public accounting firms in the United States and Canada. Much work is still required to examine how and why an individual's level of ethical reasoning influences his or her potential for career attainment and upward mobility within accounting firms. For example, future studies can explore the way the management of accounting firms observe the ethical beliefs and values of employees, and whether these observations are used by them to select, screen and advance only certain types of individuals. Other studies can examine the ways ethical or unethical behaviours can be employed by individuals to signal characteristics deemed to be acceptable to accounting firm management.

Research is also required to determine the generalizability of these findings before reaching a conclusion about the importance of ethical reasoning as an antecedent to ethical judgment and actual behaviour in audit or accounting settings. For example, future researchers could explore the connection between ethical reasoning and ethical behaviour more rigorously using decision or game theoretic models in a multiperiod setting. Such frameworks have been useful in explaining behaviour for both economic agents and principals under various social and ethical constraints (Sen [1986]). Experimental markets research also can be employed to study individual differences (in terms of ethical reasoning) on economic choice studies that attempt to simulate actual auditing conditions under a wide array of monetary incentives, social contracts and economic institutions. It is hoped that such future research will shed light on the way ethical reasoning influences an auditor's ability, motivation and action under a variety of conditions that cannot be explained by conventional experimental methods that rely on hypothetical audit cases alone.

Assuming that there is a connection between the quality of judgments rendered in the auditing domain and the individual's level of ethical reasoning, then it may be imperative to conduct pedagogical research into the most effective ways for raising the auditor's reasoning capacity — especially for those at a relatively low level of ethical reasoning. There is, however, a major limitation to such an approach. That is, ethics interventions that attempt to foster development to the post-conventional level may only be effective for those individuals eager and willing to learn (Rest [1986]). This may explain why recent studies do not find a causal link between ethics education in the accounting curriculum and the ethical development of college students in traditional accounting programs (Ponemon [1992c]; Shaub [1991]; St. Pierre, Nelson and Gabbin [1990]). A second, related problem concerns the extreme rule-orientation of accounting professionals in the United States. According to Gaa [1992], Lampe and Finn [1993] and Ponemon [1992b], the rule-orientation of accounting and auditing practice in large CPA firms may prohibit individuals from aspiring to higher levels of principled reasoning in the Kohlberg [1969] and Rest [1979a] models. As a result, the managers of these firms may perceive it as being somewhat dysfunctional to foster the cognitive development of their employees beyond the conventional level of ethical reasoning.

7.3 CONCLUDING REMARKS

An enormous amount of work needs to be done before conclusions regarding the role of ethical reasoning in the accounting or auditing domain can be drawn. Before attempting to extend the findings presented in this monograph, it would be desirable to conduct a larger replication of the experimental studies presented here, perhaps utilizing the DIT in conjunction with other domain-specific psychometrics of ethical reasoning. In addition, a study of a controlled group of public accounting practitioners over time from several nations with markedly different cultures could provide important insights into the nature and pervasiveness of the ethical socialization within the global accounting and auditing community.

The objective of this research was not to provide a definitive solution to the issue of ethical behaviour of the accounting or auditing practitioner, but instead to illustrate the importance of ethical reasoning as a cognitive determinant of judgment and decision making in the audit setting. To this end, the findings of this monograph should be of value to those interested in extending an important area of research and theory. In conclusion, this research has, it is hoped, provided the reader with a better understanding of the role of ethical reasoning in the context of an ever-changing professional practice.

Appendices

APPENDIX A

INSTRUCTION BOOKLET

DIT

DEFINING ISSUES TEST
University of Minnesota

Opinions about Social Problems

The purpose of this questionnaire is to help us understand how people think about social problems. Different people have different opinions about questions of right and wrong. There are no "right" answers to such problems in the way that math problems have right answers. We would like you to tell us what you think about several problem stories.

You will be asked to read a story from this booklet. Then you will be asked to mark your answers on a separate answer sheet. More details about how to do this will follow. But it is important that you fill in your answers on the answer sheet with a #2 pencil. Please make sure that your mark completely fills the little circle, that the mark is dark, and that any erasures that you make are completely clean.

The Identification Number at the top of the answer sheet may already be filled in when you receive your materials. If not, you will receive special instructions about how to fill in that number.

In this questionnaire you will be asked to read a story and then to place marks on the answer sheet. In order to illustrate how we would like you to do this, consider the following story:

FRANK AND THE CAR

Frank Jones has been thinking about buying a car. He is married, has two small children and earns an average income. The car he buys will be his family's only car. It will be used mostly to get to work and drive around town, but sometimes for vacation trips also. In trying to decide what car to buy, Frank Jones realized that there were a lot of questions to consider. For instance, should he buy a larger used car or a smaller new car for about the same amount of money? Other questions occur to him.

We note that this is not really a social problem, but it will illustrate our instructions. After you read a story you will then turn to the answer sheet to find the section that corresponds to the story. But in this sample story, we present the questions below (along with some sample answers). Note that all your answers will be marked on the separate answer sheet.

First, on the answer sheet for each story you will be asked to indicate your recommendation for what a person should do. If you tend to favor one action or another (even if you are not completely sure), indicate which one. If you do not favor either action, mark the circle by "can't decide."

Second, read each of the items numbered 1 to 12. Think of the issue that the item is raising. If that issue is important in making a decision, one way or the other, then mark the circle by "great." If that issue is not important or doesn't make sense to you, mark "no." If the issue is relevant but not critical, mark "much," "some," or "little" --depending on how much importance that issue has in your opinion. You may mark several items as "great" (or any other level of importance) -- there is no fixed number of items that must be marked at any one level.

Third, after you have made your marks along the left hand side of each of the 12 items, then at the bottom you will be asked to choose the item that is the <u>most</u> important consideration out of all the items printed there. Pick from among the items provided even if you think that none of the items are of "great" importance. Of the items that are presented there, pick one as the most important (relative to the others), then the second most important, third, and fourth most important.

SAMPLE ITEMS and SAMPLE ANSWERS:

FRANK AND THE CAR: ● buy new car   0 can't decide   0 buy used car

Great	Much	Some	Little	No	Item
0	0	0	0	●	1. Whether the car dealer was in the same block as where Frank lives.
●	0	0	0	0	2. Would a used car be more economical in the long run than a new car.
0	0	●	0	0	3. Whether the color was green, Frank's favorite color.
0	0	0	0	●	4. Whether the cubic inch displacement was at least 200.
●	0	0	0	0	5. Would a large, roomy car be better than a compact car.
0	0	0	0	●	6. Whether the front connibilies were differential.

	1	2	3	4	5	6	7	8	9	10	11	12
Most important item	0	0	0	0	●	0	0	0	0	0	0	0
Second most important	0	●	0	0	0	0	0	0	0	0	0	0
Third most important	0	0	●	0	0	0	0	0	0	0	0	0
Fourth most important	●	0	0	0	0	0	0	0	0	0	0	0

Note that in our sample responses, the first item was considered irrelevant; the second item was considered as a critical issue in making a decision; the third item was considered of only moderate importance; the fourth item was not clear to the person responding whether 200 was good or not, so it was marked "no"; the fifth item was also of critical importance; and the sixth item didn't make any sense, so it was marked "no".

Note that the most important item comes from one of the items marked on the far left hand side. In deciding between item #2 and #5, a person should reread these items, then put one of them as the most important, and the other item as second, etc.

Here is the first story for your consideration. Read the story and then turn to the separate answer sheet to mark your responses. After filling in the four most important items for the story, return to this booklet to read the next story. Please remember to fill in the circle completely, make dark marks, and completely erase all corrections.

HEINZ AND THE DRUG

In Europe a woman was near death from a special kind of cancer. There was one drug that doctors thought might save her. It was a form of radium that a druggist in the same town had recently discovered. The drug was expensive to make, but the druggist was charging ten times what the drug cost to make. He paid $200 for the radium and charged $2,000 for a small dose of the drug. The sick woman's husband, Heinz, went to everyone he knew to borrow the money, but he could only get together about $1,000, which is half of what it cost. He told the druggist that his wife was dying, and asked him to sell it cheaper or let him pay later. But the druggist said, "No, I discovered the drug and I'm going to make money from it." So Heinz got desperate and began to think about breaking into the man's store to steal the drug for his wife. Should Heinz steal the drug?

ESCAPED PRISONER

A man had been sentenced to prison for 10 years. After one year, however, he escaped from prison, moved to a new area of the country, and took on the name of Thompson. For eight years he worked hard, and gradually he saved enough money to buy his own business. He was fair to his customers, gave his employees top wages, and gave most of his own profits to charity. Then one day, Mrs. Jones, an old neighbor, recognized him as the man who had escaped from prison eight years before, and whom the police had been looking for. Should Mrs. Jones report Mr. Thompson to the police and have him sent back to prison?

NEWSPAPER

Fred, a senior in high school, wanted to publish a mimeographed newspaper for students so that he could express many of his opinions. He wanted to speak out against the use of the military in international disputes and to speak out against some of the school's rules, like the rule forbidding boys to wear long hair.

When Fred started his newspaper, he asked his principal for permission. The principal said it would be all right if before every publication Fred would turn in all his articles for the principal's approval. Fred agreed and turned in several articles for approval. The principal approved all of them and Fred published two issues of the paper in the next two weeks.

But the principal had not expected that Fred's newspaper would receive so much attention. Students were so excited by the paper that they began to organize protests against the hair regulation and other school rules. Angry parents objected to Fred's opinions. They phoned the principal telling him that the newspaper was unpatriotic and should not be published. As a result of the rising excitement, the principal ordered Fred to stop publishing. He gave as a reason that Fred's activities were disruptive to the operation of the school. Should the principal stop the newspaper?

DOCTOR'S DILEMMA

A lady was dying of cancer which could not be cured and she had only about six months to live. She was in terrible pain, but she was so weak that a good dose of pain-killer like morphine would make her die sooner. She was delirious and almost crazy with pain, and in her calm periods, she would ask the doctor to give her enough morphine to kill her. She said she couldn't stand the pain and that she was going to die in a few months anyway. Should the doctor give her an overdose of morphine that would make her die?

WEBSTER

Mr. Webster was the owner and manager of a gas station. He wanted to hire another mechanic to help him, but good mechanics were hard to find. The only person he found who seemed to be a good mechanic was Mr. Lee, but he was Chinese. While Mr. Webster himself didn't have anything against Orientals, he was afraid to hire Mr. Lee because many of his customers didn't like Orientals. His customers might take their business elsewhere if Mr. Lee was working in the gas station.

When Mr. Lee asked Mr. Webster if he could have the job, Mr. Webster said that he had already hired somebody else. But Mr. Webster really had not hired anybody, because he could not find anybody who was a good mechanic besides Mr. Lee. Should Mr. Webster have hired Mr. Lee?

STUDENT TAKE-OVER

Back in the 1960s at Harvard University there was a student group called Students for a Democratic Society (SDS). SDS students were against the war in Viet Nam, and were against the army training program (ROTC) that helped to send men to fight in Viet Nam. While the war was still going on, the SDS students demanded that Harvard end the army ROTC program as a university course. This would mean that Harvard students could not get army training as part of their regular course work and not get credit for it towards their degree.

Harvard professors agreed with the SDS students. The professors voted to end the ROTC program as a university course. But the President of the University took a different view. He stated that the army program should stay on campus as a course.

The SDS students felt that the President of the University was not going to pay attention to the vote of the professors, and was going to keep the ROTC program as a course on campus. The SDS students then marched to the university's administration building and told everyone else to get out. They said they were taking over the building to force Harvard's President to get rid of the army ROTC program on campus for credit as a course.

Were the students right to take over the administration building?

Please make sure that all your marks are dark, fill the circles, and that all erasures are clean.

THANK YOU.

DEFINING ISSUES TEST
University of Minnesota

IDENTIFICATION NUMBER

0 1 2 3 4 5 6 7 8 9
0 1 2 3 4 5 6 7 8 9
0 1 2 3 4 5 6 7 8 9
0 1 2 3 4 5 6 7 8 9
0 1 2 3 4 5 6 7 8 9

GREAT MUCH SOME LITTLE NO

HEINZ AND THE DRUG: ○ Should Steal ○ Can't Decide ○ Should not steal

○○○○○ 1. Whether a community's laws are going to be upheld.
○○○○○ 2. Isn't it only natural for a loving husband to care so much for his wife that he'd steal?
○○○○○ 3. Is Heinz willing to risk getting shot as a burglar or going to jail for the chance that stealing the drug might help?
○○○○○ 4. Whether Heinz is a professional wrestler, or has considerable influence with professional wrestlers.
○○○○○ 5. Whether Heinz is stealing for himself or doing this solely to help someone else.
○○○○○ 6. Whether the druggist's rights to his invention have to be respected.
○○○○○ 7. Whether the essence of living is more encompassing than the termination of dying, socially and individually.
○○○○○ 8. What values are going to be the basis for governing how people act towards each other.
○○○○○ 9. Whether the druggist is going to be allowed to hide behind a worthless law which only protects the rich anyhow.
○○○○○ 10. Whether the law in this case is getting in the way of the most basic claim of any member of society.
○○○○○ 11. Whether the druggist deserves to be robbed for being so greedy and cruel.
○○○○○ 12. Would stealing in such a case bring about more total good for the whole society or not.

Most important item ① ② ③ ④ ⑤ ⑥ ⑦ ⑧ ⑨ ⑩ ⑪ ⑫
Second most important ① ② ③ ④ ⑤ ⑥ ⑦ ⑧ ⑨ ⑩ ⑪ ⑫
Third most important ① ② ③ ④ ⑤ ⑥ ⑦ ⑧ ⑨ ⑩ ⑪ ⑫
Fourth most important ① ② ③ ④ ⑤ ⑥ ⑦ ⑧ ⑨ ⑩ ⑪ ⑫

GREAT MUCH SOME LITTLE NO

ESCAPED PRISONER: ○ Should report him ○ Can't decide ○ Should not report him

○○○○○ 1. Hasn't Mr. Thompson been good enough for such a long time to prove he isn't a bad person?
○○○○○ 2. Everytime someone escapes punishment for a crime, doesn't that just encourage more crime?
○○○○○ 3. Wouldn't we be better off without prisons and the oppression of our legal system?
○○○○○ 4. Has Mr. Thompson really paid his debt to society?
○○○○○ 5. Would society be failing what Mr. Thompson should fairly expect?
○○○○○ 6. What benefits would prisons be apart from society, especially for a charitable man?
○○○○○ 7. How could anyone be so cruel and heartless as to send Mr. Thompson to prison?
○○○○○ 8. Would it be fair to all the prisoners who had to serve out their full sentences if Mr. Thompson was let off?
○○○○○ 9. Was Mrs. Jones a good friend of Mr. Thompson?
○○○○○ 10. Wouldn't it be a citizen's duty to report an escaped criminal, regardless of the circumstances?
○○○○○ 11. How would the will of the people and the public good best be served?
○○○○○ 12. Would going to prison do any good for Mr. Thompson or protect anybody?

Most important item ① ② ③ ④ ⑤ ⑥ ⑦ ⑧ ⑨ ⑩ ⑪ ⑫
Second most important ① ② ③ ④ ⑤ ⑥ ⑦ ⑧ ⑨ ⑩ ⑪ ⑫
Third most important ① ② ③ ④ ⑤ ⑥ ⑦ ⑧ ⑨ ⑩ ⑪ ⑫
Fourth most important ① ② ③ ④ ⑤ ⑥ ⑦ ⑧ ⑨ ⑩ ⑪ ⑫

PLEASE DO NOT WRITE IN THIS BOX

05638

Printed in U.S.A. NCS Trans-Optic® MP18-73897-321

GREAT MUCH SOME LITTLE NO

NEWSPAPER: ○ Should stop it ○ Can't decide ○ Should not stop it

○○○○○ 1. Is the principal more responsible to students or to parents?
○○○○○ 2. Did the principal give his word that the newspaper could be published for a long time, or did he just promise to approve the newspaper one issue at a time?
○○○○○ 3. Would the students start protesting even more if the principal stopped the newspaper?
○○○○○ 4. When the welfare of the school is threatened, does the principal have the right to give orders to students?
○○○○○ 5. Does the principal have the freedom of speech to say "no" in this case?
○○○○○ 6. If the principal stopped the newspaper would he be preventing full discussion of important problems?
○○○○○ 7. Whether the principal's order would make Fred lose faith in the principal.
○○○○○ 8. Whether Fred was really loyal to his school and patriotic to his country.
○○○○○ 9. What effect would stopping the paper have on the student's education in critical thinking and judgment?
○○○○○ 10. Whether Fred was in any way violating the rights of others in publishing his own opinions.
○○○○○ 11. Whether the principal should be influenced by some angry parents when it is the principal that knows best what is going on in the school.
○○○○○ 12. Whether Fred was using the newspaper to stir up hatred and discontent.

Most important item ① ② ③ ④ ⑤ ⑥ ⑦ ⑧ ⑨ ⑩ ⑪ ⑫
Second most important ① ② ③ ④ ⑤ ⑥ ⑦ ⑧ ⑨ ⑩ ⑪ ⑫
Third most important ① ② ③ ④ ⑤ ⑥ ⑦ ⑧ ⑨ ⑩ ⑪ ⑫
Fourth most important ① ② ③ ④ ⑤ ⑥ ⑦ ⑧ ⑨ ⑩ ⑪ ⑫

GREAT MUCH SOME LITTLE NO

DOCTOR'S DILEMMA: ○ He should give the lady an overdose that will make her die ○ Can't decide ○ Should not give the overdose

○○○○○ 1. Whether the woman's family is in favor of giving her the overdose or not.
○○○○○ 2. Is the doctor obligated by the same laws as everybody else if giving an overdose would be the same as killing her.
○○○○○ 3. Whether people would be much better off without society regimenting their lives and even their deaths.
○○○○○ 4. Whether the doctor could make it appear like an accident.
○○○○○ 5. Does the state have the right to force continued existence on those who don't want to live.
○○○○○ 6. What is the value of death prior to society's perspective on personal values.
○○○○○ 7. Whether the doctor has sympathy for the woman's suffering or cares more about what society might think.
○○○○○ 8. Is helping to end another's life ever a responsible act of cooperation.
○○○○○ 9. Whether only God should decide when a person's life should end.
○○○○○ 10. What values the doctor has set for himself in his own personal code of behavior.
○○○○○ 11. Can society afford to let everybody end their lives when they want to.
○○○○○ 12. Can society allow suicides or mercy killing and still protect the lives of individuals who want want to live.

Most important item ① ② ③ ④ ⑤ ⑥ ⑦ ⑧ ⑨ ⑩ ⑪ ⑫
Second most important ① ② ③ ④ ⑤ ⑥ ⑦ ⑧ ⑨ ⑩ ⑪ ⑫
Third most important ① ② ③ ④ ⑤ ⑥ ⑦ ⑧ ⑨ ⑩ ⑪ ⑫
Fourth most important ① ② ③ ④ ⑤ ⑥ ⑦ ⑧ ⑨ ⑩ ⑪ ⑫

PLEASE DO NOT WRITE IN THIS AREA

GREAT MUCH SOME LITTLE NO

WEBSTER: ○ Should have hired Mr. Lee ○ Can't decide ○ Should not have hired him

○○○○○ 1. Does the owner of a business have the right to make his own business decisions or not?
○○○○○ 2. Whether there is a law that forbids racial discrimination in hiring for jobs.
○○○○○ 3. Whether Mr. Webster is prejudiced against orientals himself or whether he means nothing personal in refusing the job.
○○○○○ 4. Whether hiring a good mechanic or paying attention to his customers' wishes would be best for his business.
○○○○○ 5. What individual differences ought to be relevant in deciding how society's rules are filled?
○○○○○ 6. Whether the greedy and competitive capitalistic system ought to be completely abandoned.
○○○○○ 7. Do a majority of people in Mr. Webster's society feel like his customers or are a majority against prejudice?
○○○○○ 8. Whether hiring capable men like Mr. Lee would use talents that would otherwise be lost to society.
○○○○○ 9. Would refusing the job to Mr. Lee be consistent with Mr. Webster's own moral beliefs?
○○○○○ 10. Could Mr. Webster be so hard-hearted as to refuse the job, knowing how much it means to Mr. Lee?
○○○○○ 11. Whether the Christian commandment to love your fellow man applies to this case.
○○○○○ 12. If someone's in need, shouldn't he be helped regardless of what you get back from him?

Most important item ① ② ③ ④ ⑤ ⑥ ⑦ ⑧ ⑨ ⑩ ⑪ ⑫
Second most important ① ② ③ ④ ⑤ ⑥ ⑦ ⑧ ⑨ ⑩ ⑪ ⑫
Third most important ① ② ③ ④ ⑤ ⑥ ⑦ ⑧ ⑨ ⑩ ⑪ ⑫
Fourth most important ① ② ③ ④ ⑤ ⑥ ⑦ ⑧ ⑨ ⑩ ⑪ ⑫

GREAT MUCH SOME LITTLE NO

STUDENTS: ○ Take it over ○ Can't decide ○ Not take it over

○○○○○ 1. Are the students doing this to really help other people or are they doing it just for kicks.
○○○○○ 2. Do the students have any right to take over property that doesn't belong to them.
○○○○○ 3. Do the students realize that they might be arrested and fined, and even expelled from school.
○○○○○ 4. Would taking over the building in the long run benefit more people to a greater extent.
○○○○○ 5. Whether the president stayed within the limits of his authority in ignoring the faculty vote.
○○○○○ 6. Will the takeover anger the public and give all students a bad name.
○○○○○ 7. Is taking over a building consistent with principles of justice.
○○○○○ 8. Would allowing one student take-over encourage many other student take-overs.
○○○○○ 9. Did the president bring this misunderstanding on himself by being so unreasonable and uncooperative.
○○○○○ 10. Whether running the university ought to be in the hands of a few administrators or in the hands of all the people.
○○○○○ 11. Are the students following principles which they believe are above the law.
○○○○○ 12. Whether or not university decisions ought to be respected by students.

Most important item ① ② ③ ④ ⑤ ⑥ ⑦ ⑧ ⑨ ⑩ ⑪ ⑫
Second most important ① ② ③ ④ ⑤ ⑥ ⑦ ⑧ ⑨ ⑩ ⑪ ⑫
Third most important ① ② ③ ④ ⑤ ⑥ ⑦ ⑧ ⑨ ⑩ ⑪ ⑫
Fourth most important ① ② ③ ④ ⑤ ⑥ ⑦ ⑧ ⑨ ⑩ ⑪ ⑫

PLEASE DO NOT WRITE IN THIS AREA

GREAT MUCH SOME LITTLE NO

DILEMMA #7: ○ Pro ○ Can't decide ○ Con

○○○○○ 1.
○○○○○ 2.
○○○○○ 3.
○○○○○ 4.
○○○○○ 5.
○○○○○ 6.
○○○○○ 7.
○○○○○ 8.
○○○○○ 9.
○○○○○ 10.
○○○○○ 11.
○○○○○ 12.

Most important item ① ② ③ ④ ⑤ ⑥ ⑦ ⑧ ⑨ ⑩ ⑪ ⑫
Second most important ① ② ③ ④ ⑤ ⑥ ⑦ ⑧ ⑨ ⑩ ⑪ ⑫
Third most important ① ② ③ ④ ⑤ ⑥ ⑦ ⑧ ⑨ ⑩ ⑪ ⑫
Fourth most important ① ② ③ ④ ⑤ ⑥ ⑦ ⑧ ⑨ ⑩ ⑪ ⑫

DO NOT WRITE IN SHADED AREAS

GREAT MUCH SOME LITTLE NO

DILEMMA #8: ○ Pro ○ Can't decide ○ Con

○○○○○ 1.
○○○○○ 2.
○○○○○ 3.
○○○○○ 4.
○○○○○ 5.
○○○○○ 6.
○○○○○ 7.
○○○○○ 8.
○○○○○ 9.
○○○○○ 10.
○○○○○ 11.
○○○○○ 12.

Most important item ① ② ③ ④ ⑤ ⑥ ⑦ ⑧ ⑨ ⑩ ⑪ ⑫
Second most important ① ② ③ ④ ⑤ ⑥ ⑦ ⑧ ⑨ ⑩ ⑪ ⑫
Third most important ① ② ③ ④ ⑤ ⑥ ⑦ ⑧ ⑨ ⑩ ⑪ ⑫
Fourth most important ① ② ③ ④ ⑤ ⑥ ⑦ ⑧ ⑨ ⑩ ⑪ ⑫

PLEASE DO NOT WRITE IN THIS BOX

05638

APPENDIX B

EXPERIMENTAL INSTRUMENT: AUDITORS' PERCEPTIONS OF DYSFUNCTIONAL BEHAVIOR IN THE AUDITING SETTING

Jane is a auditor for a large international public accounting firm located in the northeast region of the country. She has recently been assigned to the XYZ Corporation to assume in-charge responsibility for the completion of its year ending 19X1 financial statement audit. The XYZ Corporation is a large, public and somewhat complex organization that has engaged Jane's firm for many years. Even though Jane is a well trained and highly competent individual, she is having extreme difficulty in meeting the preset audit time budget completed by her superiors. To date, she has exceeded the audit time budget by over 35 percent.

Jane knows that she is being evaluated by her superiors for promotion in the very near future and also believes that meeting one's time budget is an important factor for consideration in the performance appraisal and promotion process.

Based on the audit evidence collected to date and the history of clean (unqualified) audit opinions rendered in the past, Jane is certain that the remaining substantive audit procedures to be completed by her or her staff will not yield material audit findings. Jane also believes that much of her remaining work on the job, such as filing and reviewing workpapers, can be performed away from client premises.

(Subjects received only one of the following treatments)

Penalty

Jane is told by the audit partner in-charge of the XYZ engagement that he is disappointed in her performance on the XYZ engagement so far and that if budget overruns continued he would be forced to give her a negative performance appraisal.

Affiliation

Jane believes that most people in her firm have distorted their time budgets by eating time or shifting chargeable hours to another client engagement. She also believes that many auditors in her firm slack-off or prematurely sign-off on audit work in order to report that they got the job done within the prespecified audit time budget.

Each of the following four behaviors should be considered independent events. Please provide your best prediction using the 100 point continuous scale provided below each question by placing a slash (/) directly onto the 0-to-100 point line.

Assuming that Jane has the opportunity to underreport (eat) time without getting caught, will she do so?

Rate your answer using the following scale:

No Unsure Yes

0 50 100

Assuming that Jane has the opportunity to shift her time to another chargeable engagement in the audit firm without getting caught, will she do so?

Rate your answer using the following scale:

No — Unsure — Yes

0 — 50 — 100

Assuming that Jane has the opportunity to do the remaining work more quickly, but less carefully, without getting caught, will she do so?

Rate your answer using the following scale:

No — Unsure — Yes

0 — 50 — 100

Assuming that Jane has the opportunity to prematurely sign-off on much of the remaining work without getting caught, will she do so?

Rate your answer using the following scale:

No — Unsure — Yes

0 — 50 — 100

APPENDIX C

AUDITORS' PERCEPTIONS OF CLIENT COMPETENCE, INTEGRITY AND AUDIT RISK

Control: ___ Firm: ___ Client: ___ Auditor: ___ Level: ___ Date: ___ / ___ / ___

Auditor Experience: ___ Education: ___ Client Tenure: ___ Auditor Tenure: ___

Risk Assessment Level: ___ SIC Code: ___ Public ___ /Private ___ Exchange: ___

Please answer each question listed below using the scales provided. All responses will remain completely confidential. Thank you in advance of your participation.

A. Overall, you believe that the riskiness of this audit client to your firm is...

(1)	(2)	(3)	(4)	(5)
High: ___	Moderately High: ___	Average: ___	Moderately Low: ___	Low: ___

B. Provide the total number of audit engagements managed by you at present:

Total Number: ______

C. Statement on Auditing Standards (No. 47) requires the auditor to evaluate the level of audit risk that is believed to exist within the organization prior to and during the audit engagement. Audit risk is defined as the likelihood that the auditor will fail to detect material accounting error. Please provide the rank of this client relative to all other client organizations audited by you in terms of its **audit risk** to your firm. For example, if you audit ten clients, a rank of 1 (10) means that this client has the most (least) audit risk relative to all other clients. Ties in audit risk among client organizations are allowed.

Relative rank of audit risk: ___ Number of ties: ___

D. Statement on Auditing Standards states that two of the most significant characteristics of the client organization to be assessed by the auditor during the planning phase of the audit are the **competence** and **integrity** of management personnel.

D1. On average, you believe that individual managers of the client organization possess...

(1)	(2)	(3)	(4)	(5)
High: ___	Moderately High: ___	Average: ___	Moderately Low: ___	Low: ___
Integrity	Integrity	Integrity	Integrity	Integrity

D2. On average you believe that individual managers of the client organization possess...

(1)	(2)	(3)	(4)	(5)
Low: ___	Moderately Low: ___	Average: ___	Moderately High: ___	High: ___
Competence	Competence	Competence	Competence	Competence

E. Rank the **competence** of this client's management relative to all other client organizations managed by you. For example, if you audit ten clients, a rank of 1 (10) means that managers have the highest (lowest) level of competence relative to all other client managements. Ties in ranks are allowed.

Relative rank of audit risk: ___ Number of ties: ___

F. Rank the **integrity** of this client's management relative to all other client organizations managed by you. For example, if you audit ten clients, a rank of 1 (10) means that managers have the highest (lowest) level of integrity relative to all other client managements. Ties in ranks are allowed.

Relative rank of audit risk: ___ Number of ties: ___

G. The factors that influenced your response to question E were (please check only one of the four categories for each of the 15 factors listed):

Factors relating to management's competence

Degree of Influence

Great	Moderate	Little	None	
				1. Managers keep up with professional developments.
				2. Key managers are innovative.
				3. Managers finish work on time.
				4. Managers delegate responsibility to subordinates.
				5. Managers double check calculations.
				6. Accounting managers have worked for Big 8 public accounting firm.
				7. Accounting managers are members of a professional organization or society.
				8. Managers work on weekends and evenings.
				9. Managers spend much time doing irrelevant things during the workday.
				10. Managers do not pay attention to details.
				11. Managers are evasive when responding to auditors' questions.
				12. Managers put off unpleasant personnel decisions.
				13. Managers do not seem motivated to do their assigned tasks.
				14. Managers blame mistakes on subordinates.
				15. Key managers have superior educational training and are experts in their fields.

H. The factors that influenced your response to question F were (please check only one of the four categories for each of the 15 factors listed):

Factors relating to management's integrity

Degree of Influence

Great	Moderate	Little	None	
				1. Managers take credit for work done by subordinates.
				2. Managers make promises they know they cannot keep.
				3. Managers attempt to save the company money whenever possible.
				4. Managers tend to inflate per diem expense reports.
				5. Managers use corporate assets for their personal benefit.
				6. Accounting managers do not easily admit to mistakes in financial records.
				7. Accounting managers are likely to distort financial reports.
				8. Managers lie about progress to superiors.
				9. Accounting managers cooperate with auditors only when necessary.
				10. Accounting managers never juggle the books.
				11. Accounting managers are honest and trustworthy in all their dealings with the auditor and the audit firm.
				12. Key managers are likely to be fired if they breech the company's ethical norms.
				13. Accounting managers are likely to blow the whistle on corporate wrongdoing within organization.
				14. Key managers would never trade on their inside information.
				15. Accounting managers never take a vacation.

APPENDIX D

EXPERIMENTAL INSTRUMENT: AUDITORS' RECOGNITION OF DISTORTIONS TO FINANCIAL STATEMENT INFORMATION

Instructions (please read carefully):

The following scenario is based on a real life situation and selected at random from a group of fifty (50) similar cases all involving client organizations with a material accounting error within the current financial statements under audit. In exactly twenty-five cases (50 percent), the auditor failed to detect this error as a result of normal auditing procedures. In the other cases, the error was detected by the auditor.

Your job is to read your randomly selected scenario and from the information provided try to predict whether or not the auditor detected or failed to detect material accounting error. Using your professional judgment, please assign up to 100 points to each of the following categories:

A. The auditor detected error: ____________________

B. The auditor failed to detect error: ____________________

Total points: 100

Unless you are **absolutely** sure of your answer (prediction), do not allocate all 100 points to any single category. For example, if you believe that the auditor detected the error, but you are only 80% certain of your prediction, you should assign 80 points to category A and 20 points to category B. Remember, all responses will remain confidential. Again, thank you for your participation.

Case No. 31: Obsolete Inventory

John is an experienced audit manager with a large national public accounting firm. He is responsible for the 198X XYZ Corporation audit which has been an audit client of the accounting firm for five years. Unqualified audit opinions have been issued in all previous audits.

The XYZ Corporation is a minicomputer manufacturer with sales offices and plants throughout North America. Its common stock is publicly traded on a major securities exchange. XYZ also plans to issue more common stock in the first quarter of the next fiscal year for major expansion. During the past five years, normal economic conditions have prevailed in XYZ's industry. Further, XYZ revenues and income have steadily increased in all prior years.

Because of technological changes in the microchip industry, a significant amount of the XYZ inventory is **obsolete**. Further, key managers of the XYZ Corporation are aware of this problem. An inventory write-down, however, will decrease net income this year by over 10 percent.

In addition to the above facts, the audit firm requires the completion of an internal control questionnaire to assess the characteristics of management personnel within the XYZ Corporation. Two critical characteristics, the competence and integrity of key managers, were evaluated by the senior auditor during the planning phase of the engagement. She marked her assessment using a 0 to 100 percent continuous scale (x denotes level).

Version A:

Assume that the audit senior provided the following ratings for XYZ management during the planning phase of this year's audit engagement:

Rate the **integrity** of key managers within the organization:

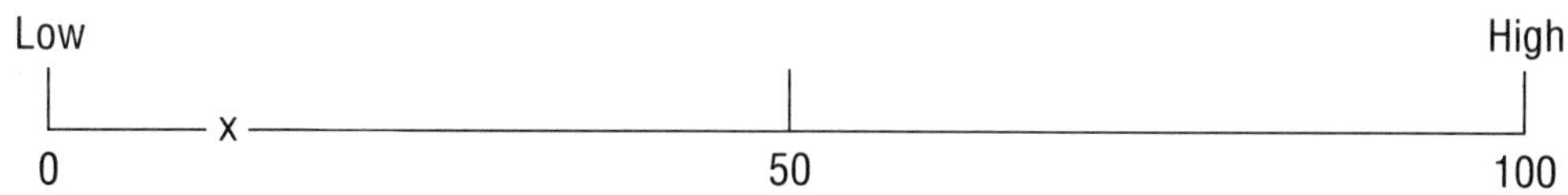

Rate the **competence** of key managers within the organization:

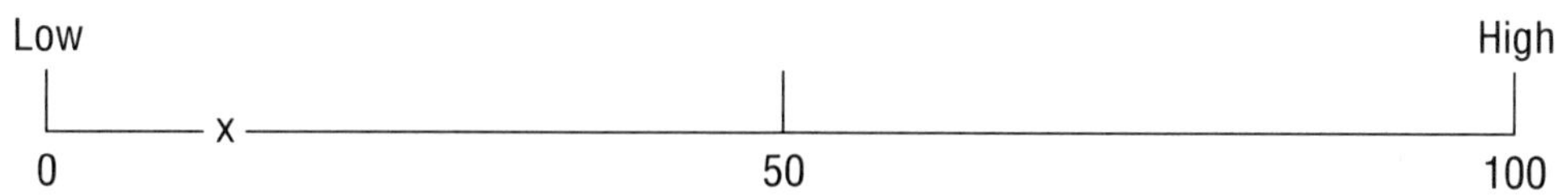

Provide your prediction as to whether or not John failed to detect a material accounting error in the XYZ financial statements during this audit.

A. John detected the obsolete inventory problem: ________

B. John failed to detect the obsolete inventory problem: ________

Total: 100 pts.

Version B:

Assume that the audit senior provided the following ratings for XYZ management during the planning phase of this year's audit engagement:

Rate the **integrity** of key managers within the organization:

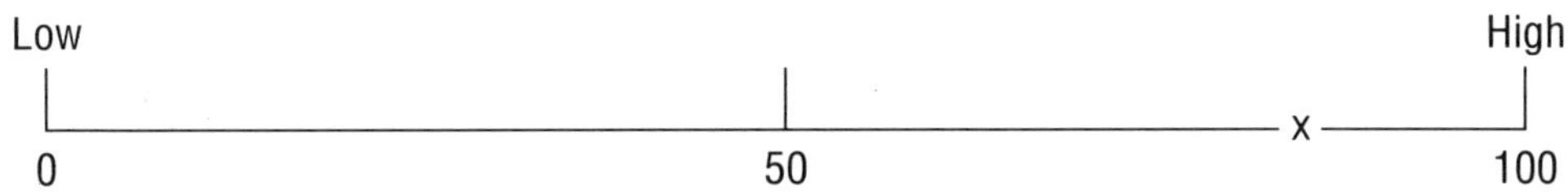

Rate the **competence** of key managers within the organization:

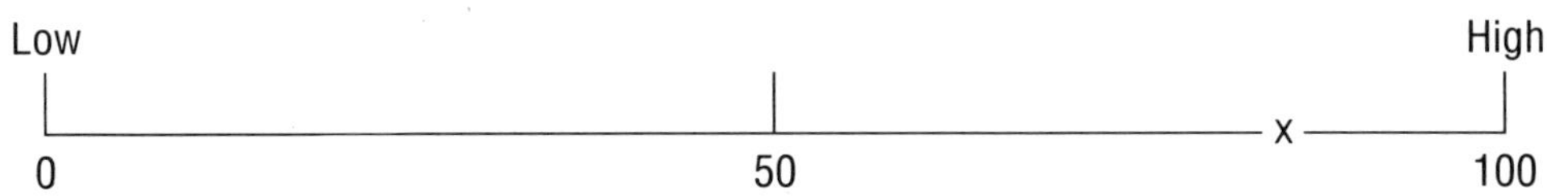

Provide your prediction as to whether or not John failed to detect a material accounting error in the XYZ financial statements during this audit.

A. John detected the obsolete inventory problem: ________

B. John failed to detect the obsolete inventory problem: ________

Total: 100 pts.

Version C:

Assume that the audit senior provided the following ratings for XYZ management during the planning phase of this year's audit engagement:

Rate the **integrity** of key managers within the organization:

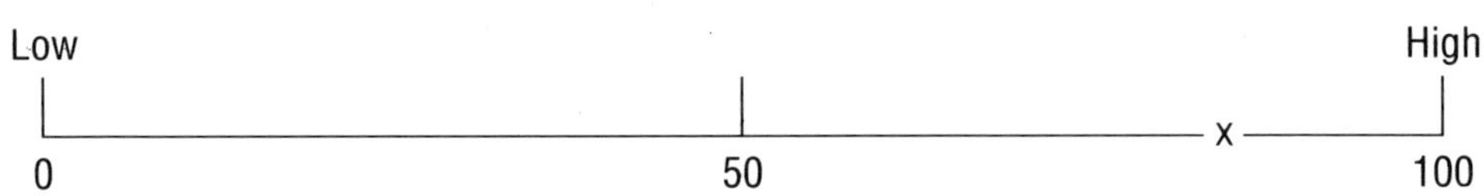

Rate the **competence** of key managers within the organization:

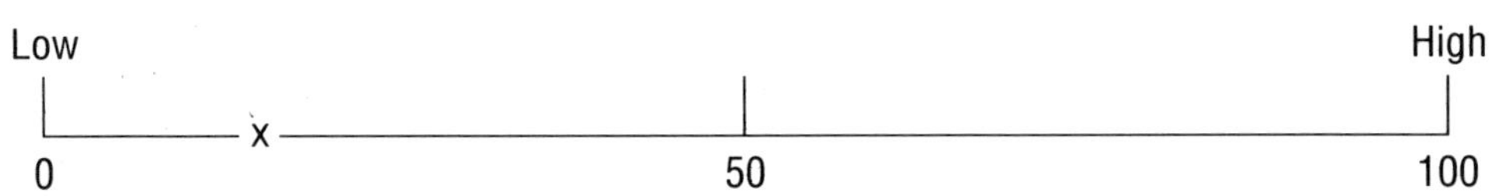

Provide your prediction as to whether or not John failed to detect a material accounting error in the XYZ financial statements during this audit.

A. John detected the obsolete inventory problem: ________

B. John failed to detect the obsolete inventory problem: ________

Total: 100 pts.

Version D:

Assume that the audit senior provided the following ratings for XYZ management during the planning phase of this year's audit engagement:

Rate the **integrity** of key managers within the organization:

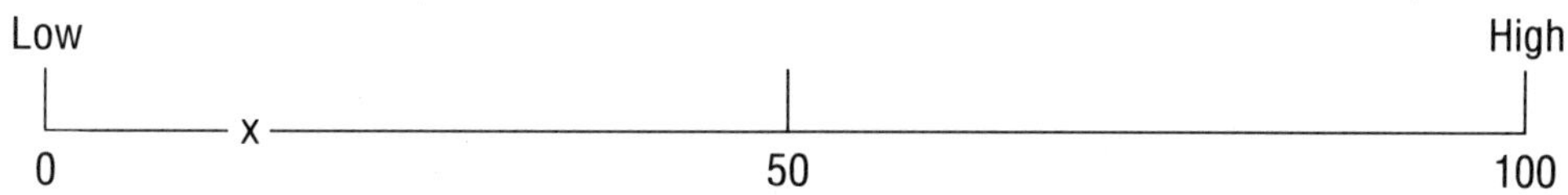

Rate the **competence** of key managers within the organization:

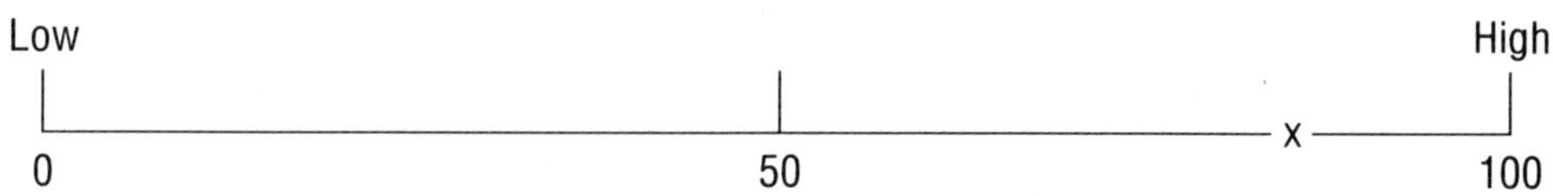

Provide your prediction as to whether or not John failed to detect a material accounting error in the XYZ financial statements during this audit.

A. John detected the obsolete inventory problem: ________

B. John failed to detect the obsolete inventory problem: ________

Total: 100 pts.

APPENDIX E

AUDITORS' MATERIALITY JUDGMENT AND THEIR SENSITIVITY
TO CONTEXTUAL AUDIT EVIDENCE

Instructions:

The following scenario is based on a real life situation and selected at random from a group of fifty (50) similar cases all involving client organizations with a potential accounting error within the current financial statements under audit. In exactly twenty-five cases (50 percent), the error was in fact material. In the other cases, the error was not material.

Your job is to read your randomly selected scenario and from the information provided try to predict whether or not the auditor detected or failed to detect material accounting error. Using your professional judgment, please assign up to 1,000 points to each of the following two categories:

A. The auditor considered the error material: ________________

B. The auditor considered the error immaterial: ________________

Total points: 1,000

Unless you are absolutely sure of your answer (prediction), do not allocate all 1,000 points to any single category. For example, if you believe that the auditor should have considered the error material, but you are only 80% certain of your prediction, you should assign 800 points to category A and 200 points to category B. Remember, all responses will remain confidential. Again, thank you for your participation.

Case No. 42: Allowance for Doubtful Accounts

John is the auditor-in-charge of the XYZ Corporation. John is a senior auditor in a national public accounting firm, ABC &Co. The financial statements of XYZ were audited by ABC for the past four consecutive years. Net income after taxes (per company books) is $6,226,000 for the current year. During this audit, normal economic conditions prevailed; that is, real GNP at four percent, inflation rate at eight percent, prime interest rate at ten percent. Dow Jones Industrial Average at 1950 and New York Stock Exchange price-earnings ratio at 14.

Normal audit procedures lead John to believe that the year-end Allowance for Doubtful Accounts should be increased. The proposed adjustment will decrease current income after taxes by 2.7 percent.

Provide your prediction as to whether or not John considered or did not consider the adjustment to the allowance for doubtful accounts as being material in terms of the XYZ financial statements during this year.

A. John considered the error material: ____________

B. John considered the error immaterial: ____________

Total: 1,000 pts.

(Subjects received only one of the following two treatments)

Positive Contextual Information

The XYZ Company management has been completely cooperative and open in all dealings with John's firm and in connection with the current audit. The company's management follows conservative accounting policies in areas of income determination and asset valuation, and its reported earnings are generally viewed as of high quality.

Negative Contextual Information

The XYZ Company management has been less than completely cooperative and open in all dealings with John's firm and in connection with the current audit. The company's management follows unconservative accounting policies in areas of income determination and asset valuation, and its reported earnings are generally viewed as of low quality.

ENDNOTES

Preface

1 The notion of auditor independence had been employed by the profession prior to the stock market crash of 1929. In this instance, however, independence implied that the accountant was neither an agent nor an employee of the client (Previts [1986]).

2 Over the past two decades, the SEC, General Accounting Office (GAO) and Congress have conducted investigations to determine the validity of public concerns regarding the auditing profession in the United States. Much of this research has aimed to uncover possible conflict areas that might seriously harm the general investment community or diminish public confidence (GAO [1989]). Examples of these examinations can be found in public hearings or the final report of the Metcalf (U.S. Senate [1977]), Moss (U.S. House of Representatives [1976]), Dingell (U.S. House of Representatives [1988]) and Wyden (U.S. House of Representatives [1992]) Committees.

Chapter 1

3 These ethical resolutions only typify the innumerable possible responses for an individual at any given stage of development.

4 An important aspect of issue scoring is the omission of Stage 6 from the system. Kohlberg and other cognitive-developmental researchers suggest that Stage 6 is the highest and most uncommon level of ethical cognition. Because of a lack of Stage 6 data from the various research data used to construct the scoring method, such interview and criterion judgments are omitted from the scoring manual. Thus, the technique fails to differentiate between Stage 5 and Stage 6 global developmental stages.

5 This eleborate scoring methodology is equivalent to a more generalized protocol analysis technique developed by Ericsson and Simon [1984]. In their methodology the issue would be classified as an environmental or situational "cue", and the norm + element would be the utilization of the cue, and termed a verbal "operator".

6 The global stage score (G^*) is a weighted average of criterion judgments (G) which specify a stated resolution for each issue k(i) in the dilemma, and is computed for every individual over the entire hypothetical case series. Let $\Phi(\cdot)$ be a functional assignment of a stage score to a stated issue, and let $\Omega(\cdot)$ be a weighted average function for each criterion cited in a dilemma. Thus, the terms can be expressed as follows:

$$G(i) = \Phi[k(i)];\ i = 1, \ldots, n \text{ and}$$

$$G^* = \Sigma_i \Omega\cdot(G(i)) = \Sigma_i \Omega\cdot(\Phi\cdot[k(i)])$$

7 Kohlberg [1984] and Rest [1986] provide summaries of literally hundreds of empirical studies of ethical reasoning and moral development, showing longitudinal cross-cultural stability in psychometric measures.

Chapter 3

8 This case was developed by Arnold and Ponemon [1987].

9 This case is adapted from Ponemon and Gabhart [1990]. For those interested in obtaining a formal definition of auditor independence as used in the context of this illustration, read Previts [1986].

10 This case is based on Fund of Funds, Ltd. v. Arthur Andersen & Co. (cite: 545 F 1314 [S.D.N.Y. 1982]). The auditors were found liable as a result of failing to use information they obtained from another client to determine which of the two clients' financial statements accurately portrayed the facts of the same transaction.

Chapter 4

11 Canadian and U.S. offices of the same international accounting firms were used to control for the influence of firm differences that according to Bernardi [1991] may also be a determinant of ethical development in audit firms.

12 Tests of late respondents did not reveal any differences in demographic or DIT characteristics.

13 Using the Kolmogorov-Smironov test (Hollander and Wolfe [1973, pp. 219-228]) Firm 1 and 2 were not significantly different in terms of DIT P scores and, hence, could be combined for purposes of analysis.

14 To avoid strict assumptions about the theoretical distribution of sample elements, nonparametric statistical tests were used to evaluate CA and CPA samples (see, for example, Hollander and Wolfe [1973] or Conover [1980]).

15 Because a firm's culture and ethical codes are typically defined by its partners, it is interesting and somewhat disturbing to find that partners have the lowest average DIT P scores among all other position levels in the firm's hierarchy. The implications of this finding are discussed in the last section of this chapter.

16 DIT P score norms reported by Rest [1979a, 1986] are based on the collective findings from many published and unpublished academic studies.

Chapter 5

17 Implicit in this framework is that underreporting will be perceived as unethical. It is possible however, that auditors may view underreporting as altruistic given that it requires them to forgo personal time, and in some cases even pay, to complete the audit within budget (Dirsmith and Covaleski [1985a, 1985b]; McNair [1991]).

18 Some may argue that post-conventional reasoning may not be a desirable characteristic for auditors because professional behavior demands compliance to an accepted set of rules or guidelines. However, recent events in the U.S. savings and loan industry, the demise of the seventh largest public accounting firm, and significant audit firm litigation suggest that the long-run interests of the profession may be better served if auditors follow their own principles instead of rules when the two conflict.

19 In a recent study, Ponemon [1992b] found a strong relationship between auditor's ethical reasoning, as measured by the DIT, and ethical action on a simulated audit exercise. While ethical reasoning and ethical action are not synonymous concepts, Kohlberg [1984] and Rest [1986] summarize the results of several studies, showing systematic relationships. Blasi [1980] also provides a critical review of the literature with respect to this issue.

20 A nonparametric X^2 test (Feinberg [1983, p. 40]) did not reveal bias in the assignment of subjects to treatment groups by DIT P scores and various demographic variables including position level, gender, firm, or country.

21 Although CPA and CA samples are different in terms of DIT P scores by position level, using the Kolmogorov-Smirnov test (Hollander and Wolfe [1973, pp. 219-228]), both samples were determined not to be significantly different in terms of response patterns to scenario questions and, hence, were combined for purposes of correlation analysis only.

22 It is important to note that high and low DIT groups in this study were classified according to the median value for each sample of Canadian and U.S. auditors. While representative of earlier DIT studies of professional accountants, subjects in this study were relatively homogeneous in terms of their DIT results. Thus, the high DIT group contained auditors with moderate and high DIT P and percentage stage scores, while the low DIT group consisted of auditors with moderately low DIT P and percentage stage scores.

23 Since treatment and country are dichotomous variables, a dummy coding scheme was used to classify these qualitative variables for purposes of regression. For treatment, 1 denotes penalty and for country, 1 denotes Canadian firms.

24 Goodness-of-fit tests did not reveal significant violations in multivariate models in terms of non-normal residuals, multicollinearity or heteroscedastic variance.

25 Along these lines, Ponemon [1992b] examined actual underreporting on a simulated auditing exercise. He found that staff level auditors with lower DIT P scores were more likely to underreport their time, under conditions of time budget and peer pressure, than staff with higher DIT P scores.

Chapter 6

26 The theoretical arguments and empirical results discussed in sections 6.1 to 6.3 of this chapter are based on a paper by Ponemon [1993b]. Section 6.4 is adopted from an earlier unpublished paper by Ponemon and Gabhart [1991]. For those interested in reading these original works, please contact the authors.

27 As noted in the *Management Reporting to External Parties* section of the draft report [1992, p. 4] by the Committee of Sponsoring Organizations of the Treadway Commission (COSO), the competence, integrity and ethical values of an organization's management are among the most critical elements of the control environment with respect to the company's objective of reliable financial information.

28 See Kohlberg [1984] and Rest [1979a] for a detailed discussion of cognitive structure in the context of ethical reasoning and moral development theory.

29 These ratios were computed by first listing all audit clients managed by the manager in ascending order from the highest competence (highest integrity) to the lowest competence (lowest integrity), and placing the total number of clients in the denominator of the ratio. The relative position or rank of the selected client was placed in the numerator of the ratio. If ties emerged among client ranks, the total number of tied observations was simply subtracted from the denominator. Thus, the ratio was a real number between 0 and 1.

30 This definition conforms with Statement on Auditing Standard (SAS) No. 47 (AICPA [1983]) which also provides a component model of audit risk. That is, the overall level of audit risk can be attributed to three underlying causes: inherent risk, control risk, and detection risk. In this study, we examine the overall level of audit risk rather than its individual components.

31 Because of possible multicollinearity among independent variables, separate regressions were compiled for competence, integrity and the interaction between competence and integrity. Goodness of fit tests on all four equations do not reveal significant biases in regression residuals.

32 Note that both slopes would equal zero if the DIT did not moderate the regression relationship, thus resulting in two flat and parallel lines. Further, when management integrity is judged to be low, high competence should result in higher assigned audit risk than low competence (see Exhibit 6.1 for an explanation). This is clearly not the case here. That is, looking at Exhibit 6.4, assigned audit risk is higher for management with low competence and low integrity for auditors with DIT P scores below 39.22 (where the two regression lines intersect).

33 The experiment was developed with the assistance of seven audit partners from one office of a large accounting firm. It is based on an actual case (presently in litigation) resulting from the auditor's over-reliance on the representations of client management regarding a questionable asset valuation.

34 The order of the treatments was randomized on a subject-by-subject basis. Response bias caused by the order of treatments was not indicated.

35 The sample median DIT P score (m = 35.70) was used to split the sample into low (n = 30) and high (n = 31) DIT P score groups.

36 The Kolmogorov-Smirnov test (Hollander and Wolfe [1973, p. 252]) revealed non-normal (heteroscedastic) residuals in the ANOVA employing posterior probabilities as the dependent variable. No violations were indicated in the likelihood model.

37 Along these lines, other researchers have found that the organization of the experiment can dramatically influence the way subjects respond to experimental tasks (cf. Joyce and Biddle [1981], Pany and Reckers [1987], Rebele, Heintz and Briden [1988]).

BIBLIOGRAPHY

American Institute of Certified Public Accountants, *Statement on Auditing Standards No. 47: Audit Risk and Materiality in Conducting an Audit*. (New York: American Institute of Certified Public Accountants, 1983).

American Institute of Certified Public Accountants, *Statement on Auditing Standards No. 53: Auditor's Responsibility to Detect Errors and Irregularities*. (New York: American Institute of Certified Public Accountants, 1988).

American Institute of Certified Public Accountants, *Statement on Auditing Standards No. 55: Consideration of the Internal Control Structure in a Financial Statement Audit*. (New York: American Institute of Certified Public Accountants, 1988).

American Institute of Certified Public Accountants, *Code of Professional Conduct*. (New York: American Institute of Certified Public Accountants, 1988).

Anderson, U. and Marchant, G., The Auditor's Assessment of the Competence and Integrity of Auditee Personnel, *Auditing: A Journal of Practice and Theory* (Suppl. 1989) pp. 1-16.

Antle, R., The Auditor as an Economic Agent, *Journal of Accounting Research* (Fall 1982) pp. 503-527.

Antle, R., Auditor Independence, *Journal of Accounting Research* (Spring 1984) pp. 1-20.

Aranya, N. and Ferris, K., A Reexamination of Accountants' Organizational Professional Conflict, *The Accounting Review* (1984) pp. 1-15.

Aranya, N., Lachman, R. and Amernic, J., Accountant's Job Satisfaction: A Path Analysis," *Accounting, Organizations and Society* (1982) pp. 201-215.

Argyris, C., Human Problems with Budgets, *Harvard Business Review* (January-February 1953) pp. 97-110.

Argyris, C., *Reasoning, Learning, and Action: Individual and Organizational* (San Francisco: Jossey-Bass, 1982).

Argyris, C. and Schon, D., *Theory in Practice: Increasing Professional Effectiveness* (San Francisco: Jossey-Bass, 1974).

Armstrong, M., Internalization of the Professional Ethic by Certified Public Accountants: A Multidimensional Scaling Approach, Ph.D. Dissertation, University of Southern California (1984).

Armstrong, M., Moral Development and Accounting Education, *Journal of Accounting Education* (Spring 1987) pp. 27-43.

Arnold, D. and Ponemon, L., Internal Auditors' Perceptions of Whistle-Blowing and the Influence of Moral Reasoning: An Experiment, *Auditing: A Journal of Practice and Theory* (Fall 1991) pp. 1-15.

Arnold, D. and Ponemon, L., Moral Judgment Perspective for the Various Auditing Judgment Issues, *Proceedings of the British Accounting Association* (April 1987).

Arnold, H., Moderator Variables: A Clarification of Conceptual, Analytic, and Psychometric Issues, *Organizational Behavior and Human Performance*, Vol. 29 (1982) pp. 143-174.

Ashton, R., *Human Information Processing in Accounting* (Sarasota, FL: American Accounting Association, 1982).

Avolio, B. and Gibbons, T., Developing Transformational Leaders: A Life Span Approach, in J. Conger and R. Kanungo (eds.), *Charismatic Leadership: The Elusive Factor in Organizational Effectiveness* (San Francisco: Jossey-Bass, 1988).

Baron, R. and Kenny, D., The Moderator-Mediator Variable Distinction in Social Psychological Research: Conceptual, Strategic and Statistical Considerations, *Journal of Personality and Social Psychology* (1986) pp. 1173-1182.

Bartlett, J., *Bartlett's Familiar Quotations* (Boston: Little, Brown and Company, 1968).

Baumhart, R., *Ethics in Business* (New York: Holt-Rinehart, 1968).

Bayles, M., *Professional Ethics* (Boston: Wadsworth, 1989).

Beauchamp, T. and Bowie, N., *Ethical Theory and Business* (Englewood Cliffs, NJ: Prentice-Hall, 1988).

Benke, R. and Rhode, J., The Job Satisfaction of Higher Level Employees in Large Certified Public Accounting Firms, *Accounting, Organizations and Society* (1980) pp. 187-202.

Benke, R. and Rhode, J., Intent to Turnover Among Higher Level Employees in Large CPA Firms, *Advances in Accounting* (1984) pp. 157-174.

Benson, G., *Business Ethics in America* (Boston: Lexington Books, 1982).

Benston, G., Accounting Standards in the United States and the United Kingdom: Their Nature, Causes and Consequences, *Vanderbelt Law Review* (1975) pp. 235-268.

Bernardi, R., Fraud Detection: An Experiment Testing Differences in Perceived Client Integrity and Competence, Individual Auditor Cognitive Style and Experience, and Accounting Firms, Ph.D. Dissertation, Union College (1991).

Blank, M., Socialization in Public Accounting Firms, Ph.D. Dissertation, Pennsylvania State University (1984).

Blasi, A., Bridging Moral Cognition and Moral Action: A Critical Review of the Literature, *Psychological Bulletin* (1980) pp. 1-45.

Bloom, R., American and Canadian Accounting Standard Setting: A Comparative Analysis, *International Journal of Accounting and Education Research* (1984) pp. 47-58.

Bloom, R. and Kantor, J., Professional Accounting Education in England, The United States, Australia and Canada: A Status Report, *Advances in International Accounting* (Summer 1991).

Bloom, R. and Naciri, M., Accounting Standard Setting and Culture: A Comparative Analysis of the United States, Canada, England, Germany, Australia, New Zealand, Sweden and Japan, *International Journal of Accounting and Education Research* (1989) pp. 70-97.

Bowie, N., Challenging the Egoistic Paradigm, *Business Ethics Quarterly* (1991) pp. 1-22.

Brabeck, M., Ethical Characteristics of Whistle Blowers, *Journal of Research in Personality* (1984) pp. 41-53.

Brenner S. and Molander, E., Is the Ethics of Business Changing?, *Harvard Business Review* (January 1977) pp. 57-71.

Briloff, A., Old Myths and New Realities in Accounting, *The Accounting Review* (July 1966) pp. 484-495.

Briloff, A., *Unaccountable Accounting* (New York: Harper and Row, 1972).

Brown, C. and Solomon, I., Auditor Configural Information Processing in Control Risk Appraisal, *Auditing: A Journal of Theory and Practice* (1990) pp. 17-38.

Brown, C. and Solomon, I., Configural Information Processing in Auditing: The Role of Domain-Specific Knowledge, *The Accounting Review* (1991) pp. 100-119.

Buchman, T. and Tracy, A., Obtaining Responses to Sensitive Questions: Conventional Questionnaire versus Randomized Response Technique, *Journal of Accounting Research* (1982) pp. 263-271.

Bullen, M. and Flamholtz, E., A Theoretical and Empirical Investigation of Job Satisfaction and Intended Turnover in the Large CPA Firm, *Accounting, Organizations and Society* (1985) pp. 287-302.

Canadian Institute of Chartered Accountants, Materiality and Audit Risk, Section 5130, *CICA Handbook* (Toronto: CICA).

Canadian Institute of Chartered Accountants, Internal Control in the Context of an Audit, Sections 5200-5220, *CICA Handbook* (Toronto: CICA).

Candee, D., The Psychology of Watergate, *Journal of Social Issues* (1975).

Candee, D., Structure and Choice in Moral Reasoning, *Journal of Personality and Social Psychology* (1976) pp. 1293-1301.

Carmella, P., Moral Judgment: A Study of Professional Business Managers, Ph.D Dissertation, University of Texas at Austin (1985).

Carmichael, H., Reputations in the Labor Market. *American Economic Review* (1984) pp. 713-725.

Chewning, G., Pany, K. and Wheeler, S., Auditor Reporting Decisions Involving Auditing Principle Changes: Some Evidence on Materiality Thresholds, *Journal of Accounting Research* (Spring 1989) pp. 78-96.

Choo, F., Job Stress, Job Performance and Auditor Personality Characteristics, *Auditing: A Journal of Practice and Theory* (Spring 1986) pp. 14-34.

Chow, C., The Effects of Job Standard Tightness and Compensation Scheme on Performance: An Exploration of Linkages, *The Accounting Review* (October 1983) pp. 667-685.

Cohen, J. and Cohen, P., *Applied Multiple Regression/Correlation Analysis for the Behavioral Sciences* (Hillsdale, NJ: Lawrence Erlbaum, 1983).

Colby, A. and Kohlberg, L., *The Measurement of Moral Judgment* (New York: Cambridge University Press, 1987).

Commission on Auditor's Responsibilities: Report, Conclusions and Recommendations (New York: AICPA, 1978).

Committee of Sponsoring Organizations of the Treadway Commission (COSO), *Internal Control-Integrated Framework* (New York: COSO, 1992).

Conover, W., *Practical Nonparametric Statistics* (New York: Wiley, 1980).

Coreless, J. and Parker, L., The Impact of MAS on Auditor Independence: An Experimental Study, *Accounting Horizons* (September 1987) pp. 25-30.

Cullen, J., *The Structure of Professionalism* (New York: BPI, 1978).

Datar, S., A Game Theoretical Approach to Auditor Independence, Ph.D. Dissertation, Stanford University (1985).

Davidson, R., Implicit Control in Public Accounting Firms, working paper, University of Calgary (1990).

Davidson, R., Selection-Socialization Control in Auditing Firms: A Test of Ouchi's Model of Control, Ph.D. Dissertation, University of Arizona (1988).

Davis, M., Conflict of Interest, *Business and Professional Ethics Journal* (1982) pp. 17-27.

Dean, R., Ferris, K. and Konstans, C., Occupation Reality Shock and Organizational Commitment: Some Evidence from the Accounting Profession, *Accounting, Organizations and Society* (1988) pp. 31-38.

DeAngelo, L., Auditor Independence, 'Low Balling', and Disclosure Regulation, *Journal of Accounting and Economics* (1981) pp. 113-128.

Derry, R., An Empirical Study of Moral Reasoning among Managers, *Journal of Business Ethics* (1989) pp. 855-862.

Dillard, J., A Longitudinal Evaluation of an Occupational Goal-Expectancy Model in Professional Accounting Organizations, *Accounting, Organizations and Society* (1981) pp. 17-26.

Dillard, J. and Ferris, K., Sources of Professional Staff Turnover in Public Accounting Firms: Some Further Evidence, *Accounting, Organizations and Society* (1979) pp. 179-186.

Dillard, J. and Ferris, K., Individual Behavior in Professional Accounting Firms: A Review and Synthesis, *Journal of Accounting Literature* (1989) pp. 208-234.

Dirsmith, M. and Covaleski, M., Informal Communications, Nonformal Communications and Mentoring in Public Accounting Firms, *Accounting, Organizations and Society* (1985a) pp. 149-169.

Dirsmith, M. and Covaleski, M., Practice Management Issues in Public Accounting Firms, *Journal of Accounting, Auditing and Finance* (1985b) pp. 5-21.

Dopuch, N., King, R. and Wallin, D., The Use of Experimental Markets in Auditing Research: Some Initial Findings, Auditing: *A Journal of Practice and Theory* (Suppl. 1989) pp. 98-127.

Donaldson J., Ethics and the Organization, *Journal of Management Studies* (1980) pp. 34-55.

Donaldson, T., *Corporations and Morality* (Englewood Cliffs, NJ: Prentice-Hall, 1982).

Donaldson, T. and Werhane, P., *Ethical Issues in Business* (Englewood Cliffs, NJ: Prentice-Hall, 1979).

Downie, R., *Roles and Values: An Introduction to Social Ethics* (Boston: Methuen, 1971).

Drucker, P., What is Business Ethics?, *The Public Interest* (1981) pp. 18-28.

Dunfee, T., Business Ethics and Extant Social Contracts, *Business Ethics Quarterly* (1991) pp. 23-52.

Dunmore, P. and Falk, H., Auditor-Client Disagreement and Auditor's Independence: The Case for Canada, working paper, McMaster University, 1992.

Ericsson, K. and Simon, H., *Protocol Analysis: Verbal Reports As Data* (Cambridge, MA: MIT Press, 1984).

Farmer, T., Rittenberg, L. and Trompeter, G., An Investigation of the Impact of Economics and Organizational Factors on Auditor Independence, *Auditing: A Journal of Practice and Theory* (Fall 1987) pp. 1-14.

Feinberg, S., *The Analysis of Cross-Classified Categorical Data* (Cambridge, MA: MIT Press, 1983).

Fellingham, J. and Newman, D., Strategic Considerations in Auditing, *The Accounting Review* (October 1985) pp. 634-650.

Ferris, K., Perceived Uncertainty and Job Satisfaction in the Accounting Environment, *Accounting, Organizations and Society* (1977) pp. 23-28.

Finn, D. and Lampe J., A Study of Whistleblowing Among Auditors, *National Conference on Ethics and the Professions* (University of Florida, January 30 to February 1, 1992).

Fisher, D., Merron, K. and Torbert, W., Human Development and Managerial Effectiveness, *Group and Organizational Studies* (1987) pp. 257-273.

Fleming, M., Implications of Budgetary Pressure in CPA Firms, DBA Dissertation, University of Southern California (1979).

Forbes, B., Early Intraorganizational Mobility: Patterns and Influences, *Academy of Management Journal* (1987) pp. 110-125.

Friedson, E., *Profession of Medicine* (New York: Dow, Meade & Co., 1971).

Gaa, J., User Primacy in Financial Reporting Rulemaking: A Social Contract Approach, *The Accounting Review* (July 1986) pp. 435-454.

Gaa, J., The Philosophy and Psychology of Auditor Independence and Objectivity *Proceedings of the 1992 Deloitte & Touche University of Kansas Symposium of Auditing Problems* (Lawrence KS: University of Kansas, 1992).

Gaertner, J. and Ruhe, J., Job-Related Stress in Public Accounting, *Journal of Accountancy* (June 1981) pp. 68-73.

Galambos, L., *The Public Image of Big Business in America*: 1880-1940 (Baltimore: Johns Hopkins University Press, 1975).

Galbraith, J., *The Affluent Society* (Boston: Houghton-Mifflin, 1976).

Gibbs, J., Kohlberg's Stages of Moral Judgment: A Constructive Critique, *Harvard Educational Review* (1977) pp. 43-61.

Gilligan, C., In a Different Voice: Women's Conceptions of the Self and of Morality, *Harvard Educational Review* (1977) pp. 481-517.

Goldman, A. and Barlev, B., The Auditor-Firm Conflict of Interest: Its Implications for Independence, *The Accounting Review* (October 1974) pp. 707-718.

Gormley, R., Developments in Accountants' Liability to Nonclients for Negligence, *Journal of Accounting, Auditing and Finance* (Summer 1988) pp. 185-212.

Graham, J., Principled Organizational Dissent: A Theoretical Essay, in L. Cummings and B. Staw (eds.), *Research in Organizational Behavior* (Greenwich, CT: JAI Press, 1986).

Greenberger, D., Miceli, M. and Cohen, D., Oppositionists and Group Norms: The Reciprocal Influence of Whistle-Blowers and Co-Workers, *Journal of Business Ethics* (1987) pp. 527-542.

Greenwood, E., Attributes of a Profession, *Social Work* (July 1957) pp. 45-55.

Hall, D., *Careers in Organizations* (Santa Monica, CA: Goodyear, 1976).

Haskins, M., Baglioni, A. and Cooper, C., An Investigation of the Sources, Moderators, and Psychological Symptoms of Stress among Senior Auditors, *Contemporary Accounting Research*, Volume 6 (Spring 1990) pp. 361-385.

Higgins, A., Powers, C. and Kohlberg, L., The Relationship of Moral Atmosphere to Judgments of Responsibility, in W. Kurtines and J. Gewitz (eds.), *Morality, Moral Behavior and Moral Development* (New York: Wiley Interscience, 1984).

Hofstede, G., *The Game of Budget Control* (Assen, The Netherlands: Koninklijke Van Gorcum and Company, N.V., 1968).

Hollander, M. and Wolfe, D., *Nonparametric Statistical Methods* (New York: Wiley, 1973).

Holmstrom, B., *The Provision of Services in a Market Economy*, working paper, University of Pennsylvania, 1984.

Holstrum, G., The Effect of Budget Adaptiveness and Tightness on Managerial Decision Behavior, *Journal of Accounting Research* (Autumn 1971) pp. 258-277.

Holstrum, G. and Messier, W., A Review and Integration of Empirical Research on Materiality, *Auditing: A Journal of Practice and Theory* (Fall 1982) pp. 45-63.

Holt, D. and Jeffrey, C., Ethical Development of Accounting Students, Business Students, and Liberal Arts Students, working paper, Iowa State University, 1991.

Hopwood, A., An Empirical Study of the Role of Accounting Data in Performance Evaluation, *Journal of Accounting Research* (Suppl. 1972) pp. 156-182.

Jaccard, J., Turrisi, R. and Wan, C., *Interaction Effects in Multiple Regression* (Newbury Park, CA: Sage Research Report, 1990).

Jansen, M. and Von Glinow, M., Ethical Ambivalence and Organizational Reward Systems, *Academy of Management Review* (1985) pp. 814-822.

Johnston, D., Lemon, W. and Neumann, F., The Canadian Study of the Role of the Auditor, *Journal of Accounting, Auditing and Finance* (1980) pp. 251-263.

Jones, T., Ethical Decision Making by Individuals in Organizations: An Issue-Contingent Model, *Academy of Management Review* (1991) pp. 366-395.

Joyce, E. and Biddle, G., Are Auditors' Judgments Sufficiently Regressive?, *Journal of Accounting Research* (Autumn 1981) pp. 323-349.

Kahneman, D. and Tversky, A., On the Psychology of Prediction, *Psychology Review* (1973) pp. 237-251.

Kelly, H. and Michela, J., Attribution Theory and Research, *Annual Review of Psychology* (1980) pp. 457-501.

Kelley, T. and Margheim, L., The Effect of Audit Billing Arrangement on Underreporting of Time and Audit Quality Reduction Acts, *Advances in Accounting 5* (1987) pp. 221-233.

Kelley, T. and Margheim, L., The Impact of Time Budget Pressure, Personality, and Leadership Variables on Dysfunctional Auditor Behavior, *Auditing: A Journal of Practice and Theory* (Spring 1990) pp. 21-42.

Kelley, T. and Seiler, R., Auditor Stress and Time Budgets, *The CPA Journal* (December 1982) pp. 24-34.

Keynes, J., *Economic Consequences of Peace* (Oxford: Oxford Press 1919 [1971]).

Knapp, M., Audit Conflict: An Empirical Study of the Perceived Ability of Auditors to Resist Management Pressure, *The Accounting Review* (April 1985) pp. 202-211.

Kohlberg, L., The Development of Modes of Moral Thinking and Choice in the Years Ten to Sixteen, Ph.D. Dissertation, University of Chicago (1958).

Kohlberg, L., Stages and Sequences: The Cognitive Developmental Approach to Socialization, in D. Goslin (ed.), *Handbook of Socialization Theory and Research* (Chicago: Rand McNally, 1969).

Kohlberg, L., *Essays on Moral Development: Volume Two: The Psychology of Moral Development* (San Francisco: Harper & Row, 1984).

Kohlberg, L., Hickey, J. and Scharf, P., The Justice Structure of Prison: A Theory and Intervention, *The Prison Journal* (1972) pp. 3-14.

Kohlberg, L. and Kramer, R., Continuities and Discontinuities in Childhood and Adult Moral Development, *Human Development* (1969) pp. 93-120.

Kohlberg, L., Levine, C., and Hewer, A., Moral Stages: A Current Formulation and a Response to Critics, in J. Meacham (ed.) *Contributions to Human Development* (Basel: Karger, 1983).

Kreps, D. and Wilson, R., Reputation and Imperfect Information, *Journal of Economic Theory* (August 1982) pp. 253-279.

Krogstad, J., Ettenson, R. and Shanteau, J., Context and Experience in Auditor Materiality Judgments, *Auditing: A Journal of Practice and Theory* (Spring 1984) pp. 54-74.

Kuhn, D., Short-Term Longitudinal Evidence for the Sequentiality of Kohlberg's Early Stages of Moral Judgment, *Developmental Psychology*, (1980) pp. 162-166.

Kurtines, W. and Grief, E., The Development of Moral Thought, Review and Evaluation of Kohlberg's Approach, *Psychological Bulletin* (1974) pp. 453-470.

Lampe, J. and Finn, D., A Model of Auditors' Ethical Decision Process," *Auditing: A Journal of Practice and Theory* (Forthcoming, 1993).

Lawrence, B., At the Crossroads: A Multiple-Level Explanation of Individual Attainment, *Organization Science* (1990) pp. 65-85.

Levinthal, D. and Fichman, M., Dynamics of Interorganizational Attachments: Auditor-Client Relationships, *Administrative Science Quarterly* (1988) pp. 345-369.

Libby, R., *Accounting and Human Information Processing: Theory and Application* (Englewood Cliffs, NJ: Prentice-Hall, 1981).

Lickona, T., *Moral Development and Behavior: Theory, Research and Social Issues* (New York: Holt-Rinehart, 1976).

Lightner, S., Adams, S. and Lightner, K., The Influence of Situational, Ethical and Expectancy Theory Variables on Accountants' Underreporting Behavior, *Auditing: A Journal of Practice and Theory* (Fall 1982) pp. 1-12.

Lightner, S., Leisenring, J. and Winters, A., Underreporting Chargeable Time, *Journal of Accountancy* (January 1983) pp. 52-57.

Loeb, S., A Behavior Study of CPAs Ethics, Ph.D. Dissertation, University of Wisconsin (1970).

Lord, A., Pressure: A Methodological Consideration for Behavioral Research in Accounting, working paper, University of Alabama, 1990.

Lyons, N., Conceptions of Self and Morality and Modes of Moral Choice: Identifying Justice and Care in Judgments of Actual Moral Dilemmas, Ph.D. Dissertation, Harvard University (1982).

Margheim, L. and Pany, K., Quality Control, Premature Signoff and Underreporting of Time: Some Empirical Findings, *Auditing: A Journal of Practice and Theory* (Spring 1986) pp. 50-63.

Marxen, D., A Behavioral Investigation of Time Budget Preparation in a Competitive Audit Environment, *Accounting Horizons* (June 1990) pp. 47-57.

Maslow, A., *Motivation and Personality* (New York: Harper and Row, 1970).

Mautz, R. and Evers, C., *Evolution of the Quality Control Inquiry Committee* (New York: American Institute of Certified Public Accountants, 1991).

Mautz, R. and Sharaf, H., *The Philosophy of Auditing* (Sarasota: American Accounting Association, 1961).

McNair, C., The Effects of Budget Pressure on Audit Firms: An Empirical Examination of the Underreporting of Chargeable Time, Ph.D. Dissertation, Columbia University (1987).

McNair, C., Proper Compromises: The Management Control Dilemma in Public Accounting and Its Impact on Auditor Behavior, *Accounting, Organizations and Society* (1991) pp. 635-653.

Merchant, K., The Control Function of Management, *Sloan Management Review* (Summer 1982) pp. 43-55.

Merchant, K., *Control in Business Organizations* (Boston: Pittman Publishing Company, 1985).

Milgrom, P. and Roberts, J., Predation, Reputation and Entry Deterrence, *Journal of Economic Theory* (August 1982) pp. 280-312.

Montagna, P., *Certified Public Accounting: A Sociological View of a Profession in Change* (Houston TX: Scholars Book Co., 1974).

Murphy, J. and Gilligan, C., Moral Development in Late Adolescence and Adulthood: A Critique and Reconstruction of Kohlberg's Theory, *Human Development* (1980) pp. 77-104.

National Commission on Fraudulent Financial Reporting (Treadway), *Report of the National Commission on Fraudulent Financial Reporting* (Washington, DC: NCFFR, 1987).

Neimark, M. and Tinker, T., The Social Construction of Management Control Systems, *Accounting, Organizations and Society* (1986) pp. 369-396.

Neter, J., Wasserman W. and Kutner M., *Applied Linear Statistical Models* (Homewood, IL: Irwin, 1985).

Nichols, D. and Price, K., The Auditor-Firm Conflict: An Analysis Using Concepts of Exchange Theory, *The Accounting Review* (April 1976) pp. 335-346.

Noreen, E., The Economics of Ethics: A New Perspective on Agency Theory, *Accounting, Organizations and Society* (1988) pp. 359-369.

Norris, D. and Niebuhr, R., Professionalism, Organizational Commitment and Job Satisfaction, *Accounting, Organizations and Society* (1983) pp. 49-60.

Nozick, R., *Anarchy, State and Utopia* (New York: Basic Books, 1975).

Nystrom, P. and McArthur, A., Organizations' Roles in Career Theory, in M. Arthur, D. Hall and B. Lawrence (eds.), *Handbook of Career Theory* (Cambridge, MA: Cambridge University Press, 1989).

Otley, D. and Berry, A., Control, Organization and Accounting, *Accounting, Organizations and Society* (1980) pp. 231-244.

Ouchi, W., A Conceptual Framework for the Design of Organizational Control Mechanisms, *Administrative Science Quarterly* (1977) pp. 833-848.

Ouchi, W., Markets, Bureaucracies, and Clans, *Administrative Science Quarterly* (1980) pp. 129-141.

Palmrose, Z., An Analysis of Auditor Litigation and Audit Service Quality, *The Accounting Review* (January 1988) pp. 55-73.

Pany, K. and Reckers, P., Within- Vs. Between-Subjects Experimental Designs: A Study of Demand Effects, *Auditing: A Journal of Practice and Theory* (Fall 1987) pp. 39-53.

Piaget, J., *The Moral Judgment of the Child* (New York: Free Press [1932] 1966).

Ponemon, L., A Cognitive-Developmental Approach to the Analysis of Certified Public Accountants' Ethical Judgments, Ph.D. Dissertation, Union College (1988).

Ponemon, L., Ethical Judgments in Accounting: A Cognitive-Developmental Perspective, *Critical Perspectives on Accounting* (1990) pp. 191-215.

Ponemon, L., Ethical Reasoning and Selection-Socialization in Accounting, *Accounting, Organizations and Society* (1992a) pp. 239-258.

Ponemon, L., Auditor Underreporting of Time and Moral Reasoning: An Experimental-Lab Study, *Contemporary Accounting Research*, Volume 9 (1992b) pp. 171-189.

Ponemon, L., Can Ethics be Taught in Accounting? *Journal of Accounting Education* (forthcoming, 1993a).

Ponemon, L., The Influence of Ethical Reasoning on Auditors' Perceptions of Management's Integrity and Competence, *Advances in Accounting*, Volume 11 (forthcoming, 1993b).

Ponemon, L. and Gabhart, D., Auditor Independence Judgments: A Cognitive Developmental Model and Experimental Evidence, *Contemporary Accounting Research* (1990) pp. 227-251.

Ponemon, L. and Gabhart, D., Auditor's Ethical Cognition: Influence of Individual Differences on Materiality Judgment, working paper, Bentley College (1991).

Ponemon, L. and Glazer, A., Accounting Education and Ethical Development: The Influence of Liberal Learning on Students and Alumni in Accounting Practice, *Issues in Accounting Education* (1990) pp. 21-34.

Powers C. and Reimer, J., Moral Atmosphere: An Educational Bridge Between Moral Judgment and Moral Action, in W. Damon (ed.), *New Directions for Child Development: Moral Development* (New York: John Wiley, 1978).

Powers, C. and Vogel, D., *Ethics in the Education of Business Managers* (New York: Hastings, 1980).

Previts, G., *The Scope of CPA Services: A Study of the Development of the Concepts of Independence and the Profession's Role in Society* (New York: John Wiley, 1986).

Raghunathan, B., Economic Determinants of Auditor Independence, Ph.D. Dissertation, University of Pittsburgh (1986).

Rawls, J., *A Theory of Justice* (Cambridge, MA: Harvard University Press, 1971).

Rebele, J., Heintz, J. and Briden, G., Independent Auditor Sensitivity to Evidence Reliability, *Auditing: A Journal of Practice and Theory* (Fall 1988) pp. 43-52.

Reeder, G. and Coovert, M., Revising an Impression of Morality, *Social Cognition* (January 1986) pp.1-17.

Rest, J., *Development in Judging Moral Issues* (Minneapolis, MN: University of Minnesota Press, 1979a).

Rest, J., *Revised Manual for the Defining Issues Test, MMRP Technical Report*, University of Minnesota (1979b).

Rest, J., *Moral Development: Advances in Research and Theory* (New York: Praeger, 1986).

Rest, J., Can Ethics Be Taught in Professional Schools? The Psychological Research, *Ethics: Easier Said Than Done* (Winter 1988) pp. 22-26.

Rhode, J., *The Independent Auditor's Work Environment: A Survey* (New York: AICPA, 1978).

Rhode, J., Sorensen, J. and Lawler, E., Analysis of Personal Characteristics Related to Professional Staff Turnover in Public Accounting Firms, *Decision Sciences* (October 1976) pp. 771-800.

Rhode, J., Sorensen, J. and Lawler, E., Sources of Staff Turnover in Public Accounting Firms Revealed by the Exit Interview, *Accounting, Organizations and Society* (1977) pp. 165-175.

Rockness, H. and Shields, M., Organizational Control Systems in Research and Development, *Accounting, Organizations and Society* (1984) pp. 165-177.

Rosenbaum, J., Tournament Mobility: Career Patterns in a Corporation, *Administrative Science Quarterly* (1979) pp. 220-240.

Rosenbaum, J., *Career Mobility in a Corporate Hierarchy* (San Francisco: Academic Press, 1984).

Scheaffer, R., Mendenhall, W. and Ott, L., *Elementary Survey Sampling*, (Boston: Duxbury Press, 1986).

Schilit, H., An Empirical Study of Auditor Independence, DBA Dissertation, University of Maryland (1981).

Sen, A., *On Ethics and Economics* (London: Blackwell, 1986).

Shaub, M., An Empirical Examination of the Determinants of Auditors' Ethical Sensitivity, Ph.D. Dissertation, Texas Tech University (1989).

Shaub, M., An Analysis of Factors Affecting the Cognitive Moral Development of Auditors and Auditing Students, working paper, University of Nebraska, (1991).

Simpson, E., Moral Development Research: A Case Study of Scientific Cultural Bias, *Human Development* (1974) pp. 81-106.

Smircich, L., Concepts of Culture and Organizational Analysis, *Administrative Science Quarterly* (1983) pp. 339-358.

Solomon, I. and Krogstad, J., Integration and Perspectives on Substantive Audit Issues. In R. Abdel-khalik and I. Solomon (eds.), *Research Opportunities in Auditing: The Second Decade* (Sarasota, FL: American Accounting Association, 1988).

Sorensen, J., Professional and Bureaucratic Orientation in the Public Accounting Firm, *The Accounting Review* (1967) pp. 553-565.

Sorensen, J., Rhode, J. and Lawler, E., The Generation Gap in Public Accounting, *The Journal of Accountancy* (December 1973) pp. 42-50.

Sorensen, J. and Sorensen, T., Comparison of 1965 and 1970 Organizational and Professional Profiles and Migration Plans of Large-Firm CPAs, in T. Burns (ed.), *Behavioral Experiments in Accounting* (Columbus, OH: Ohio State University, 1972).

Sorensen, J. and Sorensen, T., The Conflict of Professionals in Bureaucratic Organizations, *Administrative Science Quarterly* (1974) pp. 98-106.

St. Pierre, K., Nelson E. and Gabbin, A., A Study of the Ethical Development of Accounting Majors in Relation to Other Business and Nonbusiness Disciplines, *The Accounting Educators Journal* (Summer 1990) pp. 23-35.

Stedry, A., *Budget Control and Cost Behavior* (Englewood Cliffs, NJ: Prentice-Hall, 1960).

Sullivan, J., Litigation Risk Broadly Considered, *Proceedings of the 1992 Deloitte & Touche University of Kansas Symposium of Auditing Problems* (Lawrence, KS: University of Kansas, 1992).

Swieringa, R. and Moncur, R. The Relationship Between Managers' Budget-Oriented Behavior and Selected Attitude Position, Size and Performance Measures, *Journal of Accounting Research* (Fall 1972) pp. 194-209.

Thompson, B., *Canonical Correlation Analysis: Uses and Interpretation* (Newbury Park, CA: Sage Research Report, 1984).

Trevino, L., Ethical Decision Making in Organizations: A Person-Situation Interactionist Model, *Academy of Management Review* (1986) pp. 601-617.

Trevino, L. and Youngblood, S., Bad Apples in Bad Barrels: A Causal Analysis of Ethical Decision-Making Behaviour, *Journal of Applied Psychology* (1990) pp. 378-385.

Troy, H. and Jones D., *A Bibliography of Business Ethics* (Virginia: University of Virginia Press, 1982).

Tull, G., A Study of Moral Development of Selected Employees in Certain Public Accounting Firms, Ph.D. Dissertation, Louisiana State University (1982).

United States General Accounting Office (GAO), *CPA Audit Quality: Status of Actions Taken to Improve Auditing and Financial Reporting of Public Companies*, Report to the Chairman, Oversight and Investigations Subcommittee, House of Representatives (Washington DC: U.S. Government Printing Office, 1989).

United States House of Representatives Subcommittee on Oversight and Investigation of the Committee on Interstate and Foreign Commerce (Moss Committee), *Federal Regulations and Regulatory Reform* (Washington DC: U.S. Government Printing Office, 1976).

United States House of Representatives Subcommittee on Oversight and Investigation, *Published Hearings of the Dingell Committee* (Washington DC: U.S. Government Printing Office, 1988).

United States House of Representatives Subcommittee on Energy and Commerce, *Published Hearings of the Wyden Committee* (Washington DC: U.S. Government Printing Office, 1992).

United States Senate Subcommittee of Reports, Accounting and Management of the Investigation of Governmental Affairs (Metcalf Report), *Report on the Accounting Profession* (Washington DC: U.S. Government Printing Office, 1977).

Walters, R., Operation Highroad: A Plan to Restore Confidence and Balance, *Proceedings on Ethics in the Accounting Profession*, (Los Angeles: University of Southern California Press, 1986).

Watts, R. and Zimmerman, J., The Markets for Independence and Independent Auditors, working paper, University of Rochester, 1981.

Weber, M., *The Methodology of Social Science* (New York: Free Press, 1949).

Weick, K., Cognitive Processes in Organizations, in B. Staw (ed.), *Research in Organization Behavior* (Greenwich, CT: JAI Press, 1979).

Weiner, B., *An Attributional Theory of Motivation and Emotion* (New York: Springer-Verlag, 1986).

Wilensky, H., The Professionalization of Everyone, *American Journal of Sociology* (September 1964).

Willingham, J. and Wright, W., Estimation of Errors in Financial Statements, in R. Abdel-khalik and I. Solomon (eds.) *1984 Auditing Research Symposium* (University of Illinois, 1985) pp. 139-167.

Wilkins, A. and Ouchi, W., Efficient Cultures: Exploring the Relationship Between Culture and Organizational Performance, *Administrative Science Quarterly* (1983) pp. 468-481.

Whyte, W., *The Organization Man* (New York: Simon and Schuster, 1956).

Yerkes, R., Variation in Adherence to Expressed Rules of Ethics by the Accounting Profession and Some Factors Associated with Such Variation, Ph.D. Dissertation, State University of New York at Buffalo (1975).

Zind, R. and Zéghal, D., Some Characteristics of the Canadian Audit Industry, *Contemporary Accounting Research* (Fall 1989) pp. 26-47.

PROTEINS:
FORM AND FUNCTION

21.00x